Paralegal Career

2nd Edition

by Scott A. Hatch, JD, and Lisa Zimmer Hatch, MA

Authors of *LSAT For Dummies*

for **dummies**®

A Wiley Brand

Paralegal Career For Dummies®, 2nd Edition

Published by: **John Wiley & Sons, Inc.**, 111 River Street, Hoboken, NJ 07030-5774, www.wiley.com

Copyright © 2019 by John Wiley & Sons, Inc., Hoboken, New Jersey

Published simultaneously in Canada

For general information on our other products and services, please contact our Customer Care Department within the U.S. at 877-762-2974, outside the U.S. at 317-572-3993, or fax 317-572-4002. For technical support, please visit https://hub.wiley.com/community/support/dummies.

Wiley publishes in a variety of print and electronic formats and by print-on-demand. Some material included with standard print versions of this book may not be included in e-books or in print-on-demand. If this book refers to media such as a CD or DVD that is not included in the version you purchased, you may download this material at http://booksupport.wiley.com. For more information about Wiley products, visit www.wiley.com.

Library of Congress Control Number: 2019936126

ISBN 978-1-119-56491-1 (pbk); ISBN 978-1-119-56494-2 (ebk); 978-1-119-56493-5 (ebk)

Manufactured in the United States of America

SKY10032564_011722

Contents at a Glance

Table of Contents

Introduction

America has a fascination with courtroom dramas. Dozens of TV shows and hundreds of movies have been based on the legal profession. Hollywood has even made musicals with courtroom scenes! Real courtroom dramas receive nearly constant attention on the news networks, and if CNN's coverage of every detail in a trial isn't enough, there's are always continuous access to *Law and Order* reruns on numerous channels and streaming devices.

You may not have noticed, but one thing's missing from most of these legal dramas: the behind-the-scenes work of the paralegals (or legal assistants as they're sometimes called). In the media, lawyers give flawless and impassioned pleas to the jury, and the force of their arguments turns the case, or, under relentless cross-examination, the defendant suddenly admits to the crime. In reality, these events rarely happen — cases are won and lost based on what takes place outside of the courtroom even before the trial.

The vast majority of the work for a civil or criminal trial is done before the trial begins, and after a trial starts there are usually very few surprises. But just as the networks choose to broadcast the Olympics, but not the four years of training in between, so the focus of dramas is on the action in the courtroom and not all the investigation, interviewing, writing, and research that builds the case. So, when you're watching TV dramas , you'll usually see the lawyers in the courtroom, but not the paralegals whose research allows the trial to take place.

Whether you're researching the paralegal profession to see if it peaks your interest or you've worked as a paralegal since Clinton was in office, you can find a wealth of pertinent information in this book. This book is a fun and informative resource for anyone who loves the law and wants to find out more about it. You'll want it within easy reach as a reference to consult throughout your paralegal career or to explain the nuances of what you're watching on television. This book offers something for everyone.

About This Book

If being a paralegal appeals to you, you've come to the right place. Since 1980, we've instructed people from all walks of life and with a variety of goals on how to work as paralegals. This experience has shown us what information you absolutely need to know before you apply for a paralegal position and what information is best learned on the job. So, *Paralegal Career For Dummies*, Second Edition, doesn't cover things you don't need to know — we want to focus on what's *most* important.

This second edition incorporates updated information designed to help you decide whether a paralegal career is right for you. It also directs you to the current resources you need to get the right education and experience to make your dream a reality. The best part is that it actually goes into great detail to teach you the vital skills you need to work as a paralegal or to act as your own pro se litigant.

As if the amazing information in this text wasn't enough, in this second edition, we include accompanying online resources at www.dummies.com/go/paralegalcareer2e. You can access useful forms, sample resumes and cover letters, and other references, as well as links to valuable websites.

Finally, this book is a reference book, which means that you can keep it at your desk and reach for it whenever you need some more information. You don't have to read it from beginning to end — you can just dip into whatever chapter or section is most interesting to you today, and come back to the book later as your needs and interests change. Of course, if you want to read the book from cover to cover, we won't stop you!

Foolish Assumptions

We make a few assumptions about who you are, as the reader of this book.

Maybe you've always had an interest in law, but you don't want to spend the time and expense on law school. (Besides, who wants to be the brunt of all those lawyer jokes!) Or, if you don't mind the jokes, you could be considering law school, but you want to be sure that law's a good match for you before you invest in three or four more years of education. Because paralegals do almost everything an attorney does, working as a paralegal will let you know right away whether you love the law as much as we do. Plus, a job as a paralegal would be a perfect way to make money while you're in your last two years of law school. You may even decide you'd rather stick with a paralegal career, especially considering that the Department of

Labor consistently projects the paralegal career to grow much faster than the average for other professions.

Maybe you're working as a legal secretary and thinking that you could do a lot more of the legal work in the office. Wouldn't it impress your supervising attorney if you could come up with a vital piece of legal research discovered as a result of your newly honed legal research skills? Or it could be that you worked on one of your own legal nightmares either as a pro se litigant or as an assistant to your attorney. You may have had an epiphany that you could do as good a job as (or a better one than) the attorney who worked on your case and that you could actually get *paid* for your efforts!

Whatever level of interest or experience you bring to the table, this book is for you.

Icons Used in This Book

One helpful feature of this book is the icons that highlight especially significant portions of the text. These little pictures in the margins alert you to certain kinds of information:

TIP

Throughout the book, we give you insights into how you can enhance your performance as a paralegal and your knowledge of how the law works. When we highlight something especially helpful, we flag the paragraph with a Tip icon.

TECHNICAL STUFF

The language of law can be puzzling. Whenever you see one of these icons, you know that we're providing (sometime excruciating) details on a complex legal concept. If you're not as into the minutiae as we are, you can safely skip these paragraphs and get the main point.

WARNING

Working as a paralegal isn't all fun and games. As a paralegal, you can do — or fail to do — things that have devastating consequences. Heed these cautionary timebombs to avoid pitfalls that can cost you your dignity and maybe even your job.

REMEMBER

This book gives you gobs of information, and some of it's so important we may just have to say it again. When we talk about something especially important for you to remember, this icon will be nearby.

In addition to the fountain of information contained in this book, you'll find floods of handy forms and sample documents online. When we mention something that's available online at www.dummies.com/go/paralegalcareer2e, we also flag it with this icon.

Where to Go from Here

If you're new to the paralegal profession and want to see what it's all about, start with Chapter 1, which gives you a great introduction to a paralegal career. Then read the chapters in Part 2 to gain a general understanding of the field of law. From there, choose chapters that sound interesting to you to better determine if this exciting career up your alley.

If you've worked as a paralegal or legal secretary, use this book to find out more about what you do on a daily basis. For example, if your supervising attorney wants you to take on more responsibility, such as legal research (Chapter 13), document drafting (Chapters 10 and 16), and interviewing (Chapter 12), read the specific chapters that pertain to your new duties. Or if you've always wanted to know about the legal system to get a better understanding of why you do what you do, read Chapter 4.

Although we're pretty confident about the comprehensiveness of this book, you'll probably need more education if you've never worked in a law office before or if you have but don't feel confident about the depth of your skills. Enroll in a quality program through a recognized university or college (like the one we offer) and impress your instructors with the expertise you've gained from reading this book!

You may want to join a state and local paralegal association to find out more about your chosen career and gain valuable networking resources. Above all, don't be timid. Get out there and apply your newly found knowledge to a real live job. If you think you need a little experience first, volunteer your services to a local nonprofit law office, such as Sierra Club, Legal Aid Foundation, or the public defender's office in your area. You'll be surprised about how much you know with this book as your guide!

1

A Snapshot of the Exciting and Lucrative Paralegal Profession

Explore the wide variety of jobs in the paralegal profession and sample those jobs where paralegals are most in demand.

Discover the skills and education necessary to succeed in a paralegal career.

Amplify your networking success through joining paralegal associations and decide whether certification makes sense for your path.

Prepare killer cover letters and effective resumes for securing a paralegal position.

Set up your freelance paralegal business and advertise your skills to law firms and other potential legal employers.

Chapter 1

Discovering the Paralegal Profession

With so much media coverage for attorneys and so little for the equally important paralegals, you may not be entirely familiar with what a paralegal career entails. In this chapter, we tell you what paralegals do, where paralegals work, and what it takes to become a paralegal.

Almost a Lawyer: What a Paralegal Does

Both paralegals and lawyers are legal professionals. The difference is that an attorney must supervise a paralegal's work, and a paralegal can't do certain things, like give legal advice and represent clients in court.

But there are many things paralegals *can* do. Because using a paralegal instead of an attorney can save a lot of money, law firms and corporations are increasingly relying on paralegals. As a paralegal, you'll likely be doing many of the tasks that in past decades were accomplished only by licensed attorneys. We cover some of these important tasks in the following sections.

Researching and analyzing the law

Courts make decisions about current cases based on the decisions made in past cases. So, to effectively prepare a case, you have to know what the courts have decided in similar circumstances and evaluate them to figure out how they apply to the case you're working on. You find prior cases and relevant statutes through legal research.

Performing legal research can eat up gobs of time, so attorneys often count on competent paralegals to take up this duty. No matter which area of law you enter, you'll have to do legal research. If you work in areas that frequently require litigation, you'll do lots of research, but even other areas like domestic law, trusts and estates, corporate law, and entertainment law are going to require you to hit the books.

Of course, legal research has increasingly moved away from books and into computer technology. This doesn't mean that you'll be doing less research, just that you may be doing more of it from your desk rather than heading to a law library. (Chapter 13 shows you how to research the law in texts and on a computer.)

Your job doesn't stop with the accumulation of research. You also have to analyze the information by applying law to facts and probably draft memos that present your analysis for the lawyers in your firm. You may need to apply the information that you find to a corporate contract, will, or other legal document. In many cases, you may even be asked to do initial writing on motions that will actually be filed in court. So although *you* may not be speaking in court, your *work* will be.

Playing Sherlock: Interviewing and investigating

Cases aren't only about relevant statutes and case precedents; they're also about the facts. As we discuss in Chapters 11 and 12, you may interview witnesses and collect evidence in your paralegal career. Evidence gathering is especially important in any kind of litigation. Litigation results in many areas of law. For example, corporate law may involve litigation stemming from contract disputes or product liability; patent and trademark law may lead to trials over intellectual property rights; and family law features frequent litigation, especially stemming from divorce and child custody issues.

For each of these kinds of lawsuits, there are witnesses to interview and evidence to gather. For example, if your supervising attorney were working for a plaintiff in a product liability suit, you would need to gather information on the harm caused by the product, interview other people who may have been adversely affected by the product, work to determine what the company knew of the danger and when, and collect information from any additional witnesses.

TIP

Even if you aren't working in litigation, you may still need your interview and investigation skills. For example, when you help prepare a prenuptial agreement for a family law practice, you need to determine the client's assets and investigate the background of the future spouse. If you're working for attorneys in entertainment law who are reviewing a record deal for one of their clients, you may have to investigate the details of the deal or the record company. Whatever the area of law you become involved in, you'll use your interview and investigation skills.

Convening with clients

Without clients, the practice of law wouldn't exist. Tasks like legal research and document preparation may seem to be the main duties of legal professionals. But, you only engage in these and other legal tasks because you're working on behalf of a client. Establishing good relationships with clients is essential to open communication and good legal practice — and it's also important to strengthening your career.

During your paralegal career you may find that you're often the liaison between the client and the attorneys you work for, which may be one of the most important duties you have. As the liaison, you keep the client informed of how the case is progressing and work with the client to get all the relevant case information. Then you accurately relay what the client tells you to the attorney who represents the client.

REMEMBER

As a paralegal, you generally aren't allowed to have your own clients. If you tell clients that you're representing them in a legal matter, you're probably guilty of the unauthorized practice of law. So, in every case, clearly communicate to the client your status as a paralegal. All your duties are supervised by a licensed attorney, which means that you communicate everything the client tells you to your supervising attorney. Attorney-client privilege doesn't require or even allow you to keep any secrets from your client's lawyer. (You can find more on these and other ethical concerns for paralegals in Chapter 15.)

Administrating the legal environment

In some offices, you may work as a case administrator. An administrator handles the case details for a client and the attorney. For example, law firms have special accounts where they keep money that belongs to clients rather than to the firm. If a client wins a judgment or if money included in a will is being dispersed, that money passes though the accounts of a law firm. Or, you may keep track of the money bequeathed through a will if you work for a probate attorney.

In a small law office, your paralegal duties may also include administrating the entire operation, including the filing system, the calendar, and the billings. (For more on how to manage these tasks, turn to Chapter 18.)

WHY IT PAYS TO BE A PARALEGAL

Many people with dreams of working in the legal profession think first about becoming an attorney. The reality is that becoming a paralegal may make more sense than becoming an attorney. In general, paralegals don't make as much money as the licensed attorneys they work for. However, some experienced paralegals, such as those working in large corporate firms, may make considerably more money than young attorneys in other areas like criminal and family law. For the sake of comparison, consider two imaginary college students who graduate from the same college in the same year and end up working at the same midsize corporate law firm three years later.

Ann decides to attend law school after graduation. Because of her good grades and LSAT scores, she's accepted at a competitive law school, one that doesn't offer many scholarships. So Ann has to finance her education with loans. The average cost of tuition, living expenses, and books at a competitive law school is more than $45,000 per year. Federally guaranteed loans only cover about half of this, so Ann has to take the rest in private loans with higher interest rates. At the end of her three years of study and her six months of preparing for the bar exam, Ann is in debt for more than $100,000. To pay off her loans within 20 years, Ann makes monthly payments of as much as $2,200 per month. Ann also had to forgo three and a half years of wages while she was in law school and studying for the exam.

John decided after graduation to become a paralegal. He chose a course of paralegal training that took about a year, but the classes fit his schedule so that he could also work full-time as an administrative assistant at a law firm. His tuition was much lower than Ann's, and because he was working, John didn't have to take out any loans at all. After completion of his course, John stayed with the firm as a paralegal instead of an administrative assistant.

By the time Ann is hired by the firm, John has already worked there for three and half years, the last three as a paralegal. He has earned raises each year and is making $60,000 per year. Ann joins the firm at a salary of $85,000 (a good starting salary for an attorney). Ann's loan payments of $2,200 per month add up to about $26,000 per year. So, when taxes are taken into account, John actually has more disposable income than Ann! In addition, John has saved $20,000 from his three and a half years of working, while Ann still has to pay off $100,000 in debt. In terms of wealth, John is starting out $120,000 ahead of Ann! Even if Ann's salary rises faster than John's, it will probably take about 20 years for Ann to catch up with John in terms of wealth.

As this example illustrates, for many people, becoming a paralegal is a better way to get involved in a law career.

On the Job: Where Paralegals Work

Paralegals work in many different areas of the law. (For a sampling of some them, read Chapter 9.) Some paralegals choose to earn high salaries in corporate law or complex litigation. Other paralegals work for low-income clients or for public interest or environmental law firms. Some paralegals like the personal atmosphere of a small firm and others take control of their futures by starting their own paralegal businesses. There are as many different choices for paralegals as there are types of law!

The six-figure paralegal: Working for the big firm

If you think that attorneys are the only legal professionals capable of making six-figure salaries, you're wrong! In bigger cities, experienced paralegals working for large firms can make more than $100,000 per year. Two factors have a big influence on the salary you can earn as a paralegal:

>> **Your level of experience:** The longer you work as a paralegal, the more valuable you become. (That's why it's important to get started on your career as soon as possible.) As you develop your skills, you'll be given more complex tasks and get paid accordingly.

>> **Your area of specialization and the responsibilities of your job:** If you choose to specialize in corporate law or litigation, you have a high earning potential. Increased salaries usually mean more responsibility. The highest paid paralegals often supervise other paralegals or have particularly important duties within the firm.

Here are some areas of the law where paralegals often make the highest salaries:

>> **Litigation:** Paralegals working in the field of litigation have some of the most interesting, and challenging, duties available to legal professionals. Litigation can be fast-paced and complex with dozens of potential witnesses and mountains of evidence. It takes qualified and talented lawyers and paralegals to deal with complicated litigation. If you aren't afraid of intense work that often extends beyond the normal workweek, you may have what it takes to make a big salary in litigation.

>> **Corporate law:** Corporate law involves important and lucrative deals. Contracts, mergers, takeovers, and issuing of stock constitute just some of the activities of a corporate legal team. If you have an eye for detail and you're interested in business, corporate law could mean a big deal for you.

>> **Other special areas of law:** Another way to make a high salary is to special-
ize. Paralegals are always in demand in certain specialties. These specialties
require knowledge of more than just the law. For example if you have a
degree in chemistry, you could specialize as a paralegal working with the
pharmaceutical industry. Nurses find highly paid positions as consultants in
firms that specialize in medical malpractice.

Examples of areas where your interests can turn into a high paying paralegal
position include patent and trademark law, environmental protection and
other areas involving science, and medical malpractice and product liability.

Jack- or Jill-of-all-trades: Working for the small firm

Working in corporate law, complex litigation or an unusual specialty might not be
for you. Paralegals do tend to earn the most in these areas, but salary isn't everything. Working in a small firm offers many advantages, and if you don't want to live
in one of the big cities in the United States, a small firm may be your best option.

As a paralegal in a small firm, you may find yourself performing diverse tasks
while working on a wide variety of cases. You might be compiling asset information for a bankruptcy filing, interviewing witnesses for a child custody issue,
helping a client draft a will, and assisting a small business with incorporation.
Talk about multitasking!

If you like to constantly confront new challenges, if you like seeing your efforts have
immediate results for real people, and if you're flexible enough to do your best with
any assignment you're given, the small firm might be the choice for you. Plus, small
firms often offer opportunities for fledgling paralegals to get their feet in the door.

Spreading the love: The pro bono paralegal

If you're willing to sacrifice salary for public assistance, you could become a paralegal at one of the pro bono firms that work for justice rather than profit. These
firms work to help disadvantaged clients, save the environment, uphold civil
rights, and protect constitutionally guaranteed liberties. By working for one of
these firms, you'll pull in a modest salary but make a big difference!

Working for the government

A growing area of employment for paralegals is with the public sector. All levels of
government and court systems employ paralegals. The biggest federal employer
of paralegals is the Department of Justice, followed by the Social Security

Administration and the Treasury Department, but nearly every cabinet department employs paralegals. State governments have been hiring new paralegals at increasing rates. Paralegals have been replacing licensed attorneys in bureaucracies because using paralegals saves governments lots of money.

If you choose to become a paralegal in the public sector, you'll be a member of a bureaucracy. The public sector has more defined rules and procedures and more definite job descriptions and roles than the private sector does. Working for a small firm, you might be asked to perform just about any task required for a client. Working for the government, you'll likely have a strictly defined job description and a firm knowledge of exactly what you'll be doing each day.

The public sector pays less than large firms but generally more than small firms. Government employment also tends to be less risky then employment in the private sector. Government employees have more rights, including the protection of certain personnel procedures that don't allow government employees to be fired on a whim. Government jobs also tend to provide excellent benefits packages. If you favor stability, a public sector job may be right for you.

Doing it your way: The paralegal as independent contractor

On the other end of the spectrum from stable government employment is the paralegal entrepreneur. If you don't want to be tied down to a single firm, if you want the opportunity to work for different firms on different projects, or if you're comfortable taking risks and reaping the rewards that come with being your own boss, you may choose to strike out on your own as an independent contractor.

Independent contractors are paralegals for hire. If a small law firm suddenly gets involved in big litigation, it needs lots of help. Instead of hiring a bunch of employees and paying them benefits, the firm may be better off contracting with a freelance paralegal. Of course, freelance paralegals still have to be supervised by an attorney. But, by creating your own paralegal contracting service, you can take more control of your professional life than you usually can working for one particular firm. (For more information about setting up a freelance paralegal business, see Chapter 3.)

What It Takes: The Skills, Knowledge, and Training You Need

Gaining the skills you need to become a legal professional takes more than reading every John Grisham novel. Paralegals are skilled professionals. When you work as a paralegal, you won't have your own clients, give legal advice, or argue a case in court (except in specific administrative law hearings), but you can do any of the other tasks that can only be performed by a skilled legal professional. Of course, you have to become a skilled legal professional first! To succeed as a paralegal, you need the right combination of personality and education.

The paralegal personality

The legal profession is a demanding one for attorneys and paralegals. The hours can be long, deadlines tight, and stakes high. The legal profession also has a strict code of ethics — just missing a deadline can be an ethics violation.

People with many different backgrounds and personalities can and have succeeded as paralegals. However, there are certain things that nearly all successful paralegals have in common. So when we talk about the right personality for the paralegal profession, we mean the group of characteristics that successful legal professionals — both lawyers and paralegals — tend to share.

TIP

Here are some of the main characteristics you need to survive in the legal profession:

>> **You need the ability to reason.** You don't need to have aced the I.Q. test or earned a 4.0 GPA throughout your educational career to be a good paralegal. But you do need to be able to understand and analyze complex legal issues to interview witnesses, conduct legal research, or draft contracts.

>> **You need to be reliable.** The legal profession lives and breathes deadlines. In litigation, there are specific deadlines you have to meet for filing documents with the court. And you must meet these deadlines or suffer sanctions that adversely affect the client. In law, if you miss a deadline, your client may lose the case or lose the right to begin a case.

>> **Your work should be thorough.** Imagine that you provide research for the contents of a contract for a corporate client, and the contract contains a penalty if your client defaults. You think that you've found the cases that show how a court will interpret the default clause. So you decide to stop researching and submit what you have to the attorney. It turns out that another, more applicable, case gives a completely different interpretation of the default clause, and your client loses millions of dollars. The client could sue your firm, and the attorney supervising you could be disbarred because you cut corners in your research.

>> **You must be trustworthy and discrete.** Legal professionals hold a position of trust with their clients. You have access to clients' private information, like financial information and private secrets that they may not have revealed even to family members. So, the most important rules of legal ethics center

on maintaining integrity in dealing with clients. As a paralegal, you must respect attorney-client confidentiality and refrain from talking with anyone about a client. And if the people you work with lack integrity, you must be willing to report their behavior to your supervising attorney.

>> **You've got to be tough.** No matter how intelligent, reliable, and thorough you are, you'll probably experience a setback at some time in your paralegal career. Maybe, despite your very best efforts, you'll make a mistake that's damaging to a client. Even when you do your job perfectly, factors beyond your control may produce an adverse outcome for a client whom you've gotten to know well, like losing custody of a child in a divorce proceeding. You need fortitude to go beyond these disappointments and move on to the next case.

TIP

You won't always be perfect and outcomes won't always seem fair. Think about your own resilience not only when considering whether you have the right personality for the paralegal profession but also in choosing the area of law to work in. Most paralegals work in civil, rather than criminal law, so a person's life or freedom is not usually at stake, but setbacks in areas such as family law and litigation can really test your toughness.

Paralegal know-how

You need to have special skills to work as a paralegal. In the paralegal profession, there are big differences in salary based on levels of experience. Even if you don't already have the specific legal education and experience that you need to work as a paralegal, certain skills contribute to your overall ability to thrive in the paralegal profession.

TIP

Here are some of the life skills that contribute to making someone a successful paralegal:

>> **Writing skills:** One of the most important skills for a paralegal is good writing ability, including a strong command of grammar and sentence structure. (If writing presents challenges for you, check out Chapter 16 to find ways to improve your writing.)

REMEMBER

Your legal writing ability doesn't need to be perfect when you begin your career. You'll have lots of opportunity to practice your legal writing skills on the job.

>> **Research skills:** Basic research skills are essential to a successful paralegal career. In today's world, this means not only being able to skim through a mountain of academic texts in the library but also using technology. If you're already familiar with conducting online searches, legal research will come more easily to you. (Chapter 17 explains how technology fits into legal research.)

>> **Communication skills:** Most paralegal positions require lots of contact with other people. You deal with attorneys, other members of the law office, clients, witnesses, county clerks, and sometimes the media. So, being comfortable around a variety of personalities is an important career skill.

Education and experience: Two ways to train

You can learn the profession of paralegalism two ways: through formal education or on-the-job experience. Most paralegals incorporate a little of both.

Academia: Kinds of paralegal training

Currently, only the state of California mandates education requirements for paralegals. In all other states, there are no specific requirements to work as a paralegal. They leave that determination up to the attorney who hires and supervises a paralegal.

Most attorneys require some type of prior paralegal training when they hire, so most paralegals begin their careers with some sort of specialized training. Formal training is popular with employers because it gives their employees the basic paralegal skills that the employers don't have time to train them on. Formal education is attractive to future paralegals because it gives them confidence to enter the job market and a hiring advantage over someone without training or experience. You may get hired without some sort of formal paralegal training, but you probably won't be paid as much as you would if you had specialized education.

ATTEMPTS AT REGULATING PARALEGALS

Because paralegals work under the supervision of a bar-certified attorney, they're regulated under that attorney. In other words, states have regulated paralegals indirectly by regulating the attorneys who employ them. Therefore, most states don't mandate specific education and experience requirements for paralegals, but several states are in the process of considering ways to regulate or license the paralegal profession.

Currently, the exception is California. The state of California says that to call yourself a paralegal, you must have a certain level of paralegal training or job experience. The state leaves it up to the supervising attorney who hires the paralegal to make sure the paralegal meets the qualifications.

Another reason that formal education is increasingly becoming the standard for new paralegals is the availability and diversity of education programs. Paralegal programs come in a variety of shapes and sizes designed to fit the needs of future paralegals.

CERTIFICATE PROGRAMS

If you're interested in a paralegal career and have an associate's or bachelor's degree in any field or if you have legal experience as a legal secretary or law office administrator, a certificate program is perfect for you. Most certificate programs focus on the practical skills you need to work as a paralegal, so you won't waste a lot of time learning legal theory. These programs can be completed in as little as a few months or as long as two years. Because you learn specific law office procedures on the job, you don't need a program that offers you more than a foundation in legal terminology, legal research, legal documents, legal process, and ethics.

Classes often accommodate the schedules of working adults, with night, weekend, and online offerings. And some attorneys may hire you with a reputable certificate of completion even if you don't already have a college degree or prior law office experience.

TIP

We developed paralegal certificate programs through colleges and universities nationwide. You can find out more about our programs at www.legalstudies.com. For most future paralegals, a certificate fills the bill.

ASSOCIATE'S DEGREE PROGRAMS

The job market in your community may dictate that you have a degree before you work as a paralegal. Community colleges and some state and private four-year institutions offer two-year programs in paralegal studies. Many of the classes are geared towards the paralegal profession, as they are in a certificate program, but you also take the core courses required to earn your associate's degree.

TIP

If you don't have a college degree or law office experience, associate's degree programs may be the quickest way to enter the profession.

BACHELOR'S DEGREE PROGRAMS

A few colleges and universities offer a major or a minor in paralegal studies, but these programs are still pretty rare. These programs are designed around a four-year bachelor's degree and include 30 credit hours of paralegal courses. The advantage of these programs is that you earn a four-year degree and get trained as a paralegal at the same time.

If you're planning on going to college and thinking of becoming a paralegal, a bachelor's degree is a good option to explore. However, if you want to enter the paralegal profession sooner rather than later, certificate programs and two-year degrees get you into the job market faster with less education debt.

On-the-job training: Experience

Some of the most successful paralegals earned their positions by working their way up in law firms. You may start as a legal secretary, filing clerk, or mail clerk, and with time and proven ability gradually take on paralegal duties until you move into a position of performing primarily paralegal tasks. This method of entry into the paralegal profession has some obvious advantages: You don't have to pay tuition, and you start earning a salary right away.

The downside to relying completely on working your way to a paralegal position may outweigh the advantages, however:

>> **Securing an entry-level position without prior training may be difficult.** Some attorneys require that their legal secretaries have specialized training, so you may need to go to school to work in any position in a law office. Attorneys don't have a lot of time to train staff. You'll be competing for jobs with people who have legal education or experience, so they already have the specific skills you're hoping to learn on the job.

>> **Entry-level work in a law office may not interest you.** Legal secretaries, file clerks, and mail clerks offer invaluable services to attorneys, but their duties are primarily clerical. If this type of work doesn't interest you, you may be disappointed with the amount of time it takes you to acquire paralegal duties.

>> **Working your way to a paralegal position could take years.** There are no guarantees that experience will lead to a paralegal position in your law office. You may be passed up by new hires who have more education than you do and end up having to complete a certificate course to show your employer that you have what it takes to work as a paralegal.

Unless you're already working in a law office, planning to get a paralegal job without special training is probably impractical.

If you already work as a legal secretary and feel you're ready for additional responsibility, you may want to approach your employer for paralegal duties or seek a position in another firm that allows you to do paralegal work.

If you're just starting out, we recommend that you complete paralegal training. It'll make you more competent, confident, and attractive to future employers.

Chapter 2

Membership Has Its Privileges: Paralegal Associations and Their Certification Exams

Some of the decisions you make when you become a paralegal include whether to join an association of paralegals and whether to take steps to become certified. If you decided to become a member of a paralegal group, you have many types to choose from. And, because certification is voluntary for paralegals, different types of processes exist. This chapter helps you sort through your options for joining an association and becoming certified.

To Join or Not to Join

Depending upon your time, availability, and proclivity toward joining organizations, you may decide to join a local, state, or national paralegal association. But keep in mind that no one *has* to join a paralegal association to practice paralegalism.

In addition to enhancing your knowledge about new areas of law, association membership can lead to jobs by networking with other members. Because virtually all paralegal associations require that you pay annual dues and aspire to promote the ethical practice of the paralegal profession, you probably don't need to join more than one organization. A major consideration when you're figuring which one to join is whether you prefer a local, state, or national association, because each type has distinct advantages. We cover these questions in the following sections.

Characterizing the types of associations

TIP

You'll find paralegal groups on the national, state, and local level. Each level has something a little different to offer, but generally you'll probably get more out of joining a local association than you will from signing up with a national one.

Reaching out: National paralegal organizations

In terms of membership numbers, the two largest national collections of paralegals are:

>> **National Association of Legal Assistants (NALA;** www.nala.org**):** NALA represents about 18,000 paralegals as individuals and through its state and local paralegal association members.

>> **National Federation of Paralegal Associations (NFPA;** www.paralegals. org**):** NFPA is a voluntary organization of more than 50 state and local paralegal associations representing more than 9,000 paralegals who are members of those other associations, too.

Both of these national organizations publish periodicals, sponsor continuing education seminars, and offer tests for members to be named a Certified Paralegal (CP) with NALA, or a PACE Registered Paralegal (RP) with NFPA.

NALS is another national organization for paralegals and other legal professionals. It provides membership and certification to paralegals, legal secretaries, and other legal support staff.

Sticking close to home: State and local paralegal associations

Virtually every state has one or more association of paralegals, and many of them are affiliated with the large national paralegal association, NFPA. Organizations may be for residents of just one state, or they may encompass larger regions consisting of several states (like the Rocky Mountain Paralegal Association, which covers Colorado, Nebraska, South Dakota, Utah, and Wyoming). Additionally, a local organization of paralegals exists in virtually every large metropolitan area. Local groups often hold monthly brown-bag luncheons in a local law office conference room where prominent local attorneys or paralegals often speak to the group on pertinent issues of state or local interest. Dues are usually reasonable, but their primary advantage is the networking opportunities and local job leads you get during monthly meetings.

TIP

State and local paralegal groups usually offer a better organizational structure than local groups do and are more personal than the national organizations.

REMEMBER

The online content contains a list of many national, state, and regional paralegal association in the United States, so you can get involved right away.

Hanging out at the bar: Paralegal divisions of bar associations

You can also join the paralegal division of many state and local bar associations. Although bar associations cater primarily to attorneys, many have paralegal divisions that provide excellent networking and education opportunities.

The American Bar Association (ABA) is an organization primarily for attorneys. However, the individual associate category of ABA membership is aimed at attracting persons who are qualified through education, training, or work experience and are employed by a lawyer, law office, government agency, or other similar entity to perform under attorney supervision tasks that attorneys usually undertake (in another word, paralegals). An ABA member who supervises the paralegal's work may have to sign the paralegal's application for associative membership.

Weighing in on whether or not to join an association

Federal and state governments don't make it mandatory for paralegals to join paralegal associations to practice their chosen career. The federal government thus far allows virtually unfettered access to the paralegal profession. California's mandatory education requirements for paralegals focus on elevating a paralegal's qualifications and not at mandating organizational membership. So, although your supervising attorney has to be a member of the state bar to practice law, you don't have to join an association to be a paralegal.

TIP

You may choose to join an association, however. Some of the big advantages of joining one or more paralegal organizations include networking with other paralegals for purposes of social interaction, knowledge, or job advancement; getting involved in continuing legal education seminars; and having quick access to changes in local court practice

WARNING

Although these advantages make joining an association seem like a no-brainer, there are some viable reasons to opt out. First, joining can be costly. You must pay yearly dues, take time out of your day to attend meetings, and, in some cases, volunteer to commit yourself to pro bono or other association-sponsored activities. Plus, in addition to the cost, time, and commitment involved, not everyone likes joining groups.

Many paralegals, however, find that the benefits of joining outweigh the drawbacks, especially when they participate in state or local associations. Associations that are closer to home usually provide more pertinent, state-specific education opportunities and more relevant job prospects. Plus, the people you meet live in your area, so you can get together with them outside of meetings if you want. You usually meet with other members of the national organizations at yearly conventions.

Deciding Whether to Get Certified

Currently, no state requires that paralegals take a certification exam to work in their profession. So, you don't have to spend a bunch of money and a lot of time studying for an exam if you don't want to. But you may decide that taking a certification exam is the right path for you. If so, you need to determine *which* exam is best for you.

Choosing a certification exam

The two primary organizations that provide paralegal certification exams are the two major national paralegal associations: NALA and NFPA (we cover these associations earlier in this chapter). But NALS and some state paralegal associations offer certification options as well.

The CP exam

NALA calls its certification exam the CP, which stands for Certified Paralegal. So, when you pass this exam, you can add the CP designation as a professional title at the end of your name. It makes for a very fancy nameplate on your desk and adds some distinction to your resume.

WARNING

Only paralegals who have taken and passed the NALA CP exam can say that they are Certified Paralegals. Successfully completing a certificate course for paralegals without taking the CP exam doesn't allow you to say you're certified.

NALA also offers advanced certification programs that provide you with additional distinction when you successfully complete them. You can find out more about the CP exam and the advanced programs at www.nala.org.

The PACE exam

Not to be outdone by NALA, NFPA also provides an exam to certify paralegals. Successfully completing NFPA's PACE (which stands for Paralegal Advanced Competency Exam) allows you to call yourself a Registered Paralegal and designate the title with an RP at the end of your name. Only paralegals who've passed the PACE can use the RP title. NFPA also offers an exam to assess the knowledge and skill of early career and entry-level paralegals called the Paralegal CORE Competency Exam (TM) also known as (PCCE) (R).

The PACE lasts four hours, and you can take it at testing centers nationwide pretty much any time you want throughout the year. The PACE uses hypothetical situations to test general knowledge and critical reasoning. To take the exam, you have to pay a registration fee and an exam fee and meet education and experience requirements. To find out more, go to www.paralegals.org.

Other certification options

NALS (see "Reaching out: National paralegal associations) offers four types of certifications by offering several exams with different emphases. Its four-part Professional Paralegal (PP) exam is offered online to those who meet the criteria. It also provides an Accredited Legal Professional (ALP) exam for entry-level staff, a Professional Legal Secretary (PLS) exam, and a Certified Legal Professional (CLP) exam. Current PLS or CLP individuals need only take the fourth part of the PP exam to gain that certification. You can find out more details on the NALS website at www.nals.org. NALS also offers a specialty certificate program that includes more than 20 areas of legal specialization by taking at least 50 credit hours of CLE credit in a specialized area of law.

Some state and local paralegal associations provide certification designations for their members. For instance, if you meet the requirements of the North Carolina Paralegal Association, you can call yourself a North Carolina Certified Paralegal (NCCP). Some states, like Texas, offer exams in specific areas of law to recognize a paralegal's achievements. So, there may be several certification options available to you, depending on where you live. You can find out more by contacting paralegal associations and bar associations in your area.

Weighing the pros and cons of paralegal certification

Most paralegals wait until they've worked for a few years before they take a certification exam. When you decide to take on the challenge of a certification exam, it's usually for one or more of these reasons:

» **You enjoy the challenge.** The national certification exams are quite grueling, and you should feel a deep sense of accomplishment if you pass them.

» **You want recognition.** After you've achieved a level of experience and expertise in your profession, you may want documentation of it. Using a professional title tells the world that you're an expert in your field.

» **Your supervising attorney requires it.** Attorneys want their practices to be as reputable and marketable as possible. And being able to say that their paralegals are certified may help them achieve this goal. Clients may feel more confident working with a paralegal who's certified. So, some attorneys may require you to take a certification exam or provide incentives like a higher salary if you pass.

» **Your supervising attorney pays for it.** Some attorneys foot the bill for their paralegals to take certification exams, which eliminates any financial concerns a paralegal would have about getting certified.

» **You're seeking a new position.** You may want to move on to a new paralegal position in another law firm or in your current firm, and certification status may be the extra edge you need to gain your dream job, maybe in a specialized area of law or in a supervisory capacity.

Despite the perks of certification, many paralegals feel that, because certification isn't mandatory, they'd rather not incur the expense or spend the time it takes to pass an exam. Some paralegals spend months preparing for the CP or PACE exam. Some people would rather focus on their paralegal work than study for an exam. What you decide to do depends on your level of experience, the type of firm you work for, the desires of your supervising attorney, and your own professional goals.

Chapter 3

The Hunt Is On: Securing a Paralegal Position

Nothing you can do will give you a better paralegal education than hands-on experience. And the best way to get hands-on experience is to get involved in an internship or job in the legal practice area you like best.

This chapter gives you the tools you need to find a paralegal job or internship, including sources for job leads and guidelines for creating cover letters and resumes. If you have an entrepreneurial spirit, you can take advantage of our tips on how to start your own business, as well as our sample freelance rate sheet.

Finding the Perfect Job

Job hunting can be pretty challenging, but persistence and careful planning will give you the edge you need to succeed in the job search. Many different entities employ paralegals in a variety of areas, so sometimes you have to think creatively to find the best position for you. Law firms, government agencies, banks, insurance companies, and corporate legal divisions comprise the primary employers of paralegals. But other businesses, like real estate agencies, professional sports teams, and public utility companies, also need employees who know about law.

REMEMBER

Flexibility and persistence go a long way in shaping your future and solidifying your success. So, if you don't find your dream job in a traditional law office, dream a little differently.

Paralegal jobs are plentiful, but you have to know where to look for them. To help you in your search, this section provides you with some of the common and uncommon resources for finding a paralegal position. Our information isn't exhaustive, however — you may come up with a career source we haven't even heard of!

Traditional sources: Scanning the job boards and turning to placement services

Traditional job hunt resources include job boards, placement services, and bar association referral services.

The Internet provides one of the most prolific job lead sources you can find: online job boards. Enter pertinent information, and the search engine comes back with a list of prospects and contact information. Often, you can get the ball rolling by submitting your cover letter and resume by email to the employers who have posted job listings.

A couple of the most popular job search sites are Monster (`www.monster.com`) and Indeed.com (`www.indeed.com`). Law-specific board appear on `www.findlaw.com` and the American Bar Association website (`https://jobs.americanbar.org`). Many more sites are out there — just search "paralegal jobs" in your favorite search engine.

These sites give you the advantage of narrowing your search by field and location and may give you job leads in areas you haven't even considered. Usually, the bigger the search engine the better because you'll have more positions to choose from. And, if you're footloose and fancy free, you can check out possibilities in different cities and states.

REMEMBER

Check out the online content for this book to find links to and information about the most popular online employment search engines.

When you're searching the job boards, be creative; sometimes employers don't know they're looking for a paralegal, but you can help them see that that's just what they need. So, in addition to looking for a position in the "Paralegal" category, check out listings in the "Legal Assistant," "Law Office," "Administrative Assistant," and even "Legal Secretary" categories as well. Often working as a legal secretary for one or two attorneys becomes a paralegal position as your employers grow to trust you with increased responsibilities.

A placement service is another good traditional source for paralegal positions. Legal staffing agencies — like Gibson Arnold & Associates (www.gibsonarnold.com) and Colman Nourian (www.cnlegalsearch.com.com) — specialize in the legal field and usually don't charge fees to the job hunter. Some staffing agencies offer temporary positions, which provide great opportunities for you to develop experience in several different areas of law and legal environments without committing to a permanent position. Placement offices in your local colleges and universities (especially those that offer paralegal programs) may advertise paralegal positions particularly for first-time job seekers. And, most state and local bar associations provide job referral services for paralegals and may include job listings in their newsletters.

When you're looking for a job, be sure to work every angle — don't try just one or two methods.

Networking: It's who you know

The old saying that it's not what you know but who you know holds for the legal profession. Participating in state and local paralegal association meetings and enrolling in continuing legal education and paralegal courses are excellent ways to meet working paralegals and attorneys who may know of job openings in their offices. Most paralegal positions are filled by word of mouth before an employer even thinks of advertising, so associating with people who may be aware of available jobs is a good idea. And, you'll get the added benefit of meeting people with common interests and learning more about your profession.

Just in case you do hear of an opening, whenever you're attending a meeting or getting together with legal professionals, be sure to bring at least 50 copies of your resume and your freelance rate sheet. (See "Ravishing resumes" and "Setting Up Shop: Starting a Freelance Paralegal Business," later in this chapter, for more on how to prepare these tools.)

TIP

Compiling lists of local firms and agencies can reveal potential job sources for a burgeoning paralegal career. Start by creating a list of websites, phone numbers, email addresses, physical addresses, and names of personnel managers for local law firms, banks, insurance claims offices, real estate firms, and state and federal agencies. Then use this list to make at least five to ten calls a day to inquire about openings and arrange for interviews. After you contact a firm, mark the date of contact on the list and record its result.

REMEMBER

The key to this technique is patience and diligence. The time and effort you put in will eventually pay off.

Creating the Documentation

After you have your job leads, you'll need to introduce yourself. The customary way of letting people know just how great you are is through a well-written cover letter and resume. Supplement this introduction by creating an engaging LinkedIn profile. And, to prove to potential employers that you have what it takes to prepare legal documents, include a sample of a memoranda of law you've written (we show you how to draft one in Chapter 10).

TIP

Entire books are devoted to the subject of cover letters and resumes, so for even more information, check out the latest editions of *Resumes For Dummies* and *Cover Letters For Dummies*, both by Joyce Lain Kennedy, and *The Resume Kit* by Richard H. Beatty (all published by John Wiley & Sons, Inc.).

Killer cover letters

Often, the first contact you have with a potential employer is through the cover letter you send along with your resume. Paralegals usually work in fairly conservative settings and hold positions of great responsibility. So, your cover letter should reflect a conservative and dignified tone and obviously be mistake-free. Because most paralegal positions involve a lot of writing, you can bet that potential employers are checking out your writing style.

REMEMBER

Figure 3-1 gives you an example of a professional cover letter. You can find a copy of this cover letter online.

Kelley Konscientious
444 Windy Blvd.
Chicago, IL 00000
(555) 555-5555

August 11, 20__

Ms. Mary Garza
Baker, Garza and Johnson
1201 Main St., Suite 700
Chicago, IL 00000

Dear Ms. Garza:

Mr. Timothy Gibson, J.D., has informed me that you are seeking a paralegal to assist you with legal research, document drafting, client interviewing, and other duties related to personal injury litigation. I am confident that I possess the qualifications necessary to fill that position.

As outlined on the enclosed resume, I have recently completed the Paralegal Certificate Course offered by Chicago State University, through which I acquired the skills necessary to efficiently assist an attorney during the litigation process. Because of my communications background, I am especially proficient in legal writing, document drafting, and client relations. I welcome the challenge of legal research, and I am pleased with the results of my diligence in the law library. Samples of interoffice memoranda of law I composed during the course demonstrate my research and writing abilities. Interacting with the students I teach at Beales Business College has given me a broad insight into the delicacies of relating to different personalities, experience that will translate well in my associations with your clients. I realize that success in law is dependent upon adhering to strict deadlines, and my experiences as a newspaper editor and an adult education instructor have provided me with the discipline and organization essential to meeting deadlines.

I am eager to meet with you so that I may share my writing samples and discuss the possibility of assisting you. Thank you for the time that you have spent in considering me for the paralegal position in your office.

Very truly yours,

Kelly Konscientious

FIGURE 3-1:
A sample
cover letter.

Enclosure

TIP

You can get helpful tips for improving your writing style in Chapter 16. Here are some other things you can do to make sure your cover letter catches an employer's attention:

>> **Adopt a friendly but professional tone.**

>> **Let the employer know how you heard about the position.** If you were referred by a mutual acquaintance, name-drop.

>> **Demonstrate that you know what the responsibilities of the position will be.** Write just enough about yourself to give the employer a good idea of who you are in a quick sweep of the letter.

>> **Describe in detail the specific qualities you have that make you the ideal person to meet those responsibilities.** Present yourself confidently to the employer. Personalize the letter to demonstrate that you've done a little research about the potential employer and the position it has available.

>> **Thank the employer for taking the time to consider your application.**

>> **Have a friend proofread your letter before you send it.** The letter should look neat, balanced, well-organized, and error-free. Employers may toss sloppy looking letters and the resumes that come with them without ever reading them.

Ravishing resumes

You introduce yourself with a cover letter, but what really interests the employer is your resume.

TIP

Supply the most current and specific resume possible. A potential employer for a paralegal position doesn't want to see the resume you used to try to get a position as a circus ringleader (although at times the two positions do resemble each other). Your resume should include your

>> **Career objective:** State your career objective briefly and specifically. Avoid phrases like "To find a career where I can use my talents and grow mentally and emotionally," which focus on you and say nothing about the job at hand. Ideally, you should change the objective to match each job you apply for. But if that's too time-consuming, opt for one as specific as possible, something like "To secure a position in a law office where I can offer my research and communication skills."

>> **Work experience:** List your work experience in reverse chronological order, starting with the most recent position you've held. If you're young and have held only a few positions, list all your work experiences. If you're considering a career change after a few decades in the workforce, focus your list to your most recent and most relevant experience. Potential employers probably don't care that you moonlighted during the summer of your senior year digging for earthworms for the local bait shop.

Describe your work experience and skills with illustrative action verbs. If you have limited work experience, use your resume to highlight your related skills and education.

TIP

Consider getting involved in a paralegal internship to see how a law practice operates and to show prospective employers that you have experienced the law firsthand.

>> **Special skills:** Highlight skills you've acquired that pertain to a paralegal career. You may have developed an affinity for research, client relations, organization, or administration while working in unrelated fields. Perhaps you're especially gifted with understanding computers and related technology. These skills are especially suited to a paralegal position, so show them off in your resume, like the example in Figure 3-2 of a resume that highlights skills.

>> **Education:** List your education in reverse chronological order, starting with the degree or education you received most recently. If you haven't had a lot of related education, your resume should highlight your relevant experience. You may need to enroll in some paralegal courses to round out your resume.

>> **Honors and distinctions:** List distinctions you've received for achievements related to the work environment, such as your membership in the Phi Beta Kappa honor society or your nomination for corporate employee of the year. Don't include the third place ribbon you won in the fifth-grade science fair for your exploding volcano or the honorable mention you received in the national refrigerated-dough bakeoff recipe contest.

>> **References:** Many job seekers don't list references on their resumes because the list increases the number of pages of your resume. But potential employers want to check references, so if you don't include references at the end of your resume, make a list (on a separate sheet of paper) of several past employers and personal references who can vouch for you, and take that list with you to the interview. Employers often check your references right after your interview, and what they learn can either make or break your chances for getting hired. Your reference list should include addresses, phone numbers, and email addresses.

Kelly Konscienctious
444 Windy Boulevard
Chicago, IL 00000
kellykonscienctious@emailaddress.com
(555) 555-5555

CAREER OBJECTIVE:

To secure a position in a law office that utilizes my communication, research, and organizational skills.

EDUCATION:

07/20__   Chicago State University, Paralegal Certificate Course

05/19__   University of Colorado, Boulder, CO
B.A. English, Top 1/3, GPA 3.5

COMMUNICATION SKILLS:

Teach writing and grammar skills to adults attending a two-year business program. Conducted community writing seminars on weekends and established a successful tutorial program and writing lab for a business school.

Edited and managed *The Voice*, the University of Colorado's college newspaper, which was awarded first place in the 1998 and 1999 Press Association's college newspaper competition and first place in the National Collegiate Association's 1999 student newspaper competition.

Edited business correspondence for errors in vocabulary, spelling, diction, and usage.

RESEARCH SKILLS:

Researched the law as it related to the preparation of draft leases and other legal documents for an office management company.

ORGANIZATIONAL SKILLS:

Organized curricula for writing seminars. Set up and managed a writing lab for adults.

Managed all the functions of an office management company. Proficient in typing (75 wpm), filing, word and data processing (WordPerfect and Microsoft Word, Lotus 123, and DBase).

EMPLOYMENT:

9/19__ –present   Business Writing Instructor, Beales Business College, Chicago, IL
5/20__–7/20__   Administrative Assistant, Office Management Company, Inc., Chicago, IL
9/19__–5/20__   Editor, *The Voice*, University of Colorado's student newspaper

DISTINCTIONS:

Distinguished Student Member of the Colorado Press Club, Denver, CO
National Honor Society, University of Colorado, 19__, 19__, and 19__

WRITING SAMPLES AND REFERENCES ATTACHED

FIGURE 3-2:
Sample resume that highlights skills over law office experience.

Although employers generally prefer one-page resumes, don't be afraid to use two pages if you need that much space to highlight your skills. (A law school dean we once hired needed 26 pages to convey the most remarkable highlights of his law career!)

REMEMBER

We provide you with a copy of the resume in Figure 3-2 and another sample resume online. The other resume emphasizes employment for someone who has more law-related experience than education.

Developing an online profile

After you assemble your work history and skills, you can broadcast your qualifications online. Creating a LinkedIn profile potentially increases your network and introduces you to prospective employers. Business cards are often lost, but an online presence is perpetually available. Here are tips for setting up an effective profile:

>> **Personalize your profile with pictures.** Upload a clear headshot photo for the front picture and a background picture that conveys your personality or career goals, for instance, a shelf of law books.

>> **Use key words in your headline.** State your position clearly. The headline isn't the place to show off your creativity. If you present yourself as a "Legal Document Engineer," you won't appear in searches for paralegals.

>> **Create a personalized Profile URL.** LinkedIn allows you to change your URL from a list of arbitrary numbers to a unique designation. Include your name and title. If you have a common first and last name, distinguish yourself with a middle name or more specific title, for example, www.linkedin.com/in/ chris-middleton-smith-paralegal. You can include this URL on your business cards and email signatures.

>> **Write a thoughtful summary.** Within the introduction, you have the opportunity to define yourself and your skills. Show off your writing skills and produce three or four paragraphs to describe your overall personality and qualifications. Your summary is searchable, so include key search terms in your carefully crafted sentences.

>> **Expand your resume.** The Experience and Education sections allow you to provide detail about your prior positions that may not fit in a standard one-page resume. Highlight skills, personal attributes, and specific coursework that apply to a legal career.

» **Add media.** LinkedIn gives you the ability to add photos, videos, presentations, and websites to your introduction, experience, and education details. Go ahead and upload that presentation video of you during your local paralegal association meeting or photos of you shaking hands with the governor.

» **List all applicable skills.** The Skills & Endorsements section allows you to list everything you're good at. Start with as many as apply. Endorse the skills of other members you know, and they'll likely endorse yours.

» **Seek recommenders.** Ask former co-workers and bosses (if appropriate) to write a quick recommendation on your profile. Reciprocate by recommending them.

» **Network.** Search for groups that interest you. You can join general paralegal networks and groups that address more specific fields. Follow paralegal-related organization, such as NALA, NFPA, and the ABA. Read posts to stay in touch with current issues and add your own posts in your areas of expertise.

Regularly update your profile and add posts to forums to keep your profile front and center. Your initial goal may be to secure employment, but LinkedIn supplies a wealth of information and contacts after you're employed.

Setting Up Shop: Starting a Freelance Paralegal Business

You may be one of the many paralegals who enjoy the freedom of self-employment. Instead of being an employee of one legal entity, most freelance paralegals contract their services to several different law firms or attorneys. This situation benefits both the attorney and the paralegal: National studies indicate that freelance paralegals earn significantly more than other paralegal professionals, and attorneys that contract with a paralegal get the convenience of quality paralegal services without having to commit to or pay benefits to a new employee. Some states license independent contractors to prepare documents for clients. If you meet the state requirements, you can set up shop to do limited legal work without the supervision of an attorney. Working as an independent contractor gives the freedom to set your own hours and work from your own home or office. You can actually prepare briefs in your briefs!

Going freelance sounds great, but there are a few things you have to consider before going into business for yourself. You must be willing to accept the financial responsibility of self-employment. As with any new business, you need to have enough money to set up your business and keep it running until you've built up a large client base and the money is steadily flowing in. You're responsible for your own office supplies and equipment, health insurance, and Social Security taxes. To keep Uncle Sam happy, you need to engage in careful bookkeeping (or hire someone else to do it) and you need to pay quarterly estimated federal and state (if applicable) income taxes. You're also responsible for maintaining liability insurance, which is relatively inexpensive but very important for practicing freelance paralegals.

If you've already worked in law firms or the court system, you probably have contacts for potential clients, and you can also compile a client base by taking advantage of the resources we discuss earlier in "Finding the Perfect Job." Set up a LinkedIn profile to network (see "Developing an online profile"). After you create a personal profile, you can add a page for your paralegal business where you can present photos, lists of services, and samples of your work.

Before you approach a prospective client, create a freelance rate sheet that explains the types of services you provide and the hourly cost for each service. Your new businesses should start by charging a comparatively low hourly rate, such as $35 to $45 per hour, depending on what part of the country you live in. As your business grows and you become more experienced, you may charge as much as $75 or more per hour, depending on factors like what your specialty is, the size of your community, and what type of work you perform. You can find a sample freelance rate sheet online.

Print up some business cards and stationery to give yourself a professional image. Your business cards and letterhead must clearly state that you're a paralegal and not an attorney.

A great resource if you're considering life as a freelancer is *Freelancing For Dummies* by Susan M. Drake (John Wiley & Sons, Inc.).

2

Important Legal Concepts Every Paralegal Should Know

Harken back to your high school U.S. History course to review the American system of checks and balances, the hierarchy of U.S. judicial systems, and the concept of the jury system.

Discern the similarities and differences between the practice of administrative, criminal, and civil law.

Walk through the steps of taking criminal and civil courses through the litigation process.

Follow the proper system of legal procedure and know the rules regarding securing and preserving evidence.

Distinguish between primary and secondary legal authority as you build a client's case built on statutes and prior case law.

Explore specific areas of law and find out what roles paralegal play in each.

legal precedence

» Reviewing the three branches of the U.S. system of government

» Identifying the various forms and levels of government and their courts

» Grasping the important differences between trial by judge and trial by jury

Chapter **4**

"All Rise": The American Judicial System

The study and practice of paralegalism is exciting because the law reflects society's changing modes of conduct. So, the law has to be flexible and evolve with society. Despite its flexibility, however, the law has specific theoretical and historical origins, and before studying paralegalism, it's good to know the theoretical and historical context from which the U.S. legal system has evolved.

TECHNICAL STUFF

Law has two main interpretations: One is based on the concept of *natural* (or God-made) law, and the other is a *secular* (or nonreligious) interpretation. The more ancient of the two interpretations is Aristotle's cosmic law theory. Aristotle believed that there was a law inherent in the universe that was more important than the laws made by people. In contrast, the more recent secular, or common law, theory holds that law develops from the history of a nation and that legal experts only interpret the historical drift of a nation.

TIP

Although there are two fundamental bases of the law, U.S. society is most firmly grounded in the secular, or common, law. This law is the kind that's created by court decisions, which we discuss in more detail in the following section.

To become a good paralegal and understand the basis of your daily responsibilities, you need to be familiar with these background concepts of the U.S. legal system.

Spend a little time getting acquainted with the configuration of the U.S. government, the different levels and types of its courts, and the way these courts are set up.

Everything Old Is New Again: The Importance of Legal Precedence

Law is relatively easy to study and understand, because most of the issues that crop up in court every day have been decided in previous trials. U.S. law didn't materialize overnight. Our legal system has been around for a long time, but it's also constantly evolving. The U.S. system of justice is based upon the doctrine of *stare decisis* (pronounced *stare*-y di-*sigh*-sis), which means that past court decisions (known as *precedent*) largely determine the outcome of future cases. As long as the facts and issues of a precedent case are pretty much the same as those of the current case, and as long as the court that *rendered* (made) the decision in the precedent case is within the same system as and higher than the present court, the present court must adhere to the decision of the precedent case as authority in rendering its decision. (Say *that* ten times fast.)

In other words, say the U.S. Supreme Court says that police have to advise suspects of their rights whenever the suspects are taken into custody. The doctrine of stare decisis says that this rule will be followed in any other court that considers the same issue in a criminal case. That's because all other courts in the United States, whether state courts or federal courts, are lower than the Supreme Court. They essentially have to rule as the Supreme Court did.

TIP

The notion of stare decisis means that a court will follow prior precedent and decide similar cases the same way unless there is a good reason for the court to reject that prior legal precedent.

Stare decisis consists of statutory law and prior case decisions and provides paralegals, attorneys, and judges with security, certainty, and predictability in researching the law. The paralegal's goal is to find the most applicable case precedent (case law) and statutes, integrate that authority into a memorandum of law (a *brief*), and present that memo or brief to the supervising attorney. (For more on a paralegal's duties in the trial process, check out Chapter 14.) The attorney then argues the applicability of that particular stare decisis to the court.

The vast majority of cases that you'll research are based upon facts and issues that have already been decided. Public policy has already been set. However, as society's modes of conduct change, so do laws. So, there are times when you'll find very little, or no, stare decisis for a case because of the uniqueness of that case's facts and issues.

For example, as of the early 1950s, the law in 17 states and the District of Columbia allowed racial segregation in school facilities. Among the precedent cases interpreted to permit segregation was *Plessy v. Ferguson*, where the U.S. Supreme Court upheld a Louisiana statute that provided that "separate but equal" accommodations in railroad cars was constitutional. The stare decisis at that time favored segregation, and there was no precedent favoring school integration.

When Thurgood Marshall and the National Association for the Advancement of Colored People (NAACP) argued to the Supreme Court in 1952 that the separate but equal doctrine was unconstitutional, they had very little legal precedent to support their position and had to rely on sociological and psychological data to advance the cause of integration. On May 17, 1954, the U.S. Supreme Court rendered its decision in the watershed case of *Brown v. Board of Education*, where the Court held that the separate but equal doctrine had no place in public education and that separate but equal educational facilities were inherently dissimilar. New evidence won out over past judicial precedent.

Although the vast majority of cases are rooted in stare decisis, a few occasions arise when precedent is nonexistent. A *case of first impression* is one where there is no prior precedent or stare decisis to guide the court in its decision making. In these cases, the courts really have to scratch their collective heads to come up with what the law should be. Courts often resolve cases of first impression on the basis of nonlegal traditions, which consequently forms the foundation for future precedent.

TECHNICAL STUFF

The evolution of the law of comparative negligence is just one example where the courts have learned to feel their way to what the law should be. Prior to the latter half of the 20th century, if the defendant wrongdoer was 99 percent at fault and an injured party was only partially negligent — even only a mere 1 percent — the injured party could not recover any money damages due to her own contributory negligence. Over time, the courts viewed the concept of contributory negligence as an extremely harsh outcome. So, the courts fashioned a remedy for the party who was partially negligent and dubbed the concept *comparative negligence.* Now, instead of being completely barred from recovering damages from the defendant under the old doctrine of contributory negligence, the partially negligent party could have her money damages reduced by only her proportionate share of fault. (You can find out a lot more about negligence in Chapter 5.)

Checks and Balances: Branches of U.S. Government

REMEMBER

To understand the U.S. legal process, you need to know about the structure of the U.S. government. As you probably learned in high school U.S. history class, the United States operates under three branches of government:

>> **Legislative branch:** The legislative branch makes the laws.

>> **Executive branch:** The executive branch enforces the laws.

>> **Judicial branch:** The judicial branch interprets the laws.

Each of these branches has its own function, and each branch of government provides checks and balances on the other branches so that no one branch of government becomes too powerful. The country's Founding Fathers feared the power of the kings of Europe and even the Parliament's stranglehold over England. As a result, no single branch of government in the United States can control the country without running up against another branch.

The three branches of government show up in the federal (national) government and in state governments. Dividing power between the federal government and the state governments is known as *federalism.* The national and state governments all have their own forms of legal *sovereignty* (or power) over what happens in society. For example, only the federal government has the power to mint money or declare war. States, on the other hand, regulate such things as driver's licenses, car registrations, marriages, and divorces. And both the national and state governments have authority over criminal conduct. States can outlaw crimes that occur within their borders, while the federal government can prosecute these same crimes that cross state boundaries (that is, if the crime affects interstate commerce).

Figure 4-1 shows a complete listing of all three branches of the federal government, including the major administrative agencies. As you can see, administrative bodies tend to get lumped under the executive branch, which is by far the most widespread and bureaucratic of the three branches.

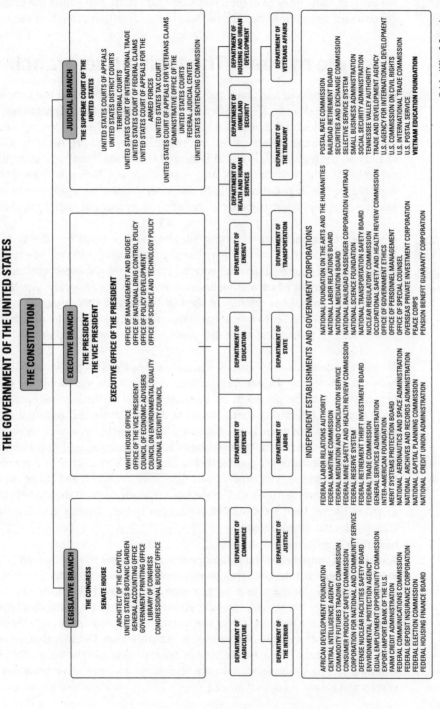

THE GOVERNMENT OF THE UNITED STATES

THE CONSTITUTION

LEGISLATIVE BRANCH

THE CONGRESS

SENATE HOUSE

ARCHITECT OF THE CAPITOL
UNITED STATES BOTANIC GARDEN
GENERAL ACCOUNTING OFFICE
GOVERNMENT PRINTING OFFICE
LIBRARY OF CONGRESS
CONGRESSIONAL BUDGET OFFICE

EXECUTIVE BRANCH

THE PRESIDENT
THE VICE PRESIDENT

EXECUTIVE OFFICE OF THE PRESIDENT

WHITE HOUSE OFFICE
OFFICE OF THE VICE PRESIDENT
COUNCIL OF ECONOMIC ADVISERS
COUNCIL ON ENVIRONMENTAL QUALITY
NATIONAL SECURITY COUNCIL

OFFICE OF MANAGEMENT AND BUDGET
OFFICE OF NATIONAL DRUG CONTROL POLICY
OFFICE OF POLICY DEVELOPMENT
OFFICE OF SCIENCE AND TECHNOLOGY POLICY

JUDICIAL BRANCH

THE SUPREME COURT OF THE UNITED STATES

UNITED STATES COURTS OF APPEALS
UNITED STATES DISTRICT COURTS
TERRITORIAL COURTS
UNITED STATES COURT OF INTERNATIONAL TRADE
UNITED STATES COURT OF FEDERAL CLAIMS
UNITED STATES COURT OF APPEALS FOR THE ARMED FORCES
UNITED STATES TAX COURT
UNITED STATES COURT OF APPEALS FOR VETERANS CLAIMS
ADMINISTRATIVE OFFICE OF THE UNITED STATES COURTS
FEDERAL JUDICIAL CENTER
UNITED STATES SENTENCING COMMISSION

DEPARTMENT OF AGRICULTURE

DEPARTMENT OF COMMERCE

DEPARTMENT OF DEFENSE

DEPARTMENT OF EDUCATION

DEPARTMENT OF ENERGY

DEPARTMENT OF HEALTH AND HUMAN SERVICES

DEPARTMENT OF HOUSING AND URBAN DEVELOPMENT

DEPARTMENT OF THE INTERIOR

DEPARTMENT OF JUSTICE

DEPARTMENT OF LABOR

DEPARTMENT OF STATE

DEPARTMENT OF TRANSPORTATION

DEPARTMENT OF THE TREASURY

DEPARTMENT OF HOMELAND SECURITY

DEPARTMENT OF VETERANS AFFAIRS

INDEPENDENT ESTABLISHMENTS AND GOVERNMENT CORPORATIONS

AFRICAN DEVELOPMENT FOUNDATION
CENTRAL INTELLIGENCE AGENCY
COMMODITY FUTURES TRADING COMMISSION
CONSUMER PRODUCT SAFETY COMMISSION
CORPORATION FOR NATIONAL AND COMMUNITY SERVICE
DEFENSE NUCLEAR FACILITIES SAFETY BOARD
ENVIRONMENTAL PROTECTION AGENCY
EQUAL EMPLOYMENT OPPORTUNITY COMMISSION
EXPORT-IMPORT BANK OF THE U.S.
FARM CREDIT ADMINISTRATION
FEDERAL COMMUNICATIONS COMMISSION
FEDERAL DEPOSIT INSURANCE CORPORATION
FEDERAL ELECTION COMMISSION
FEDERAL HOUSING FINANCE BOARD

FEDERAL LABOR RELATIONS AUTHORITY
FEDERAL MARITIME COMMISSION
FEDERAL MEDIATION AND CONCILIATION SERVICE
FEDERAL MINE SAFETY AND HEALTH REVIEW COMMISSION
FEDERAL RESERVE SYSTEM
FEDERAL RETIREMENT THRIFT INVESTMENT BOARD
FEDERAL TRADE COMMISSION
GENERAL SERVICES ADMINISTRATION
INTER-AMERICAN FOUNDATION
MERIT SYSTEMS PROTECTION BOARD
NATIONAL AERONAUTICS AND SPACE ADMINISTRATION
NATIONAL ARCHIVES AND RECORDS ADMINISTRATION
NATIONAL CAPITAL PLANNING COMMISSION
NATIONAL CREDIT UNION ADMINISTRATION

NATIONAL FOUNDATION ON THE ARTS AND THE HUMANITIES
NATIONAL LABOR RELATIONS BOARD
NATIONAL MEDIATION BOARD
NATIONAL RAILROAD PASSENGER CORPORATION (AMTRAK)
NATIONAL SCIENCE FOUNDATION
NATIONAL TRANSPORTATION SAFETY BOARD
NUCLEAR REGULATORY COMMISSION
OCCUPATIONAL SAFETY AND HEALTH REVIEW COMMISSION
OFFICE OF GOVERNMENT ETHICS
OFFICE OF PERSONNEL MANAGEMENT
OFFICE OF SPECIAL COUNSEL
OVERSEAS PRIVATE INVESTMENT CORPORATION
PEACE CORPS
PENSION BENEFIT GUARANTY CORPORATION

POSTAL RATE COMMISSION
RAILROAD RETIREMENT BOARD
SECURITIES AND EXCHANGE COMMISSION
SELECTIVE SERVICE SYSTEM
SMALL BUSINESS ADMINISTRATION
SOCIAL SECURITY ADMINISTRATION
TENNESSEE VALLEY AUTHORITY
TRADE AND DEVELOPMENT AGENCY
U.S. AGENCY FOR INTERNATIONAL DEVELOPMENT
U.S. COMMISSION ON CIVIL RIGHTS
U.S. INTERNATIONAL TRADE COMMISSION
U.S. POSTAL SERVICE
VIETNAM EDUCATION FOUNDATION

© *John Wiley & Sons, Inc.*

FIGURE 4-1: Branches of the federal government.

We provide some links to helpful websites that clarify and define the branches of government and their duties at www.dummies.com/go/paralegalcareer2e.

The rule makers: The legislative branch

At the federal or national level, the legislative branch is called the *Congress.* It's made up of two chambers — the Senate and the House of Representatives. Sometimes, members of the House of Representatives are called *congresspersons,* while members of the Senate are called, not surprisingly, *senators.* Because it has two chambers, the legislature is called *bicameral* (*bi* means "two" and *camera* means "chamber"). The U.S. Congress and every state but Nebraska have bicameral legislatures. The legislatures at both the federal and state levels create *statutory law,* the rules and regulations we all have to follow to avoid liability or arrest.

A *statute* isn't some giant structure standing with a torch on Liberty Island in New York Harbor. It's a law that is written by the legislative branch of government. So be careful in your legal writing because lawyers and paralegals commonly refer to *statutes* as *statues* when writing briefs that refer to statutory law. Another common spelling mistake is mixing up the words *trial* and *trail.* Although a trial is a journey, you can't refer to it as a trail. Your spell checker won't catch these mistakes, either. (You can find more tips about legal writing in Chapter 16.)

To enact a statute, the bicameral legislature must pass a proposed bill through both the House and the Senate and then send it to be signed by the executive branch, which is the president on the federal level or the governor on the state level. Getting a bill through both houses of the legislature and getting it signed by the president or governor is a lot of work! The bill gets introduced in each house and is referred to a committee that considers its particular subject matter. If it's a bill that has to do with the courts, then it likely gets sent to the judiciary committee in each chamber. The committee might hold hearings, and if the committee chair or the committee doesn't like the bill, it can die there. If the bill gets changed in either house, then a conference committee in both houses gets together and tries to iron out any differences.

After the bill passes out of both chambers in substantially the same form, the chief executive signs it into law. This means that the president signs those bills that come out of the Congress, and the governor signs those bills enacted by the state legislature. After it's signed, the bill becomes statutory law. If the chief executive vetoes the bill, the bill dies unless the legislature can muster enough votes to get a *supermajority* to override the executive branch's veto. Usually, that means that two-thirds of each house has to vote in favor to override the veto. (This kind of situation is one example of how the legislative and executive branches act as checks and balances on each other.)

The Founding Fathers designed the three branches to keep government power in check. The legislature votes to pass a bill, which is then either signed or vetoed by the executive. The legislature may then override the executive's veto. In this way, the legislative and executive branches keep each other in line.

A statute is sometimes called an *act,* such as the Freedom of Information Act or the Federal Communications Act. Given all the hassle that's required to enact legislation, the expression that "It's going to take an act of Congress to get that done" makes a lot of sense. Enacting even simple legislation is, in many cases, an uphill battle.

The state legislatures follow pretty much the same procedure the federal government does when enacting legislation. You can find a super-simple illustration of how a typical bill becomes law at www.usa.gov/how-laws-are-made.

The enforcers: The executive branch

In addition to signing bills into law, the executive branch also enforces the laws enacted by the legislature. The president or the state governor obviously can't accomplish the task of enforcement alone. Consequently, the legislature has created a multitude of administrative agencies that are empowered to assist the chief executive in the role of enforcing and administering the laws created by the legislature.

You may have heard the term *alphabet soup* to refer to the names of administrative agencies (for example, HUD, EPA, DEA, CIA). Administrative agencies exist on the federal, state, and local levels of government. They're often referred to collectively as the *bureaucracy.* Examples of state agencies are the Transportation Department that builds state highways and the Department of Licensing that provides licenses for your car as well as your doctor (the names of these agencies vary from state to state). Some common examples of local administrative agencies are your community's fire department, the city police department, and the county sheriff's office.

Administrative agencies also have some legislative power, and they can create the law in certain instances. Often, the statute that creates these agencies and empowers them to enforce laws also enables the agencies to regulate the public. Agencies exert their control through the process of administrative *rulemaking,* and the laws these agencies write are called *administrative regulations.* For example, the IRS was created to implement the tax code. If Larry has a problem with his federal income taxes, he contacts the IRS. Larry can appeal his case in the court system only after the IRS renders an administrative determination about Larry's problem. He would have to exhaust administrative remedies before he could take his case to federal court.

Administrative agencies may even act like courts when they engage in *quasijudicial* proceedings known as *adjudicatory hearings.* In adjudicatory hearings, the agencies make decisions that affect the rights of individuals, much like a court of law.

(You can find more information about administrative agencies and administrative law in Chapter 5.)

The interpreters: The judicial branch

The court system stems from the third branch of government, the judicial branch. The duty of the judicial branch is to interpret the laws that the other two branches of government create and enforce. When courts interpret the statutes enacted by the legislature, it's sometimes said that the courts actually make law. This judge-made law appears in the form of judicial opinions.

As intended by our founders, the judicial branch acts as a check and balance on the other two branches of government. One example of the judiciary's power over the legislature occurs when a court declares a statute unconstitutional. The statute then has to be thrown out and becomes unenforceable. But don't feel too sorry for the legislature — it can place a check on the courts by enacting a statute that says that courts don't have the authority to hear specific types of cases. Courts may not be completely stripped of their judicial authority, but their *jurisdiction* (their power and authority to hear a particular type of case) can be narrowed to a significant degree. Historically, Congress has tried to find ways to narrow the jurisdiction of the federal courts in this manner. One recent example involves proposals to strip federal courts of their ability to decide cases dealing with abortion. The president can also act as a check and balance on the courts by refusing to enforce the court's orders.

Because most paralegals deal with the judicial branch more than the other two branches, you should become very familiar with the structure of the U.S. court system.

Playing Fair: Levels of the U.S. Judicial System

Each of the three branches exists in the three levels of U.S. government. Each of the levels of government — federal, state, and local — has an executive branch, a legislative branch, and a judicial branch. As a paralegal, you'll be working primarily within the judicial branch.

The United States employs a unique blend of federal, state, and local court systems to get its judicial work done. Each court system is a separate entity, but they work together to form the case law that attorneys and paralegals rely on to develop their cases. Depending on your area of practice or interest, one level of courts may be more relevant to you than another.

The federal judicial system

The types of cases that may be heard in the federal court are limited. They must meet *one* of these qualifications:

» **Controversies that involve the U.S. government, the U.S. Constitution, or federal laws:** This is called the *federal question* jurisdiction.

» **Disputes between two different states or between the United States and a foreign government.**

» **Cases that involve *diversity of citizenship* of the litigants:** Diversity of citizenship means that the disputes are either between parties from different states or between a party from the United States and someone from a foreign country, and the amount of damages must exceed the amount set forth in federal statutes.

» **Matters that involve bankruptcy.**

If you work with the federal court system, you'll deal with three levels of adjudication: the courts of original jurisdiction, the courts of appellate jurisdiction, and the courts of last resort. Federal cases originate in the U.S. District Courts.

In the beginning: Courts of original jurisdiction

The U.S. District Courts comprise the federal courts of original jurisdiction. These courts are geographically situated throughout the country, in Washington, D.C., and in the territories of the Northern Mariana Islands, Puerto Rico, Guam, and the Virgin Islands. There's at least one federal district court in every state and territory of the United States. Federal district courts have a large caseload because they happen to be located where a significant amount of federal litigation begins. The U.S. Constitution requires that federal judges be appointed for life and that their pay can't be reduced while they're in office. This is just one more check and balance against the president and Congress so that federal courts can't be completely stripped of their authority.

TIP

Every state, U.S. territory, and the District of Columbia includes at least one U.S. district court. These courts are the basic units of trial courts, or courts of original jurisdiction, in the federal court system.

Federal litigation that doesn't begin in the U.S. District Courts originates in the specialized courts of original jurisdiction: the U.S. Court of International Trade, the U.S. Tax Court, the U.S. Bankruptcy Court, and the U.S. Court of Claims. Because these courts are highly specialized, you'll find that, depending on your area of practice, you'll either spend almost all your time working with one of these types of courts or you'll spend none of your time there. If you choose to specialize and become an expert in federal court matters, you'll need to gain a thorough understanding of federal court jurisdiction and other federal matters. (We explain how to research federal court matters in Chapter 13.)

The U.S. Supreme Court, affectionately known as "the highest court in the land," also has original jurisdiction in all cases involving ambassadors, consuls, and public ministers and in all cases where a state is a party. The Supreme Court must have original jurisdiction in those cases where one state sues another state, like the late-1990s dispute between New York and New Jersey (see the nearby sidebar, "*New Jersey v. New York:* Who's got the dirt on Ellis Island?").

NEW JERSEY V. NEW YORK: WHO'S GOT THE DIRT ON ELLIS ISLAND?

In 1834, the state of New York entered into an agreement with the state of New Jersey. That interstate compact determined that New York owned Ellis Island as it currently existed, while New Jersey retained sovereign rights over the submerged lands on the New Jersey side of the island.

Ellis Island was the receiving house for immigrants during the late 1800s and the first half of the 20th century. During that time, in order to manage the growing immigration enterprise, the federal government increased the size of Ellis Island by filling in an extra 24.5 acres of land on the shoreline toward New Jersey's side. In 1954, after the U.S. government no longer used Ellis Island for immigration purposes, the two states disputed the ownership of the additional 24.5 acres of land.

Finally in 1993, New Jersey filed a lawsuit against New York for ownership of the extra land. Where do you think the case was filed? If you guessed the U.S. Supreme Court, you'd be absolutely right. The Supreme Court has exclusive original jurisdiction over disputes between two states. The case didn't involve simply enforcing a contract between two states. The interstate *compact* (or agreement) between New York and New Jersey was ratified by the Congress, and as such it became a law of the United States, just as if it were a treaty between the United States and a foreign country.

Five years later, in the case captioned *New Jersey v. New York,* the Supreme Court sided with New Jersey, relying on the plain language of the interstate compact as well as the common law doctrine of avulsion. As you can imagine, the fees for attorneys and paralegals probably cost more than the land was worth!

Very appealing: Courts of appellate jurisdiction

If you don't like the result of your trial in the U.S. District Courts or one of the many specialized courts, you can appeal your case to the U.S. Courts of Appeals, which is comprised of 13 units of jurisdiction called *circuits*. Circuits 1 through 11 are numbered and regionally arranged; the other two circuits are the D.C. Circuit and the Federal Circuit, both located in the nation's capital. The first appeal from the U.S. District Courts is heard at the circuit court (or U.S. Courts of Appeals) level.

REMEMBER

The 13 circuits of the U.S. Courts of Appeals, with some specific exceptions, generally hear appeals from the district courts within their geographic area. Each circuit hears appeals that originate within the geographic confines of its borders. In the online content, you can find a map illustrating the geographic location of the various districts and circuits of the U.S. federal court system. Appeals from the U.S. Court of Claims or the U.S. Court of International Trade are most commonly heard by the Federal Circuit Court. However, the circuit court that has jurisdiction over the party involved in the suit hears appeals that come from the U.S. Tax Court. So, if Alice lives in Colorado, her appeal from the U.S. Tax Court is heard in the 10th Circuit Court of Appeals, which has jurisdiction over Colorado.

TECHNICAL STUFF

An appeal to the U.S. Supreme Court is technically called a *Petition for Review* or a *Petition for Certiorari*. An *appeal* (review) at the Supreme Court level is not automatic. The Supreme Court may agree to hear the case by granting a *writ of certiorari*. This is also known as *granting cert.* One little-known fact about appeals that go to the Supreme Court from states: The U.S. Supreme Court can review a case from the supreme court of any state if the case involves a federal question, but the U.S. Supreme Court can also review a case from a state trial court if that state's supreme court refuses to hear the matter upon appeal.

WARNING

Although you can appeal a case you've lost at the trial court level to one of the appellate courts, your chances of winning on appeal are very slim but not impossible. In fact, the odds are about 4-to-1 against getting a court decision overturned on appeal.

The final chance: Courts of last resort

In the United States, the court of last resort is the U.S. Supreme Court. The Supreme Court provides final review on appeal of any case that emanates from the U.S. Courts of Appeals. The Supreme Court may also review decisions appealed from each state's supreme court.

The U.S. Supreme Court has a somewhat temperamental view of what cases it chooses to hear, however. In fact, the Supreme Court receives about 8,000 petitions for review every year and hears arguments on perhaps only about a hundred of those appeals. The Court selects the cases it wants to hear from the circuit courts or the state supreme courts.

Historically, the Court has levied a great amount of discretion in deciding which cases to hear. Sometimes, it takes cases because the justices want to rule on a topical controversial issue. Or, the U.S. Supreme Court reconciles conflicting decisions from among differing jurisdictions on questions of how to interpret federal law.

Here's an example: Suppose the Congress passes a law that outlaws burning the American flag, and a New Yorker faces trial in the U.S. district court for the District of New York for breaking this law. Then, suppose that the court of appeals for the Second Circuit Western District of New York rules that a person can be prosecuted for flag burning, but a conflicting Ninth Circuit decision holds that enforcing this law is unconstitutional because it violates the First Amendment's guarantee to free speech. A person could get away with flag burning in the nine states way out west (as well as in Guam and the Northern Mariana Islands), but the federal government could throw the book at the same person for burning the flag in Connecticut, Vermont, or New York. To have uniformity among the same federal laws throughout the United States, the Supreme Court could accept an appeal from the Second Circuit court of appeals in order to resolve this conflict among the circuits.

REMEMBER

How often have you heard of someone saying, "I'm going to take this case to the highest court in the land"? In most cases, you can take an appeal as a matter of right to the next level (that is, to the U.S. Court of Appeals). The U.S. Supreme Court doesn't have to hear any appeal from a lower court unless it wants to. Kind of a nice job being a Supreme Court justice, eh?

State judicial system

State courts handle specific types of cases. Here are just some of the matters that state courts hear from their citizenry:

>> Almost all divorce and child custody cases

>> Probate and inheritance matters

>> Contract disputes

>> Traffic violations

>> Real estate issues

>> Juvenile matters

>> Personal injury suits

>> Criminal cases

>> Matters involving diversity of citizenship with potential damages less than the jurisdictional threshold, which changes frequently

In many states, the court structure looks pretty much like that of the federal system. Apparently, it was much easier for our founders to copy the federal system than it was to come up with something different after the new nation was created. States have courts with original jurisdiction, intermediate appellate courts, and courts of last resort. However, in about half the states, there's only one level of appeals. In those states, the trial court decision is appealed directly to the highest court in the state, in most (but not all) cases known as the state supreme court.

WARNING

Be sure to check the particular names of courts in your own state. Trial courts in state systems have many different names throughout the United States. A district court in the federal system can mean something entirely different in one state and something else in another state. One confusing example is that the Supreme Court in the state of New York is a general trial court; the highest court in that state is called the New York Court of Appeals.

Initiation: State trial courts

The trial courts in state judicial systems have original jurisdiction over a myriad of cases that come before them, and these cases come in many flavors. Quite often, state trial courts are two-tiered. The lower level of state trial courts often decide civil cases involving money below a certain dollar amount as well as lower-grade criminal cases known as misdemeanors. The lower-level state trial courts are called *courts of limited jurisdiction*. Depending on the state, these lower courts might be known as *county courts, district courts, justices of the peace,* or any number of other different names to signify their status as a lower-tiered court. These lower-level state courts have far greater caseloads than any of the higher-tiered courts. Procedures are also generally less formal in these lower-tiered courts. For this reason, a court of limited jurisdiction is often referred to as the *people's court.*

REMEMBER

State trial court systems generally break down into two levels. The lower courts, or *inferior courts,* as they're sometimes called, are known as *courts of limited jurisdiction,* while the upper-level courts are referred to as *courts of general jurisdiction.*

The upper-tiered courts at the state level are courts of general jurisdiction, and they similarly have many different names to signify their status. Often, these courts are referred to as the *superior courts, state courts, circuit courts,* or a variety of other names. Interestingly enough, in the state of New York, the upper-tiered trial court is called the supreme court. The cases heard by upper-tier state trial courts involve anything from criminal felony prosecutions to civil matters where unlimited amounts of money are at issue. These upper-level state courts may also hear appeals from the state's inferior courts of limited jurisdiction.

Hear it again: Intermediate courts of appeals and courts of last resort

About half of our 50 states have intermediate courts of appeals. These intermediate appellate courts compare to the U.S. Courts of Appeals for the various circuits in the federal system. Like the federal appellate courts, the intermediate courts of appeals in states generally hear matters appealed from the trial courts within their geographical region. So, they might hear only those cases appealed from the trial courts of certain counties located within their region, while another division of the same intermediate court of appeals located elsewhere in the state would hear appeals from counties in its own particular region.

Parties who don't like the outcome of their trials can file their appeals with one of these intermediate appellate courts as a *matter of right.* This means that a person has an absolute right to have a higher court review his appeal from the lower court. After an intermediate court hears a case on appeal, the appealing party generally can't appeal any farther up the chain unless the next higher court grants a request for review. This type of appeal is called *discretionary review,* where the higher court has discretion as to whether it will even hear the case. In states that don't have intermediate appellate courts, the losing party can appeal from the trial court of general jurisdiction directly to the state supreme court as a matter of right.

REMEMBER

There are two types of appeals from a lower court to a higher court. One type is called an *appeal as a matter of right,* where the party is always entitled to at least one level of review by a higher court. The second type of review is known as a *discretionary review,* where the appellant must seek permission from the higher court to actually hear the appeal.

One aspect of appeals that losing parties don't like to hear about is that an *appellant,* or losing party, generally doesn't get to have the case heard all over again. The appellate court's duty is to decide issues of errors of law that the appellant argues were made by the lower court. The appellate court can overturn the lower court usually only if the inferior court made an *error of law,* such as a mistake on the admissibility of evidence. This differs from a *trial de novo,* where in some cases, the trial can be heard all over again at the appellate level. If the trial judge (or jury) chooses to believe one party's witnesses over the other party's witnesses, then usually the losing party is out of luck and doesn't get to have the appellate court second-guess the lower court's decision based on the credibility of witnesses. The appellate courts don't get to re-decide the facts of the case.

With some exceptions, an appeal from the highest court in a state may be heard by the U.S. Supreme Court. To help you keep it all straight, Figure 4-2 diagrams the general federal and state judicial systems, where you can study the court's hierarchy.

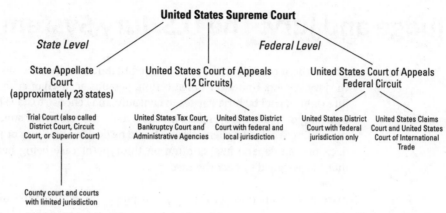

United States Supreme Court

State Level | Federal Level

State Appellate Court (approximately 23 states)

United States Court of Appeals (12 Circuits)

United States Court of Appeals Federal Circuit

Trial Court (also called District Court, Circuit Court, or Superior Court)

United States Tax Court, Bankruptcy Court and Administrative Agencies

United States District Court with federal and local jurisdiction

United States District Court with federal jurisdiction only

United States Claims Court and United States Court of International Trade

County court and courts with limited jurisdiction

FIGURE 4-2: The federal and state judicial systems.

© John Wiley & Sons, Inc.

Local judicial systems

Local court systems are similar in many ways to the lower-tiered state courts. Depending on the state, these courts are sometimes called *city courts, municipal courts, town courts, village courts,* or some other name to indicate their status as the local court system. Local courts generally have jurisdiction or authority to hear only those violations of the laws of cities, towns, or counties. Laws passed by local legislative bodies are called *ordinances.* Ordinances are analogous to the *statutes* enacted at the state and federal level, but ordinances only affect the conduct of citizens located within the boundaries of the local government.

REMEMBER

Local governments may adopt laws called *ordinances* which have legal effect only on people who violate these local codes within the boundaries of the city, town, or county where they're adopted.

Generally, all local-level criminal cases are petty or misdemeanor offenses. States retain exclusive authority to prosecute state felony violations, and local governments share the prosecution of misdemeanor offenses like drunk driving and shoplifting that occur within the local government's boundaries. Local governments usually prosecute violations of zoning ordinances or building codes because these matters are nearly always matters of local concern. Local courts may also enforce local traffic regulations that occur within the city, town, or county limits.

The loser in a case that starts in the local judicial system usually has an appeal as a matter of right to the next court level. This usually means that the appellant can take his case to the court of general jurisdiction in the state court system. To appeal the case any higher in the system, the party generally has to seek discretionary review from the higher court. The loser at the lower court may be stuck with the lower court's original decision. This often happens with a plaintiff who loses in a small claims court, which handles matters involving small money damages (which could be anywhere from $1,000 to $100,000 depending on the municipality).

Judge and Jury: The U.S. Jury System

One of the more important and unique attributes of the U.S. system of justice is the jury system. Under the Constitution, persons accused of crimes have an absolute right to trial by jury. Parties to civil suits may choose to have their cases heard by a jury, or a judge only. As a paralegal, you may assist your supervising attorney in deciding whether a client's case should be decided by a jury or just a judge. This decision can depend just as often on the type of case being heard as on which judge is assigned to hear the case.

At trial, the functions of the jury and judge are significantly different. A judge decides issues of law, such as how a statute or ordinance should be properly interpreted and applied. A jury, on the other hand, has the duty of deciding questions of fact, such as whether a party to a lawsuit acted reasonably in proceeding through a yellow caution light. The jury is required to follow the law, but sometimes juries ignore the law that the judge set forth. This situation is known as *jury nullification*, where the jury in essence nullifies the law the court presents. Jury nullification often happens when the jurors feel that a law is unjust or is being applied unfairly in the particular circumstances of the current case.

REMEMBER

In trial, the judge decides issues of law, and the jury applies the law as given by the judge to the facts in a particular case.

JURY NULLIFICATION: A ZINGER FOR ZENGER?

Throughout U.S. (and English) history, juries have been known to engage in the practice of jury nullification. Most commonly when this occurs, the jury acquits a criminal defendant it knows to be guilty of violating a law because it thinks that the law is either unjust or should not be applied to the defendant on trial. One famous early example is the trial of John Peter Zenger.

In 1735, the government charged Zenger with the crime of seditious libel for printing bad things about the colonial governor of New York. Although there was no doubt that Zenger did print the offensive material and that he was factually guilty of the crime, the jury nonetheless let him off the hook and Zenger walked away a free man. Some historians and political scientists have deemed the practice of jury nullification to be an additional check and balance of the people on the government. In fact, widespread jury nullification of criminal defendants charged with liquor violations in the 1920s is partially responsible for the repeal of Prohibition.

Order in the court: The bench trial

Although most trial court cases in the United States — especially criminal matters — are decided by a jury with a judge presiding over the case, some of the cases are more effectively argued to a judge without a jury. In cases where the right to a jury is waived, the judge decides both the issues of law and the issues of fact. A trial by a judge alone is also known as a *bench trial.*

REMEMBER

When you refer to judges collectively, you usually refer to them as the *bench* (just as you refer to attorneys collectively as the *bar*). All members of the bench are also members of the bar (but that doesn't mean they drink heavily!).

Usually, an attorney requests a bench trial in cases, like complex contract disputes, where the facts are pretty straightforward but the law is complicated. For these cases, the parties need a judge to interpret complex law and determine whether someone breached the law.

Other reasons for requesting a bench trial concern time and money. As you might imagine, a jury trial takes much longer to conduct than a bench trial, sometimes as much as 40 percent longer! The trial backlog in the U.S. justice system is generally much greater for jury trials than bench trials, and jury trials cost more to conduct. The loser in a lawsuit usually ends up paying the opponent's court costs by law in most cases. But often, neither of the parties recoup what they spend on legal fees, and the longer the trial, the greater the fees! (There are two notable exceptions to this general rule: When a law provides for payment of legal fees to the winning party, such as lawsuits involving civil rights violations, or in contract cases where the contract itself has language that specifies that the losing party must pay reasonable attorney fees and costs to the prevailing party.)

Petition to your peers: The jury trial

Worldwide, approximately 95 percent of all jury trials take place in the United States. Many paralegals who have served as jurors express the same feelings of pride and satisfaction articulated by others who have been involved in the jury system. Participating in the jury process is an unequaled lesson in democracy, and if you haven't served on a jury, you should plan to sit through a jury trial or two to get some firsthand knowledge about judicial procedure.

TIP

A party's attorney and paralegal should sit through a hearing or trial in the judge's courtroom before appearing before that judge. This way they'll be prepared for the judge's courtroom etiquette and rulings on evidentiary issues.

In most states and counties, jurors are chosen at random from several different computerized lists, like voter registrations, motor vehicle registrations, driver's license records, and property tax rolls.

The jury's responsibility is to sort through the facts presented by both sides at trial and decide what's true and what's not. A jury determines things like whether a witness is credible or not. It then renders a verdict based on its decision.

In most state criminal trials, juries have to unanimously agree on whether the accused is guilty. The prosecutor, or district attorney or attorney general, must present enough evidence to the members of the jury to convince them that the accused committed the crime charged *beyond a reasonable doubt.* So, every juror (all 6 or 12, depending on the trial) must agree beyond a reasonable doubt with the verdict of guilty. If they don't, the accused is deemed to be innocent. In death penalty cases, the jury's sentencing recommendation also has to be unanimous. In a civil case, the burden of proof is usually by a *preponderance of the evidence,* meaning that plaintiffs must convince the jury (or judge in a bench trial) that it's "more likely than not" that their version of the facts is true.

Either the plaintiff or the defendant may request a jury. If the plaintiff doesn't file a jury demand and include the required jury fee, the defendant may do it. In any case, a jury request is rarely granted if it's not made before, or shortly after, the close of pleadings. In other words, a jury demand usually must be filed no later than ten days after service of the last pleading.

TIP

As always, you should consult your state and local rules of court to figure out the last day allowed for filing of a jury demand. You wouldn't want to miss this critical deadline! Usually, plaintiffs' attorneys request a jury at the same time they file the complaint, and, if the plaintiff has not previously requested a jury, defense attorneys demand a jury when they file their answer.

Attorneys often consult with paralegals about whether to try a civil case to a jury or just a judge. The tactical decision of whether to argue a civil action to a jury is among the more important decisions to be made in the litigation process.

Chapter **5**

The Big Three: Categories of Law

I n your paralegal career, you need to know the difference between *procedural law,* which governs the processes of how the law is applied through courts and other tribunals, and *substantive law,* which consists of the actual rules that govern society. You can find out about procedural law in Chapters 6 and 7, but this chapter focuses on the three general areas of the substantive law: administrative, criminal, and civil.

Administrative law concerns the operations of agencies within the executive branch of government, like social services, worker's compensation, and unemployment benefits. Criminal actions occur when the federal or state government (or both, if someone has been really, really bad!) files charges against a person alleged to have committed a public offense and an injustice against the "peace and dignity" of the "people of the state."

Civil law consists of personal actions used to compel payment, such as money damages, or some other action. A significant difference between a criminal and a civil suit is that plaintiffs bring civil lawsuits as private citizens against other private citizens or entities to find a remedy for a perceived wrong that was done to them. Almost all civil law actions fall under two major categories: torts and breaches of contract. And these areas provide most of the work for paralegals.

Cutting Through the Red Tape: Administrative Law

Administrative law is still one of the fastest growing areas of governmental activity. The number of administrative agencies has increased dramatically since their inception, and especially since President Franklin D. Roosevelt initiated the New Deal in the 1930s.

Building the bureaucracy: Government agencies

Legislatures pass laws to govern society, and provisions of those same laws create agencies to administer them. Administrative agencies aren't mentioned in the Constitution, and critics often speak of them as the "fourth branch" of government with too much power and no basis in the law.

At the federal level, the president's cabinet contains the best-known agencies. The Department of the Treasury, for example, touches just about everyone's life through its very own sublevel agency, the Internal Revenue Service. The Treasury Department also oversees minting currency. Over the years, Congress has created 15 cabinet-level departments to assist chief executives in carrying out their duties. The president appoints the cabinet heads, who are subject to Senate confirmation. These agencies undergo constant reorganization as the president reorders priorities and sets the agenda for the administration of the executive branch of government.

In addition to the 15 cabinet departments, which could change with new presidential administrations, the federal government also has dozens of independent agencies that oversee and regulate various activities. Examples of these agencies are the Federal Trade Commission (FTC), the Social Security Administration (SSA), and the Federal Communications Commission (FCC). Although the president appoints the directors of these agencies just like cabinet officials, these agency directors have a bit more independence. They have set terms of office and can't be removed just because the president has tired of them. Thus, they don't answer directly to the chief executive as say, for example, the Secretary of State, the Secretary of Defense, or the Attorney General do.

REMEMBER

For a chart of the federal cabinet departments and other administrative agencies, see Chapter 4. The online content (www.dummies.com/go/paralegalcareer2e) contains a PDF of the chart as well as links to other related websites.

The federal government doesn't hold the patent on administrative agencies. State and local governments have their slice of the bureaucratic pie as well. The functions and even the names of state and local departments are similar to federal agencies, but there are some striking differences, too. Only the federal government has agencies that provide for national defense and the military (Department of Defense), minting money (Treasury Department), and regulating nuclear energy. Sometimes, the federal and state governments share their administrative authority in areas such as environmental regulation and labor relations.

Generally, state agencies deal with matters of local concern, like licensing cars and drivers and providing professional licensing for doctors and lawyers. State administrative agencies deal also with other local issues such as alcoholic beverage regulation and voting, usually through the state office of the secretary of state. But sometimes this state authority is delegated to the local (county) elections departments.

Local governments have their own unique concerns as well. You can find local administrative agencies at work when you get a building permit or marriage license, or when you file a crime report with your local police or sheriff's department. State and local administrative agencies have experienced greater growth rates than their federal counterparts, especially since the 1960s. No, Virginia, the government bureaucracy isn't ready to get off your back any time in the near future!

Your paralegal work requires you to interact with administrative agencies. State and local governments have their own brand of administrative agencies to implement state statutes and local ordinances, and these bureaucracies have grown much more over the last 40 years than their federal counterparts have.

Playing by the rules: Administrative law practices

Although administrative agencies seem to be growing nonstop, there is some method to what might appear to be another trip for Alice through Wonderland. With the rise in the number and variety of these agencies, people began to fear the power of bureaucratic government officials who didn't have "legitimacy" in the Constitution, weren't elected by the people, and pretty much had no limits on their authority. As a result, Congress enacted the Administrative Procedure Act (APA) and made it part of the U.S. Code in 1946. The APA applies only to federal agencies (and some federal agencies are exempt), but most states have adopted their own mini versions of the APA.

Under the APA, Congress delegated two kinds of powers to administrative agencies: legislative rulemaking and quasi-judicial adjudicatory hearings. The APA also allowed courts to rule on administrative decisions through the power of judicial review. *Rulemaking* is the technical term for administrative agencies making laws that govern society. Adjudicatory hearings are a lot like court proceedings and that's why they're called quasi-judicial proceedings. Adversarial parties appear before the agency and argue their respective positions, and the agency determines the rights and responsibilities of parties.

Making rules: Administrative legislation

Agencies engage in rulemaking every time they create laws through their legislative authority. Many areas of the law are so complex that congressional legislation doesn't cover all the possibilities that could ever come up. It's difficult to get a majority of the 535 members of Congress to agree on what to serve for dinner let alone pass major legislation! For example, the laws regarding income tax collection are quite voluminous, and you could say that Congress missed a few spots when it wrote the Internal Revenue Code. To fill in the blanks, Congress gave the Internal Revenue Service (IRS) the authority to write rules covering more specific situations.

REMEMBER

The rulemaking authority of administrative agencies is not without checks and balances. The legislative branch sets standards for administrative rulemaking. If the agency rules do not meet the legislative parameters, the courts have the power of judicial review and can strike down the rules. Congress also retains the power to veto an administrative rule in a process called *legislative oversight,* which means that if it doesn't like the rules that an agency writes, Congress can override the rules by legislation.

Taking it to the judge: Administrative hearings

Quasi-judicial adjudicatory hearings give adversarial parties their "day in court" when an administrative agency determines the rights of citizens and other entities under the law the agency administers. For example, if a Social Security recipient is denied benefits, that person can have his case heard by an unbiased administrative law judge.

Agency hearings are a bit less formal than court. But when an agency requires someone to appear at a hearing, the APA ensures that the decisions aren't arbitrary. The applicant has certain *due process* rights, including the right to notice of the hearing, the right to call witnesses and cross-examine the government's witnesses, and the right to counsel or other representation, if desired. In addition, losing parties have the right to judicial review of the agency's decision, which means they can appeal their cases to court. The APA also provides for *judicial review*. In other words, if a party doesn't like the agency's decision, that party can appeal it to court.

Although paralegals generally may not represent clients in court, they can get firsthand experience advocating for clients by going to bat for them in many types of administrative hearings. Administrative hearings are some of the few venues where paralegals may actually represent clients, especially because paralegals are less expensive than attorneys and the APA doesn't make provisions for persons who can't afford representation.

WARNING

Paralegals can represent clients in certain cases before administrative tribunals, but it may not always be allowed. Finding out if the agency allows paralegals to represent clients, either by its own rules or by some other law, is important. If you represent a client when doing so is not allowed, you could be found guilty of the unauthorized practice of law, a crime in many states.

Getting your way: Informal and formal advocacy

If parties don't like the outcome of a quasi-judicial or adjudicatory administrative decision, they can always appeal it to the civil court. But first, they have to show the court that they've exhausted their administrative remedies, which means they have to do everything they can to resolve their cases at the administrative level before they jump into the civil court to try to get judicial review of the decision. This stipulation gives paralegals plenty of opportunity to engage in informal and formal advocacy to resolve agency disputes.

Advocacy simply means trying to persuade someone to go along with what you want. In the legal context, advocacy involves trying to influence the person with decision making authority to rule in favor of the client. In the case of administrative law, you try to convince the agency official or administrative tribunal to rule your way. The big difference between *formal* and *informal* advocacy often simply depends on whom you're dealing with.

Casual contact: Informal advocacy

Informal advocacy takes on many characteristics, and your approach can be as varied as the agency official you're dealing with. For example, suppose you're trying to get a public record like a birth certificate from an agency. Sometimes a phone call or a letter gets a positive response. It's often said that the shortest distance between two points is a straight line, and that's what informal advocacy is all about.

Because you might encounter many different agency personnel with just as many personalities, you need to be perceptive enough to know what kind of person you're dealing with and flexible enough to change your tactics depending on the response you get. For example, you may encounter officials who are sticklers for rules. If these types tell you that you have to jump through a set of hoops to obtain a particular type of record, you could ask them to show you the specific regulations that they're relying on. If their rule isn't written down somewhere, insist that they not require the particular hoop jumping in your case. Or appeal to their sense of equity, justice, or common sense to see if they may be willing to grant an exception in your unique case.

At other times, an emotional approach may be just the ticket to solving your client's problem. As silly as it may sound, you may get away with using emotions to address a situation, depending, of course, on the personality of the person sitting at other end of the telephone or desk. Some bureaucrats may respond more positively if you let them know you're upset, while that same approach may have the opposite effect on others. Depending on how well you read the situation, you may find that a government official responds better to flattery.

And don't forget the old adage that you can get more flies with honey than you can with vinegar. You can be quite effective with informal advocacy by simply developing a rapport with an official you need to negotiate with. Approach officials directly, treat them with kindness, and always be honest. Sometimes, if you deal with the same person over and over again for different clients, you can develop a good working relationship built on mutual trust and respect, which can work miracles in many instances.

Systematic means: Formal advocacy

If the direct approach to the agency doesn't do the trick on an informal basis, you may have to take the client's matter to a higher level. *Formal advocacy* occurs when you go beyond the agency official behind the desk to a more official setting, like an administrative tribunal. The more your situation begins to look like you're in a courtroom setting, the more it becomes formal advocacy. For instance, formal advocacy could consist of adversarial parties arguing their respective positions in front of an administrative law judge or a hearing examiner. You may also have a case where witnesses to the conflict testify under oath and get cross-examined by the opposing side. The officer for these quasi-judicial hearings must in most cases produce a written decision in favor of one party over another.

The techniques and skills you apply in formal advocacy resemble the same approach an attorney may take when litigating a matter in court: conducting a pre-hearing investigation of the client's case, conducting legal research, drafting memos, organizing evidence for the hearing, and developing strategies to present the case to the hearing examiner. (You can find more about these specific litigation procedures and methods in Chapter 6.)

When you've appealed your request without satisfaction as far up the administrative agency chain of command as you can — from the front desk clerk, to the supervisor, to the agency head, and finally to an administrative law judge or hearing officer — you've exhausted all administrative remedies. At this point, the matter is ripe for judicial review, which means you may appeal it to a civil court. Even if you were able to represent the client at the administrative level, the client will almost always require attorney representation at court hearings.

REMEMBER

As a paralegal, you may advocate both formally and informally on behalf of a client in many types of administrative proceedings. Be sure to exhaust all administrative remedies before the client brings the case to court for judicial review. As we always say, "Court should be your last resort."

Eliminating Any Reasonable Doubt: The Nature of Criminal Law

The government (usually referred to as "the people of the state" in a state prosecution or "the United States" in a federal criminal violation) brings criminal charges against persons accused of public law violations that affect the peace and tranquility of living in orderly society. Crimes usually involve a perpetrator and a victim. The perpetrator in a criminal case is the party who commits the bad act and is referred to as the *defendant* in the case. And although the victim of the criminal act is very similar to a plaintiff who may bring a civil suit against a defendant, the true plaintiff in a criminal case is the governmental agency that presses charges.

Paralegals working in the criminal arena find employment either with the public prosecutor (called the *district attorney* or *attorney general*) who brings charges against defendants or with the public defender or private law firm who defends the defendants.

TIP

This section defines criminal law for you. If you want to find out more about the specific procedures you follow in a criminal law case, turn to Chapter 6.

Building blocks: Elements of criminal liability

To help you understand the nature of criminal law, we can break down crimes into their essential elements, which is otherwise known as establishing a prima facie case. The elements of a criminal case usually involve proving the identity of the defendant and the time of, nature of, and reason for the offense. So, similar to a game of Clue, you need to establish who committed the crime, with what, and how. Additionally, you need to determine why a crime was committed by establishing a motive. To convict someone of a crime, the prosecution has to provide proof that the elements of the crime really happened as it alleges. The defense's job is to cast doubt on any one or all aspects of the prosecution's case.

Prove it: The prosecutor's burden

In any criminal prosecution, the defendant has a *presumption of innocence,* which means the defendant has no obligation to prove her innocence. Instead, the government has the burden to prove that each element of the crime charged really happened *beyond a reasonable doubt.* Otherwise, the defendant will be *acquitted* (that is, she will be found not guilty of the crime charged). The standard for proving beyond a reasonable doubt is the highest burden of proof in the law. It's not exactly proving with 100 percent scientific certainty, but it's close. The prosecutor has to show that any reasonable person would believe that the defendant is guilty.

It wasn't my fault: Affirmative defenses

To counteract the prosecution's case, defendants try to disprove the evidence brought against them either by showing that they didn't commit the crime or that they shouldn't be held responsible for committing the crime. To prove the latter and attempt to defeat criminal liability, they raise *affirmative defenses.* You're probably familiar with some of these defenses from watching crime shows:

- >> **Self-defense:** A common defense in assault, battery, and homicide cases is *self-defense.* Defendants may argue that they were justified in reacting with reasonable force against the victim because they needed to defend themselves from the victim's assault and/or battery on them.

- >> **Diminished capacity:** Defendants may argue their actions are excusable, either by insanity or by some form of *diminished capacity.* This means that they didn't have the ability to actually form the intent to commit the crime.

>> **Entrapment:** A defense used often in drug prosecutions is *entrapment.* The defendant argues that law enforcement officers enticed the defendant into committing the crime.

>> **Duress:** *Duress* is another, less common, defense. Defendants arguing entrapment state that they had to commit the crime to prevent a greater harm from occurring. The classic example is when a defendant argues that he had to steal property because he was starving.

High crimes and misdemeanors: Classes of crimes

Crimes come in two classes: *felonies* and *misdemeanors.* Felonies, the more serious of the two, usually result in longer, harsher sentences. Less severe misdemeanor offenses generally result in relatively milder sentences, like a shorter term in a county jail or a term of probation without jail time.

Hitting the big time: Felonies

Felonies consist of more serious offenses such as murder, rape, and robbery. Convicted felons generally don't receive the proverbial "slap on the wrist" for these crimes. Instead, they're more likely to get shipped off to the big house: the state penitentiary. The most serious felonies are crimes against persons as opposed to crimes against someone else's property. Here are descriptions of many of the felony crimes against persons.

WARNING

Although the following is a list of general classifications of crimes, you should always check the laws in your own state and municipality to determine the actual elements of any crime and the laws of jurisdiction (that is, federal, state, local) where you're working.

>> **Homicide:** Homicide, the most serious of all felonies, occurs when a defendant kills another person. Types of homicide range from murder to manslaughter based on the defendant's degree of responsibility. The degree of crime depends on whether the defendant intended to kill the victim or whether it was accidental. The degree of the crime depends, therefore, on whether the elements include intentional, reckless, or negligent acts.

  • *Murder* is generally an *intentional* or *knowing* killing of another person. If the defendant plans out the crime ahead of time, it's called *premeditated murder,* and it can carry a sentence of the death penalty or life without parole in many states.

- *Manslaughter* or *negligent homicide,* depending on the terminology of the specific state, occurs when someone's death results from someone else's recklessness or negligence but not an intentional killing. Punishments for these crimes are less severe.

  Regarding intent, many states have a *felony murder rule,* which states that if defendants commit certain felonies and, in the course of committing these felonies a person dies, the defendant is also guilty of felony murder.

» **Rape:** The crime of *rape* occurs when the defendant engages in sexual intercourse with a victim against her will. When the defendant perpetrates sexual contact rather than intercourse, the defendant commits crimes that are sometimes referred to as sexual assault or *indecent liberties.* Other crimes of this nature include *child molestation, child rape,* and *stalking.*

» **Felony assault:** *Felony assault,* or *aggravated assault* as it's sometimes called, occurs when someone attacks another person with the intent to inflict severe bodily harm, usually by strong enough means to cause death or permanent injury.

REMEMBER

An assault occurs whenever someone places another person in imminent fear of his well-being.

» **Robbery:** *Robbery* occurs when a defendant uses force either to steal property (including money) or to maintain control over that property. It's considered to be a crime against a person because, even though the defendant steals only property, it's a harrowing experience for the victim.

» **Burglary:** *Burglary* involves entering someone's dwelling or some other building, with the intent to commit a crime, usually theft or assault. The prosecution must prove intent to commit a crime inside the building. If there was no intent to commit a crime, it's a matter of *criminal trespass,* which is usually a misdemeanor.

» **Kidnapping:** *Kidnapping* occurs when a defendant takes a person somewhere against the person's will. If the wrongdoer inflicts injury or uses a weapon, the crime is usually more serious. Similar crimes include *false imprisonment,* where the victim is unwillingly held in some location, and *coercion,* where the defendant forces the victim to do something.

» **Arson:** When a defendant knowingly or intentionally sets fire to a building or car, it's *arson.* Arson is more serious when a person is in the building, if the defendant sets fire to a *dwelling* (rather than just any old building), if someone (such as a firefighter) dies in the fire, or if the defendant sets a fire to collect insurance money. If the fire doesn't involve a building or car, the crime might be classified as *reckless burning.*

There are other, less serious, felonies involving crimes against only property. They become felonies because they involve either a significant amount of property or because of the character of the property involved. Examples include auto theft, gun theft, forgery, identity theft, or theft of anything worth more than a certain amount of money as defined by state law. Some states place this minimum threshold at $250. Other property crimes, like writing bad checks, possessing stolen property, and *criminal mischief* (vandalism), become felonies when the amount of property involved exceeds the threshold.

Other miscellaneous felony offenses include crimes such as *bribery, perjury, drug offenses, gambling, money laundering,* and *prostitution.* These crimes are often referred to as "victimless crimes," but critics of this characterization point out that the victims of these crimes are either the social order or the person who engages in the specified conduct.

The punishments meted out for felony offenses depend on the nature of the crime and each state's laws regarding sentencing. Some states may allow first-time offenders convicted of lower-level felonies to do little or no jail time or serve a suspended sentence with probation. More likely, though, the punishment for felonies ranges from at least some jail time for property crimes to lengthy prison sentences for the more serious property offenses and felony crimes against a person.

The lesser of two evils: Misdemeanors

Misdemeanors fall at the other end of the spectrum in terms of the seriousness of the conduct and severity of the potential punishment. Misdemeanors include offenses like shoplifting, drunk driving, and assault where little or no injury results or could result. Misdemeanor convictions receive lesser sentences, and defendants serve their time in county jails rather than in the state prison system.

Most crimes against a person are felonies because society places a higher premium on personal freedom, and these crimes invade another person's basic human rights to be free from injury and annoyance. So, misdemeanor crimes against the person may include assault where the victim suffers or could suffer little or no injury, harassment in the form of verbal threats, and violation of a court's restraining order.

The majority of misdemeanors are crimes against property. Shoplifting and other, less serious theft crimes make up a significant number of the misdemeanors you're likely to encounter as a paralegal in a criminal law practice. The main element that makes these crimes misdemeanors is the amount of money involved. Generally, if the amount stolen falls below a certain threshold (in many states $250 and under), you're dealing with a misdemeanor. Other misdemeanor property offenses that use a threshold include bad check writing and criminal mischief, where someone intentionally damages property.

Traffic offenses make up a large portion of misdemeanor offenses. These include driving under the influence of alcohol or drugs (DUI), reckless driving, driving on a suspended license, and lacking vehicle registration. Most states don't consider minor traffic infractions, like speeding, running a stop sign, failing to signal properly, and committing equipment violations, to be criminal offenses. So, violators of these laws usually don't get jury trials or jail sentences.

Maintaining Polite Society: Civil Law

Plaintiffs bring civil lawsuits against defendants to seek the reimbursement of monetary damages resulting from harm that defendants have caused to an individual or group. Plaintiffs can also seek equitable relief from the defendant. The great bulk of cases in our trial courts today are civil and traditionally involve an individual, business, or governmental agency that's seeking relief from another individual, business, or governmental agency. These cases are based upon tort law (in Latin *ex delicto*) and contract law (*ex contractu*) and include product liability actions, personal injury suits, probate actions, and domestic relations (also known as family law).

The victor's spoils: Equitable relief and money damages

Plaintiffs, sometimes known as *complainants,* can sue defendants, sometimes referred to as *respondents,* in two ways: by bringing a suit in equity or by suing the defendant for a legal remedy, which generally means monetary damages. Equitable relief suits don't generally seek a money award, and they usually aren't tried before a jury. Instead, equity suits petition the courts for an injunction or specific performance.

An ounce of prevention: Injunctions

An *injunction* is a request to the court to order that certain wrongful conduct be prevented or discontinued right away. Environmental groups commonly seek injunctions to prevent the development of forests and wetlands. Another common example is a *restraining order.* You see this a lot in divorces where one party wants to restrain the other party from spending marital assets like there's no tomorrow (prior to the court hearing on final division of property) or skipping town with a child of the marriage (before the hearing to determine custody of the children).

Just do it: Specific performance

A plaintiff seeking *specific performance* requests the court to compel certain action. For example, the plaintiff may ask the court to order another party to perform its obligation on a contract to sell real estate or unique personal property. A court grants a request for specific performance by forcing the defendant to transfer real property according to the terms of the sales agreement. Similarly, the court can also order a losing party to transfer items of personal property, such as a one-of-a-kind Babe Ruth baseball card, pursuant to the terms of the parties' original agreement.

Show me the money: Monetary damages

The vast majority of civil actions don't involve a request for equitable relief. Instead, plaintiffs in most cases seek good old-fashioned money damages from the defendant. These breach-of-contract and tort actions find their source in Anglo-Saxon common law, or judge-made law. In this justice system, each cause of action requires the plaintiff to prove actual damages caused by the defendant, or *tortfeasor.*

Much of civil law deals with the substantive law of torts and contracts. To work successfully in the area of civil law, you'll need to be familiar with both areas.

Beyond dessert: Tort law

Tort laws govern wrongs done to other people and their property, and many torts would be criminal acts if the government prosecuted the tortfeasors. In the civil arena, though, the tort system allows plaintiffs to be compensated for the wrongs they endure at the hands of others. Paralegals who work civil law are extensively involved in the prosecution and defense of tort actions. In general, representing plaintiffs in tort law actions can be very lucrative for attorneys and, ultimately, the paralegals who work for them.

TECHNICAL STUFF

To meet the criteria of certain tort matters, plaintiffs have to establish a *prima facie* case (from Latin meaning "first face"). This means that the complaint must allege all necessary elements of the tort. The complaint is complete "on its face," at first blush, because it fulfills all the necessary elements.

The tort system is comprised of six general areas: intentional torts, quasi-intentional torts, negligent torts, strict liability, product liability, and nuisance. The purpose of tort law is to make the plaintiff whole again, as if the wrongdoing never occurred.

You meant to do that: Intentional torts

The one element of intentional torts that makes them stand out is the intent of the actor, or *tortfeasor*. For a tort to be intentional, the one who commits the tort has to intend to do whatever injury is prohibited. The actor must be certain, or substantially certain, that his actions will have a detrimental effect on others or their property. So, there are two separate categories of intentional torts: intentional harm to a person and intentional harm to property.

INTENTIONAL HARM TO A PERSON

In each of the torts involving intentional harm to a person, the plaintiff injured by another's act can bring a lawsuit to determine if a wrong has been caused and to provide compensation for that wrong.

Each of the four torts discussed in this section varies according to what type of harm it's designed to guard against:

>> **Assault:** *Assault* actions are brought to protect individuals from threat of harmful or offensive contact. An assault occurs whenever the tortfeasor places the plaintiff in imminent fear for his well-being, such as when the tortfeasor takes a stick, brandishes it over the head of the plaintiff, and shouts "Your money or your life!" The tortfeasor doesn't need to strike the plaintiff in order for the tort of assault to occur.

>> **Battery:** *Battery* is the wrongful touching of another person. Battery actions seek to compensate the plaintiff who actually gets hit with the stick, mentioned in the preceding example. Because assault and battery often occur in the same action, the plaintiff usually alleges both actions together in a complaint.

>> **False imprisonment:** If a tortfeasor unreasonably detains a plaintiff against her will for an undue length of time, the plaintiff can bring a *false imprisonment* action. Plaintiffs bringing this tort action include people who've been held hostage, who've been detained by the police without just cause, or who can prove that a tortfeasor detained them in an injurious manner. Injuries in a false imprisonment action may be both physical and emotional.

>> **Intentional infliction of emotional distress:** Another intentional tort against a person, *intentional infliction of emotional distress* covers actions that force a plaintiff to experience a particularly gruesome event. For example, plaintiffs can also bring this tort if they are unfortunate enough to see their loved ones suffer injury or death at the hands of another.

INTENTIONAL HARM TO PROPERTY

Torts involving intentional injury to property are concerned with protecting a person's property from willful destruction by others or protecting a person's rights to use his own property to its full enjoyment.

Here are some of the kinds of intentional property torts you'd deal with as a paralegal working in a civil law practice:

>> **Trespass to land:** *Trespass to land* covers the unauthorized entry on or use of land. If tortfeasors enter land that doesn't belong to them, the owner of the land may bring a trespass to land action. Even if the tortfeasor merely drops some debris on the land, the owner has a right to bring an action. Littering on someone's private property would qualify as a trespass to land, and repeated trespass could become a nuisance.

>> **Trespass to chattels:** The *trespass to chattels* tort covers property owners' exclusive use of their property. Personal property has the same protection as land in tort law. The only difference between trespass to land and trespass to chattels is that land covers only real estate, whereas chattels include all other kinds of physical property, like farm animals and cars.

>> **Conversion:** The tort of *conversion* concerns stolen or wrongly possessed property. It provides the owner of stolen or converted property with the means to recover that property. The tort of conversion is the civil claim that directly corresponds to the crime of theft.

TECHNICAL STUFF

A plaintiff who wants to get a trespassing defendant off of her land may bring an action in *ejectment*. A plaintiff who wants to recover his personal property from the defendant who has converted the property can bring an action in *replevin*.

Accidents do happen: Negligent torts

Intentional torts pertain exclusively to deliberate actions of the defendant. Over time, however, the tort system has evolved to cover not only intentional harm but also harmful situations that may be unintentional. These unintentional torts form a general category of wrongs that are tested by the standard of *negligence*.

Negligent torts are the most common and the most varied torts in our civil law system. A common example of a negligent tort is personal injury, where a defendant's negligence results in injury to the plaintiff.

As a paralegal, you'll assist in the development of each of the four elements of the prima facie case for negligence because if a court or jury finds that the plaintiff's attorney has proven each of these four elements, then the jury can award damages. So, having a good understanding of each of the following is pretty important:

>> **The defendant owed a duty of care to the plaintiff.** The element of duty is based on the belief that each person owes a duty to others to refrain from hurting them. For example, John owes a duty to Mary to drive carefully and to refrain from hitting her vehicle while driving his car. Duty is often judged by the "reasonable person" standard. Society would consider John's hitting Mary with his car unreasonable, and John has a duty to act reasonably. Therefore, he's negligent if he hits Mary. The jury has to determine whether defendants have acted as reasonable persons in negligence cases.

>> **The defendant breached that duty.** When John hit Mary with the car, he breached the duty of care he owed to Mary. Breach of duty is the second element that requires proof in a negligence action. In order to prove breach, the attorney can prove that either the instrument that caused the injury was within the exclusive control or possession of the tortfeasor (*res ipsa loquitur*, "the thing speaks for itself") or the actor violated a statute or ordinance covering the situation (negligence per se).

Proving either *res ipsa loquitur* or negligence per se usually results in proving that the defendant breached a duty. If John violated a statute when he hit Mary with his car, it would be fairly easy to prove that he breached his duty to Mary. After the plaintiff proves a breach of duty, her attorney progresses to proving proximate cause, which is usually the most difficult element to prove.

>> **The defendant's breach of duty was the *proximate cause* of the plaintiff's injury (in other words, if the defendant hadn't breached the duty, the plaintiff wouldn't have suffered).** To show proximate cause, the attorney must prove not only that the defendant actually caused the injury, but also that the defendant was the legal cause of the injury. The attorney, through the assistance of the paralegal, must show that the injury was foreseeable and that there were no other intervening causes of the injury. In the example, Mary's attorney must prove that "but for" John's actions, the accident never would have happened. The attorney must also prove that the accident happened without any superseding causes, such as an earthquake's forcing John's car to hit Mary. Next, Mary's attorney must prove that the result of the accident was foreseeable and that there were no intervening events that caused the accident, such as another car's hitting Mary first and causing the damage.

>> **The plaintiff suffered damages.** If the defendant's negligence is found to be the proximate cause of the plaintiff's injuries, the defendant has to pay damages to the plaintiff. The plaintiff establishes damages by introducing evidence that indicates *special damages* (expenses you can show receipts for,

like hospital bills and car-repair bills), *general damages* (damage you can't show receipts for, like pain and suffering), and other categories of damages, including *punitive damages* (to punish the defendant) and *consequential damages* (which are damages arising as a result of the wrongdoing). In every case, the plaintiff has the duty to take reasonable steps to *mitigate* (or reduce) any damages.

To be successful in a negligence action, the plaintiff must establish each of the four elements of the prima facie case. Paralegals are instrumental in defining the facts that are vital to establishing and proving their offices' clients' cases.

The defendant who is alleged to have committed a negligent tort may respond with several different defenses. These defenses include the following:

>> **Contributory or comparative negligence:** Under the doctrines of *contributory or comparative negligence,* damages may be diminished or may not be awarded at all if it can be shown that the injured party contributed to the accident. If Mary was not wearing a seat belt at the time of the accident with John, she could be found to be contributorily negligent. John, therefore, may not have to pay damages, or the amount of damages for which he is responsible may be limited.

The modern trend is to move away from the strict standard of contributory negligence and move toward a standard of comparative negligence. Under the doctrine of comparative negligence, the judge or jury examines each party's negligence and decreases the damage award by the percentage of negligence that was caused by the plaintiff. In Mary's case, if she were found to be 30 percent at fault, and John were found to be 70 percent at fault, the damages for which John would be responsible would be decreased by 30 percent. The specific elements of this rule depend on the law of the state where the action is tried.

>> **Joint and several liability:** Actions for negligence can be further complicated by the concept of joint tortfeasors, known as *joint and several liability.* If two people act together in concert to produce the harm, both may be held liable for the injury, or one may solely be held liable. Even if the two tortfeasors perform different deeds but the responsibility for the resulting injury is inseparable, they're still held jointly liable. The issue of joint and several liability may become especially important in cases involving numerous defendants. Let's say a plaintiff sues for injuries sustained in an auto accident that occurs on a poorly designed road. The jury may award this plaintiff a judgment against numerous defendants, but only the "deep pocket" (the defendant with the big bucks, often the local government) may end up satisfying the judgment.

>> **Vicarious liability:** The concept of *vicarious liability* relates to the liability one person has for another person's actions. If John were to hit Mary while delivering a pizza for his employer, his employer may be held liable for the injuries that Mary sustained. This is a case of *respondeat superior,* a Latin phrase meaning "let the master respond." In this case, Mary would bring an action against both John and the pizza company. Vicarious liability applies to other relationships besides that between employer and employee; it also applies to parent/child relationships and owner/user relationships.

WARNING

Vicarious liability doesn't apply when the employee is acting outside the course and scope of his employment. In the preceding example, if John wasn't working at the time of the accident but was driving the pizza delivery truck on a frolic and a lark to party, he's responsible for Mary's damages, and his employer is probably off the hook.

A little bit of both: Quasi-intentional torts

Quasi-intentional torts defy categorization because they consist of actions that are a mix of intentional and negligent torts.

Quasi-intentional torts include defamation, invasion of privacy, intentional misrepresentation, and wrongful institution of legal proceedings. The courts are rapidly taking the protection that these tort actions offer more seriously.

>> **Defamation:** Defamation consists of making false statements about another. To establish a prima facie case for defamation, the plaintiff must prove that the defendant, either through written means or broadcast *(libel)* or through injurious spoken comments *(slander),* conveyed untrue remarks to a third party that harmed another's reputation. An accused may defend a defamation action by proving that the injurious comments were actually true or, if aimed at a public figure, were made non-maliciously or in jest, as in late-night talk show host monologues.

>> **Invasion of privacy:** Invasion of privacy occurs in several ways:

- When someone uses another person's name or picture for commercial advantage without consent

- When someone unreasonably pries into another person's private affairs

- When someone unreasonably and publicly discloses another person's private matters (***Note:*** The damages in privacy invasion actions usually include emotional distress, and the main defense is that the plaintiff consented to disclosure.)

>> **Intentional misrepresentation:** *Intentional misrepresentation* torts allege that the defendant has committed fraud against or deceived the plaintiff. To establish a prima facie case, the plaintiff must prove all the following:

- The defendant falsely represented herself

- The defendant knew that the representation was false

- The defendant intended the plaintiff to act in a particular manner based on the reliance on the defendant's representation

- Damage resulted from this reliance

For instance, let's say that Jerry has never gone to law school and never passed a bar exam, but he places an advertisement in the newspaper stating that he's a practicing attorney. If you hire Jerry and he loses your case in court, you may very well have a cause of action against him for intentional misrepresentation.

>> **Wrongful institution of legal proceedings:** *Wrongful institution of legal proceedings* or *malicious prosecution* covers the wrongful prosecution of a defendant in criminal cases or the wrongful suing of a defendant in a civil action. To establish a prima facie case for malicious prosecution, the plaintiff must prove that there was a criminal proceeding against the plaintiff that was decided in favor of the plaintiff, that there existed a lack of probable cause for the proceedings, that the purpose of bringing the criminal proceedings against the plaintiff was one other than to serve justice, and that the plaintiff suffered damages.

No excuses: Strict liability

There are no defenses for strict liability cases. From the plaintiff or plaintiff's attorney's point of view, these are the slam dunks and home runs of the legal field. The primary issue in strict liability cases isn't about who's responsible but what the damages are. In these cases, the defendant has an absolute duty to make sure the plaintiff is safe. Examples of strict liability cases include actions involving vicious animals and ultra-hazardous activities. Owners of known vicious animals or vicious breeds of dogs may be held strictly liable for the damage their animals cause, and persons who offer abnormally dangerous activities that can never be perfectly safe, such as bungee jumping and blasting with dynamite, are strictly liable for any injury that occurs as a result of engaging in that activity.

Buyer beware: Product liability

Product liability is closely related to strict liability (see the preceding section). Plaintiffs bring product liability actions against manufacturers and sellers of defective or potentially harmful products, products that are unreasonably dangerous when they enter the stream of commerce. Liability in product cases may be determined by the defendant's conduct and is established when the defendant breaches a duty of care owed to its customers in producing the product.

Many product liability cases are brought in the form of a *class action suit* because the product affects many people in a similar manner. In these cases, a few harmed individuals or one individual represent the entire group in the action. Typically, a single law firm serves as the counsel for this large group of plaintiffs. Recent examples of product liability cases have involved exploding gas tanks on cars and problems with Vioxx and related drugs.

A big bother: Nuisance

Nuisance involves more than just an annoying younger sibling or a pesky fly. A plaintiff brings a *nuisance* action against a defendant who interferes with the plaintiff's reasonable use and enjoyment of property. A defendant may cause either a public or private nuisance. Mary can bring a *private nuisance* action against her neighbor, John, if his excessively loud stereo at night caused her nocturnal hamsters to die. Mary or her local government could bring a *public nuisance* action against John if his factory emitted pollutants into a stream and Mary's livestock got sick from drinking the water downstream.

In a nuisance action, the court can award either money damages or injunctive relief. When awarding money, the court determines an amount that provides restitution for those who are injured. *Injunctive relief* allows the court to prevent the injuring party from causing further damages. This relief assists in controlling companies from polluting the air or land and also allows for a free-market resolution of damages.

Sealing and unsealing the deal: Contract law

Contract law is another area of civil law you should know about when you work as a paralegal. And it's pretty easy to master as a pro se plaintiff, too. A contract is an agreement between competent parties to do or abstain from doing some act in exchange for something of value. Attorneys and their paralegals are involved in both the drafting of contracts and the litigation that results when a contract isn't honored.

TECHNICAL STUFF

In legal terms, a contract is an agreement between competent parties and involves bargained-for consideration. *Consideration* is the material element of the contract. A contract may be simply defined as *quid pro quo*, which means "something for something."

Making a pact: The elements of a valid contract

TIP

To be valid, a contract must include an offer, an acceptance of that offer, a mutual manifestation of an agreement to be bound by the offer and acceptance, and consideration. If a contract is missing any of its four elements, it isn't valid. The following brief explanation of the four elements of a contract will help you to better understand the law of contracts:

>> **An *offer* initiates a contract.** The offer may be phrased as, "I will give you $500 in return for two DVD players," or it may be simply phrased as, "Here is $500," when the intention is that the $500 is being traded for two DVD players. Making an offer is fairly simple, so it's easy to enter into a contract. A valid offer essentially requires that the offering party intend that her proposal be legally binding and that the proposal be complete.

>> **A valid *acceptance* of an offer consists of three elements:**

   ● An intent on the part of the acceptor to be bound by the terms of the offer

   ● An unconditional demonstration that the acceptor intends to be bound by the terms of the offer

   ● A mutual agreement of the parties

   If John says that he will give Sam $500 for two DVD players and Sam agrees to John's offer, Sam's agreement to the offer is an acceptance. If Sam accepts the valid offer and Sam indicates that his acceptance of the terms of the offer is unconditional, Sam and John have formed a contract under the common law requirements of forming a valid contract.

>> **Both parties must *manifest* assent, which means they have the actual belief and intent that they're mutually bound by the terms of their agreement.** It's difficult to accurately understand a person's thoughts and intentions at the time a contract is formulated, but both parties' actions should reasonably show that they intend to be bound by the terms of the contract. From Sam and John's behavior at the formation of the contract, it's apparent that they wanted to be bound by their agreement. However, if Sam shrugged and said, "I don't think we should be doing this," the manifestation of assent and acceptance could be questioned.

>> **The final prerequisite of a valid contract is *consideration*.** There must be an exchange of something of value. One party cannot merely give the other party the offered item. This would constitute a gift rather than a contract. Consideration may consist of an item of value (such as money), a legal detriment (such as forbearance), or a legal benefit (such as a monetary loan). Under Sam and John's agreement, the $500 and the DVD players represent the contract's consideration.

Undoing the deal: Types of contract litigation

It's said that contracts are made to be broken, and if that happens, paralegals are there to assist in the prosecution and defense of lawsuits bought under the law of contracts. The three major types of contract litigation you should know about are

» **Breach of contract:** *Breach of contract* results when one of the parties fails to fulfill the contract's written or oral commitments. This action is the most common one under contract law. If two parties entered into a valid contract and one party didn't fulfill the terms of that contract, the result is a breach of contract. The party who didn't receive fulfillment of the agreement may bring an action against the party who breached the contract.

» **Bad faith:** Entering into an agreement with no intention of fulfilling its terms is called *bad faith.* Usually the court compels the party who entered into the agreement in bad faith to pay the other party the amount that he may have lost due to the other's bad faith. That amount could be the total cost that the injured party incurred or the total profit that the injured party lost, depending on the situation. Many states, for instance, allow recovery for bad faith against insurance companies that don't properly pay benefits to the insured as promised in the original agreement.

» **Breach of fiduciary duty:** A *breach of fiduciary duty* is the failure to act in the best interest of a party when there exists an obligation to do so. This breach most often occurs with someone who makes investments for others. Stockbrokers, bankers, and other investors owe their customers a fiduciary duty to invest their money safely and act in their best interests. If an investor breaches this duty, the injured client may seek remedy through contract litigation.

Chapter **6**

Taking a Case to Trial: The Litigation Process

P aralegals assist their supervising attorneys with cases from start to finish. This chapter gives you the nuts and bolts of how to help your supervising attorney bring your firm's criminal and civil cases through the maze of litigation.

Constructing the Criminal Case

Criminal law paralegals may work in the public sector for either the prosecution or the public defender, or they may provide services for a private defense law firm that defends those who can afford to pay for their own lawyers. No matter which side of the fence you're on, your career in criminal litigation will be extremely busy. You have to concentrate on staying on top of the constant flow of cases and making your supervising attorney look good. We focus on procedure in this chapter, but you can find out more about the nature of criminal law in Chapter 5.

Charging the defendant

Paralegals who work in a federal, state, or local prosecuting attorney's office make sure that their supervising attorneys file the proper criminal charges against criminal defendants. The attorney begins the process by reviewing police reports of suspected criminal activity. He may even assist law enforcement in the process of obtaining a search warrant.

Police officers may arrest a suspect based on *probable cause,* which is a reasonable belief — based on all the facts available to the officer given her special training and experience — that a crime has been committed. For charges like drunk driving, misdemeanor assault or theft, and malicious mischief charges, police officers often arrest individuals suspected of committing crimes and turn the case that they have filed in court over to the prosecutor. For felony cases, law enforcement often investigates criminal activity and then refers the matter to the prosecutor without first making an arrest.

WARNING

To file criminal charges, the prosecution must have more than probable cause. The prosecution must also be reasonably satisfied that sufficient admissible evidence exists to justify a conviction by a reasonable fact finder, such as the judge or jury.

So, although law enforcement authorities may develop a case against an individual for prosecution, the prosecutor alone decides which criminal charges to file, especially with major criminal matters such as felonies. The prosecuting attorney, with the assistance of the paralegal, reviews the police reports, and decides upon two things:

>> Probable cause exists to charge the defendant.

>> A reasonable likelihood exists that there's enough evidence to convince a jury that there's enough evidence to convict the defendant.

TIP

As a paralegal, you're in an excellent position to assist your supervising attorney in determining the appropriate charges to file against a criminal defendant. You need to know enough about criminal law to intelligently discuss evidence with your supervising attorney, but your common-sense viewpoint may provide wisdom that the lawyer may otherwise overlook when deciding on the ultimate filing decision. You can offer a perspective that lets the lawyer know how a jury may view the same evidence.

When prosecutors are reasonably satisfied that they can get a conviction in court, they file a charging document against the defendant. The prosecutor charges the defendant either by indictment or complaint.

Charging documents come in two varieties:

>> Indictments, handed down by grand juries

>> Complaints (also known as *information*), charged by the prosecutor

Getting an indictment

Many types of felony cases on the federal level and in those states with grand juries are initiated by an indictment. An *indictment* document charges a defendant with a felony. The indictment just states that there's probable cause to charge the defendant based on the evidence. It doesn't imply that the prosecution has met the burden of proving its case beyond a reasonable doubt.

A prosecutor presents evidence to a group of citizens, called a *grand jury,* which then returns a decision based on its review of the prosecutor's case. Grand juries exist on the federal level and in most state judicial systems. If the grand jury thinks there's enough evidence to charge the defendant, it returns an indictment (or *true bill*); if there isn't enough evidence for an indictment, the grand jury returns *no bill.*

The grand jury's indictment alleges that the defendant has committed each element of the crime charged. An indictment is enough to bring a defendant to trial.

Filing a complaint

A famous quip declares that, at least in those states without a grand jury, you need only two things to file criminal charges against a defendant: a prosecutor and a pen! That's pretty close to the truth. In many states, a prosecutor can file criminal charges against a defendant by putting his signature on a charging document called a *complaint.* Sometimes, the complaint is also called an *information* (that is, it informs defendants about the criminal charges against them).

Like an indictment, the complaint or information must, on its face, state each of the elements of the crimes charged. If it doesn't, the defendant can bring a motion to dismiss for failure to allege all elements of the crimes in the charging document. If the defendant successfully gets the court to dismiss the complaint or information, the prosecutor may choose to refile the charges to accurately reflect the defendant's conduct.

In some cases, the prosecution must present the facts to a judge in a hearing to determine whether there's probable cause to put the defendant on trial. This stage of the proceedings is called a *preliminary hearing.* The preliminary hearing is like a mini-trial. The defendant doesn't put on a case, and the judge decides whether the state can go forward with the evidence that the prosecution has presented.

TIP

Regardless of whether the prosecutor files a complaint or charges the defendant by grand jury indictment, a paralegal working for a firm that represents criminal defendants should review the charging documents and confer with the supervising attorney as soon as feasible to determine whether there are any fatal defects in the documents, as well as whether the client should raise any defenses to the charges.

You can view a sample criminal summons and complaint online at www.dummies. com/go/paralegalcareer2e.

Pushing through criminal pre-trial procedures

As a paralegal, you play an instrumental role in getting a criminal case ready for trial. In fact, if prosecuting attorneys had to do all the pre-trial preparation them-selves, they'd have little time to manage their large caseloads. The same is true for offices specializing in criminal defense. Paralegals relieve attorneys from han-dling time-consuming pre-trial matters and allow them to focus on actually prosecuting or defending their cases.

Early on you'll visualize what the trial notebook will look like for a particular case. Everything you do before trial potentially ends up in the notebook to assist the attorney at trial. (You can find more about trial notebooks in Chapter 14.) Your duties for both the prosecution and defense may include collecting police reports and other data, collecting and organizing evidence, interviewing witnesses and preparing them for trial, preparing discovery documents, assisting with pre-trial motions and briefs, and maintaining a schedule of deadlines.

Gathering police reports

As a paralegal, you gather police reports. Normally, law enforcement sends reports to the prosecutor's office, but it's not unusual for reports and other items not to make it to the prosecutor's files. The paralegal should contact the police detective, sit down with him, and compare the reports in the detective's files with the reports in the prosecutor's files. That's the only way to know whether the prosecutor's case file is complete. Often, detectives may perform follow-up investigation, and the paralegal needs to ensure that the prosecutor's case file is always up to date when new information comes in.

In addition, you should request other reports that may not ordinarily show up in the detective's investigative case file. The nature of these reports depends on the type of case. If you're dealing with a drunk driving case, you'll need to make sure you get the report showing that the breath testing machine was properly calibrated. If you're dealing with a homicide, you as the paralegal should order the autopsy report from the medical examiner. If someone called in the crime on 911, ask the emer-gency call center to reproduce a copy of the recording for later use in trial.

Often, 911 call centers don't retain recording forever. After 120, 90, 60, or even fewer days (depending on the specific policy of the law enforcement agency), the critical recording of the person calling in could disappear forever if it's not prop-erly preserved shortly after the time of the incident.

Be on the lookout for other reports as well. Examples might include crime lab reports for forensic evidence such as DNA, fingerprints, ballistics, fiber analysis, handwriting analysis, and so on.

In addition, begin creating a log for all photographs, photomontages, property, and evidence. After the documents and evidence are gathered, you can organize and compile it into a meaningful trial notebook.

Meeting with victims, clients, and witnesses

One of your pre-trial duties when you work for the prosecution is to contact crime victims and witnesses (those who are favorable to the prosecution and those who aren't). Try to arrange a meet-and-greet with the victim as soon as possible after the defendant has been charged.

TIP

Meet with victims and witnesses early on! Get their statements in writing while their memories for details are fresh and before they've had a chance to ponder their stories and change their minds as to what happened.

A crime victim has undergone a traumatic experience, especially in cases concerning a major assault, robbery, rape, or kidnapping, and the effects of the crime may go well beyond any monetary loss to the victim. In homicide cases, you need to arrange to meet with the family of the decedent. You need to be extremely sensitive to their emotional needs. Not surprisingly, they may be quite angry, upset, or distraught. They want information about how the case will proceed through the system, and many times they just need someone to listen to them. Often, the victim needs professional counseling, and you can help line up that kind of assistance.

TIP

Quite often, you're the first line of contact between the crime victim and the prosecuting attorney, and maintaining that rapport with the victim as you assist him through the legal maze may be your most important duty.

Correspondingly, if you work for the defense, you need to meet with your client as soon as you can. If the defendant is in custody, you may have to plan several trips to the jail. In many ways, meeting with the criminal defendant is as critical to the defense as is meeting with the victim for the prosecutor. In your initial meetings, remind the defendant of the attorney's advice not to discuss the case with anyone. The "friends" your client makes in the next cell could be the people who will sell her up the river in return for some perceived preferential treatment from the authorities in their own cases.

WARNING

Meet with your client in criminal cases as early and often as reasonably necessary to ensure a good defense and to make sure the client doesn't feel like she's being ignored. If the criminal defendant thinks the attorney isn't including her in the defense process and ends up in prison or paying a hefty bill, she may dislike the judge, but — worse for your office — she may file a complaint against your firm with the state bar association.

In addition to meeting with the crime victim or client, you also need to meet with witnesses early, regardless of which side you're on. The police reports give a summary of what witnesses might potentially testify to in court. However, written summaries often don't do justice to the witness's true story. When police officers interview witnesses at the scene of a crime, their time is limited. Officers can't possibly get all the important details of the incident when conducting an investigation in the hubbub and immediate aftermath of a criminal act. In their quest to solve the crime as quickly and efficiently as possible, law enforcement officials might gloss over information that's critical to winning the case in court. Sometimes, you may need to conduct follow-up witness interviews to uncover facts that were missed the first time around.

You also have an advantage over law enforcement when meeting with witnesses. You're probably not as intimidating as an officer in uniform with a badge and a gun. You can take your time to meet with victim's witnesses to obtain a fuller, more detailed statement. Through careful interviewing techniques, one witness interview may lead to additional witnesses whose names weren't uncovered when the police officer first took the report. (We talk more about interviewing skills in Chapter 12.) After you conduct initial interviews and provide a summary to your attorney, the lawyer can determine whether she needs to interview witnesses further.

Obtaining tangible evidence

Paralegals are often instrumental in seeking out and organizing evidence in criminal cases. (We discuss some of the ways you may go about obtaining evidence in Chapter 11.) As a paralegal for the prosecution, you'll probably help the victim determine what the restitution will be if the defendant gets convicted. Medical records may be critical to proving the case against the defendant, so you may ask the victim to sign a release of medical records. This allows the prosecutor to do follow-up contact with any medical personnel to decide whom to subpoena to testify in court. It also assists the prosecutor in determining the amount of restitution the defendant will owe in the event of a conviction. You determine whether the victim suffered any other financial loss as well. Typical losses include property damage, lost wages, and identity theft losses. Because crime victims deal with the trauma brought on by the criminal act, they especially need your support and guidance to help them gather receipts and other evidence of loss.

The paralegal in the prosecutor's office should also contact law enforcement to get a rap sheet on the defendant, the victim, and all witnesses. Knowing the criminal records of all the witnesses allows for their effective *impeachment* (impugning of their credibility) at trial. And it's also a good idea for the defense team to probe the backgrounds of their witnesses to prepare for any challenges the prosecutor may bring.

Based on the evidence and potential witnesses, the prosecution may opt to offer the defendant a *plea bargain,* which is an attempt to settle the case, usually by reducing or dismissing some of the charges against the defendant or reducing the severity of the punishment in exchange for a no contest or guilty plea from the defendant. With a *no contest* (or *nolo contendere*) plea, a defendant neither admits to nor denies guilt for the charges. It essentially means that, although the defendant professes innocence, he concedes that he may be found guilty of the charges if the case were to go before a jury. Through plea bargaining, many criminal cases settle before they go to trial.

Keeping track of deadlines and documents

During the pre-trial stage, you enter on a calendar all the important dates for the attorney — everything from the *arraignment* (where the court advises the defendant of the charges and defendant enters a plea) to the actual trial date. In between, there may be hearings for bond reductions, pre-trial motions to suppress evidence from a search warrant or unlawful arrest, settlement conferences, readiness hearings, and discovery compliance hearings. As the paralegal, you make sure the attorney knows about these dates and isn't surprised by anything on the calendar. When matters get continued, you generally run draft copies of orders around to other attorneys to get signatures and file these papers with the court.

About a month prior to the trial date, you develop a final witness list and prepare subpoenas the attorney will send out to all witnesses for trial. Scheduling witnesses can be a real challenge because you have to deal with individuals' schedules as well as the court's. And, trial dates can and often do change when the court grants a continuance, so you may have to reschedule everyone all over again. Whenever the trial date is moved, you need to advise prospective witnesses accordingly. If a witness is unavailable on the trial date, you need to advise your attorney so alternative plans can be made. A witness contact list is critical in order to communicate with the witnesses in a timely manner. (You can find a sample witness contact sheet in Chapter 14.)

TIP

In addition to sending out subpoenas well in advance of trial to make sure witnesses get notice of the date, you may also want to send them a short letter advising them that the subpoena is on its way. This gives the witnesses a heads-up so they don't freak out if a sheriff's deputy or process server comes to their doors.

Engaging in other pre-trial activities

You may be in charge of making sure your attorney has made appropriate demands for discovery and has responded to the other side's discovery demands. In criminal law, the prosecutor and defense attorney have an ongoing duty and obligation to continuously respond to discovery as new information becomes available. You may further assist the attorney in drafting pre-trial motions and trial briefs, which requires you to conduct legal research to support your positions. (We cover legal research techniques in Chapter 13.) Naturally, the attorney does a final review of any such documents and signs off on them before you file them with the court. Eventually, you'll put everything pertinent to the criminal case into the trial notebook for the lawyer.

Tackling criminal trial procedure

If a criminal case isn't settled through a plea bargain, a jury usually hears the case and it proceeds to the trial phase. About ten days prior to the trial date, your attorney usually attends a readiness hearing to declare that the matter is ready for trial. After the court notifies your office that a judge and courtroom are available to hear your trial, it's time to rock 'n' roll. You'll probably accompany your supervising attorney to the courtroom where your attorney may want you to assist with jury selection. Chapter 14 explains your role in this process in more detail, but essentially your observations give the attorney valuable perspective as to the types of people he should look for to sit on the jury.

You probably provide the prosecuting attorney's main contact with the victim and witnesses as they're called to court to testify. If the rule on witnesses is invoked (which means that witnesses aren't allowed to hear others' testimonies), you make sure that witnesses remain outside the courtroom until it's their turn to take the stand. This ensures that witnesses don't hear each other's testimony and thereby have a tainted version of the incident when they testify. You certainly don't want the opponent's witnesses hearing what your witnesses say in court so they can tailor their testimony. In addition, you don't want the jury to think that your own witnesses have sat through the trial and had a chance to conform their testimony as well.

TIP

If time permits, you may want to bring the witnesses to the courtroom ahead of time, show them around the courthouse, and help ease any butterflies they may have.

You're also the eyes and ears of your supervising attorney when she must focus attention on the judge and witnesses as the drama of the trial unfolds. Taking notes on witness testimony — especially on any significant deviations a witness makes from what he told you in pre-trial statements — is critical. Also jot down the jury's reaction to testimony as it comes in, whether it's positive or negative.

Your own take on what happens during the trial is invaluable to your attorney as she constantly tailors the trial strategy to meet new developments and challenges.

During trial, your attorney may need you to grab a court file from the clerk's office, or he may request that you conduct some quick legal research of any new or unanticipated issues that arise. The attorney can't easily leave the courtroom or perform research during the trial, so you're the runner to make sure that things go smoothly for the lawyer. If a mistake occurs during trial — such as a witness who fails to appear — it's often the paralegal's job to resolve this courtroom crisis, which is almost impossible to anticipate but must be rectified to avoid losing at trial, and on appeal. Your job is to help the attorney make sure the job gets done right the first time, so when your side *does* win the case at trial, the favorable outcome can withstand a challenge on appeal.

Tying loose ends with criminal post-trial procedure

If you work for the prosecutor, the worst words you'll hear at the end of trial are, "We the jury find the defendant not guilty on all counts." Perhaps the only sound worse is if you work for the defense and you hear the presiding jury utter a guilty verdict. But hearing the verdict doesn't mean the case is over. Regardless of the outcome, you still have work to do.

Polling the jury

TIP

Immediately after the jury verdict, whether your side wins or loses, you or your supervising attorney will likely meet with the jurors for a debriefing. Jurors may tell you why they decided the case the way they did. The education you receive from their feedback may help the next case your office handles.

Jurors may tell you which witnesses were believable, what evidence persuaded them, and which arguments made sense. You may also learn which witnesses, evidence, or arguments turned them off. A visit with the jurors after trial is like getting free advice from 12 jury consultants.

Appealing the decision

At the conclusion of the trial, either side may bring *post-trial motions,* including a motion for a new trial or motion to set aside the jury verdict. Generally, the defendant brings these types of motions. The prosecution usually doesn't have the right to appeal a guilty verdict. Sometimes, if the court hands down a sentence that doesn't comply with the law, either party may appeal that decision.

The party that appeals the decision of the lower court is called the *appellant* or *petitioner*. The party who defends the case on appeal is called the *appellee* or *respondent*. No consistent relationship exists between the plaintiff or defendant and the appellant and appellee. The plaintiff brings the original action in court, but that doesn't mean the plaintiff brings the appeal, too.

If your supervising attorney's side wins the trial court case, then you've already taken the first step toward winning the case on appeal. The odds favor the side that wins at the trial level in an appellate case. If you work for the prosecution, it's extremely unlikely that the attorney can appeal an unfavorable decision. If the jury comes back with a not-guilty decision, you're stuck. The constitutional prohibition against double jeopardy forbids trying a defendant for the same crime twice. If the case experiences a *hung jury* (that is, if it couldn't agree on a verdict), the prosecution must decide whether to bring the defendant to trial again. You may assist your supervisor in the decision making process. Information gained from talking to jurors after the trial helps immensely.

If your attorney decides to file an appeal, check the state statutes or court rules to determine how much time you have to file a notice. Generally, the defendant has 30 days to file a notice of appeal after the court has pronounced the sentence. Of course, this timeframe varies depending on federal, state, and local rules.

The best way to think of a notice of appeal is that it has the same function as the original complaint but has a much simpler format. You can draft the notice of appeal for your attorney, and the pleading can be as simple as a one-line notice filed with the court that the defendant appeals the judgment and sentence of the trial court.

WARNING

Filing the notice in the timeframe specified by law is important — if you fail to do so, the client loses his right to appeal forever.

You may not know that the appellate court doesn't hear the case all over again. One common mistake that new paralegals make is to assume that, because an appellate court is a higher court, it's free to do whatever it wants. But the higher court only considers whether the lower court made an error of law. The court considers only the record of the case from the trial level. The record consists of a transcript of the witness testimony, the exhibits the trial judge admitted into evidence, and any pleadings, briefs, or other documents the parties have filed with the trial court.

After your supervising attorney has filed the notice of appeal, you help designate those portions of the record that are relevant to the appeal. If you need a transcript of the trial testimony, you may make arrangements with the court reporter to transcribe the testimony as soon as you can. If you're working for the appellee, you look at the parts of the record designated by the appellant to decide if you should supplement the record with additional material because the appellant may designate only those portions of the record that would help its side.

When the transcript is ready and each side has supplemented the record as needed, the court of appeals sends out a notice to the parties that the record is complete. The court then sets a briefing schedule, or timeframe, for when the parties must submit their briefs to the court. The appellant goes first and writes the *brief of the appellant.* The appellee then submits a *brief of appellee,* and the court of appeals sets very strict timelines that the parties must conform to.

Appellate briefs are crucial because the appeals process doesn't proceed like a complete trial. There's no discovery phase, no jury, no witnesses, and no testimony. There's usually more than just one judge sitting on an appellate court. Often, there are *panels* consisting of three or more judges. Sometimes, the higher court may hear the appeal *en banc*, meaning the entire body of the higher court hears and decides the appeal.

With very few exceptions, most courts in the United States are part of a three-level system: a large number of trial courts, a smaller number of intermediate appellate courts, and one supreme court.

TECHNICAL STUFF

Some states have only two levels of courts; some have four. Not every state calls its highest court the supreme court. New York State is one such example; there, the supreme court is the name for trial courts of general jurisdiction and the highest court is called the New York Court of Appeals.

Although every party has an absolute right to appeal from a trial court to the first level of appellate court, they don't get an automatic appeal to the highest court. If a plaintiff or defendant wants to appeal to the next level of appellate court, she must file a *petition for review.* The higher court either grants or denies the petition. After the parties have exhausted all levels of appeals, the decision becomes final, and the highest court that heard the appeal issues a *mandate* (a written order of the court that terminates all review in the matter).

Carrying Through a Civil Case

In many ways, the civil action closely resembles a criminal procedure. Cases follow a pre-trial, trial, and post-trial schedule, and the court documents are similar. As with criminal cases, many civil cases settle before trial, so they don't even enter a trial phase. Chapter 5 defines civil law for you, so here we explain how a civil action makes its way from beginning to end.

Initiating the civil process

A person, group of people, or business entity that seeks restitution from another usually consults with an attorney in an effort to resolve the dispute and obtain equitable relief or money damages. (Chapter 4 contains more-specific information about the kinds of legal and equitable remedies available in civil cases.) The attorney, often with the help of the paralegal, conducts an extensive interview with the client to ascertain the underlying facts and circumstances of the problem. From those facts and information gained from interviewing witnesses and performing legal research, the attorney and staff decide whether the prospective client has a *cause of action* (grounds to sue the other party).

If the attorney decides that the prospective client has a legitimate cause of action against the wrongdoer, the attorney and client begin the attorney/client relationship by executing the *retainer agreement* (a contract that says the attorney represents the client). After the attorney and client execute the retainer, the plaintiff becomes a client of the firm and all privileges and obligations pertinent to that relationship begin.

Sending the demand letter

After the attorney and client establish a relationship, the plaintiff notifies the defendant of the damages she has sustained as a result of the defendant's negligence through a demand letter prepared by the attorney. The attorney often delegates the letter-writing task to you, the paralegal. The demand letter spells out how much time the defendant has to answer the plaintiff's allegations and requests a specific sum of money as restitution. If the defendant doesn't answer the demand letter within the specified time period or if the defendant refuses to pay the requested amount of damages, the parties prepare for trial.

REMEMBER

You can see a sample demand letter in Chapter 10 and online.

Determining jurisdiction

If you send the demand letter and the prospective defendant hasn't responded in the required amount of time, the plaintiff's side prepares for litigation by gathering as many of the facts bearing upon the case as possible. Before the plaintiff initiates litigation, the attorney and paralegal select the proper court to file the case in. So, they have to establish proper jurisdiction.

TIP

Jurisdiction determines which type of court has the authority to hear a case. A court has no authority to render a judgment in any case unless it has jurisdiction over the person or property involved. In fact, a court can throw out a case if the plaintiff files it in an improper court. For instance, bankruptcy matters can be tried only in the U.S. Bankruptcy Court.

Civil courts can exercise three types of jurisdiction over parties:

» *In personam,* which is jurisdiction over a person

» *In rem,* which is jurisdiction over property

» *Quasi in rem,* which combines a little of both

If a court exercises *in personam* jurisdiction, it has the authority to determine the rights or duties of the parties involved in the dispute. The court also has the power to bind the parties personally to a settlement agreement or other court remedy. A court has *in personam* jurisdiction if it meets one of the following qualifications:

» The defendant resides in the county in which the court has jurisdiction.

» The defendant is present in the county in which the court has jurisdiction. The defendant must be personally served with proper process while in the confines of the county.

» The defendant and the plaintiff consent to a specific jurisdiction. The defendant's consent is key in this qualification.

Under *in personam* jurisdiction, the plaintiff must serve the defendant with proper and timely notice of the impending action. The plaintiff's attorney has the responsibility of serving the defendant while the defendant is present in the county or when the defendant can be contacted to consent to jurisdiction. Generally, the notice of the impending action can't take on a form other than personal service and can't be made by publication. (For more about the rules concerning service of process, see Chapter 7.)

In personam actions fall into one of two categories:

» **Local:** The plaintiff's attorney may file a local action only where the subject matter of the litigation is located. For example, a party suing to foreclose a mortgage on real property must file the action in the county where the property is situated.

» **Transitory:** Transitory actions are much broader than local actions. The plaintiff may bring a transitory action in any county in any state where the defendant may be found and served with process. An action for personal injuries resulting from a defective bottle of beer is an example of a transitory action.

In the present court system, the law determines *in personam* jurisdiction through mutual consent of the parties much more heavily than it used to. Corporations who do business in a state and motorists who drive across a state are said to have consented to the jurisdiction of that state's trial court under the long-arm statute, which makes it easier for a state to prosecute lawbreakers who don't reside in the state where they violated the law.

All *in rem* jurisdiction actions are local. A court with *in rem* jurisdiction can rule on property that's located within its county and matters that occur within its county. Notice to satisfy *in rem* jurisdiction may be made by publication, most commonly by legal notice in the locality's officially designated newspaper. As long as a matter occurs within or involves property located within the county's limits, that court has *in rem* jurisdiction.

Quasi in rem jurisdiction is exercised rarely, usually only in cases where a court is "grasping at straws" to obtain jurisdiction. A court may have jurisdiction over a party to an action if that party owns some property, such as real property or municipal bonds, within its confines even if that property is not involved in the dispute, as long as a judgment can be satisfied by that property.

Courts may also determine jurisdiction by the subject matter of the case. In general, cases originate at either the state or federal level. Federal courts try to severely restrict access to their process when parties want to bring a typical state claim. Specific requirements dictate jurisdiction at the federal level. Courts with specific limited jurisdiction include the U.S. Bankruptcy Court, the U.S. Tax Court, the U.S. Court of International Trade, and the U.S. Claims Court.

To originate in the U.S. District Court, a case must meet one of the following requirements:

>> The United States is a party to the case.

>> The matter arises under the U.S. Constitution or a statute of the United States, such as civil rights matters.

>> The case involves a *diversity of citizenship,* which means the controversy is between citizens of different states or between a U.S. citizen and a *foreign national* (a citizen of a foreign country who resides in the U.S.). These cases must present a claim for damages that exceeds a set amount, currently $75,000.

State statutes determine the jurisdiction requirements at the state level. Factors include the amount of monetary damages sought and the type of matter that the court will hear. In many states, matters asking for damages exceeding $25,000 originate in the trial court. There are also courts with specific jurisdiction like water courts and family law courts.

TIP

An understanding of the types of jurisdiction and the jurisdictional requirements provides you with the information necessary to determine the proper court for clients' cases.

Deciding on venue

After you determine proper jurisdiction, you choose the trial's *venue* (location). Generally, the venue for the trial is chosen for the convenience of the defendant, because venue plays an important role in allowing defendants to receive an impartial jury and a fair trial.

The bases for determining the venue of each dispute are as follows:

>> **Residence of one of the parties:** Statutes commonly allow the plaintiff to bring the action in the county where the defendant resides.

>> **Defendant's place of doing business:** Plaintiffs often sue corporations in the county or district where they do business.

>> **Site of the subject matter:** The plaintiff must bring suit in the county where the property is located if the lawsuit involves specific property.

>> **Site of the cause of action:** Plaintiffs may bring some actions where the cause of the dispute occurred. For example, an assault case that occurred in Denver County involving a defendant who resides in Arapahoe County may be heard in either the Denver County Court or the Arapahoe County Court, depending on the consent of the defendant. Similarly, a negligence case that occurred in Orange County involving a defendant who resides in Los Angeles County may be heard in either Orange County Superior Court or Los Angeles County Superior Court, depending on the consent of the defendant.

Note: Where the venue rules allow a choice of venue, the plaintiff usually gets to make the choice. For example, if the defendant resides in Orange County and the cause of action arose in Riverside County, the plaintiff usually has the right to decide whether to bring the lawsuit in Orange County or Riverside County.

Either party may request a change of venue to another county or district. The defendant usually is the party that requests a change of venue. Where the case has received wide publicity before trial, a party may seek a change of venue in an effort to secure jurors who haven't formed an opinion about the case or to provide a neutral forum not charged with local bias. The parties might also request a change of venue for the convenience of witnesses. Finally, a party might request a change of venue based on that party's claim that the judge hearing the case has a conflict of interest that would prevent that judge from being completely unbiased during the trial. This formal request is traditionally called a *motion to recuse*.

Proceeding through pre-trial tasks

If initial attempts to negotiate are unsuccessful, the plaintiff initiates the cause of action by serving the defendant with a *summons and complaint.* (In some states, a *complaint* is termed a *petition,* and a *summons* is called a *citation.*) Chapter 10 contains detailed hints on drafting the more common documents of the pre-trial stage of litigation, like these pleadings and motion documents:

» **Complaint:** The *complaint* (also know as a *petition*) is a pleading that states the facts of the plaintiff's action against the defendant and sets forth the damages, judgment, or other relief sought. The complaint must contain enough information to state a claim upon which relief may be granted for the plaintiff. The defendant may begin his defense by filing one or more of the following pleadings and motions.

» **Answer:** In response to a complaint, the defendant usually files a pleading called an *answer* that either admits or denies each of the allegations in the plaintiff's complaint or admits all and pleads an excuse. The defendant's answer may also contain *affirmative defenses* that the defendant argues will serve to diminish or mitigate his liabilities to the plaintiff. A defendant may also include in his answer a cross claim against a codefendant or a counterclaim against the plaintiff, or both.

» **Counterclaim:** The defendant often files a *counterclaim* as part of her answer to the complaint. The counterclaim consists of a cause of action in its own right that requests relief or damages that the defendant suffered at the hands of the plaintiff. A plaintiff usually files an answer to the new allegations raised in the counterclaim in the same manner that a defendant files an answer to the complaint.

» **Cross claim:** A defendant may allege a *cross claim* against a codefendant concerning matters raised by the plaintiff in the complaint. The primary purpose of a cross claim is to establish affirmative relief against the codefendant or plaintiff (or both) on the part of the defendant who submits the cross claim.

» **Motion to quash service of summons:** A *motion to quash service of summons* questions whether the defendant has been properly served with process.

» **Motion to strike:** A *motion to strike* asks the court to eliminate allegations in the plaintiff's complaint or petition that the defendant deems to be irrelevant, prejudicial, or otherwise improper. If the court agrees with the defendant, the court may order the matter to be deleted from the complaint.

» **Motion for a more definite statement:** A *motion for a more definite statement* requests that the court require the plaintiff to set forth the facts of the complaint more specifically, or to describe the injury or damages in greater detail so that the defendant can answer the complaint more precisely.

This motion is similar to a *motion for a bill of particulars,* which is also designed to assist the defendant in preparing an answer to the complaint by providing more detailed information regarding the plaintiff's cause of action.

>> **Motion to dismiss:** A *motion to dismiss* requests that a plaintiff's complaint be dismissed on the grounds that it does not state a prima facie case against the defendant. This means that even if, for the sake of argument, the defendant admits that all the facts alleged by the plaintiff are true, the plaintiff has not alleged sufficient facts to obtain relief from the court. (In some states, a motion to dismiss is termed a *demurrer.*) Generally, a defendant asks the court to dismiss the plaintiff's complaint *with prejudice* so that he can't file it again in the same court. The plaintiff can only appeal this dismissal to a higher court. The plaintiff, on the other hand, doesn't want the complaint to be dismissed, but if there's a defect with the pleading, the plaintiff will more readily accept a dismissal *without prejudice* because the plaintiff need only amend the error noted by the defendant and refile the complaint with the same court.

>> **Reply:** The plaintiff may file a reply in response to new assertions raised in the defendant's answer to the plaintiff's complaint.

You can view sample pleadings and motions online.

Dealing with discovery

After the filing and service of the last pleading allowed by court rules, the parties begin the *discovery* period. Paralegals assist their supervising attorneys in the discovery process. Discovery assumes two very similar forms: oral and written. Oral discovery consists of depositions, and written discovery consists of interrogatories, request for admissions, request for production of documents, and request for mental or physical examinations.

Either party to a lawsuit may request discovery in an effort to ascertain the facts necessary to prepare for trial, prevent surprises at trial, and, ideally, settle the action. Without a court order, written discovery can only be served upon parties to the lawsuit, but the parties to a lawsuit can require both parties and non-parties to undergo a deposition.

Because paralegals create many of the questions for written discovery, and because so much of written discovery is easily stored in the law office's computers, attorneys like to explore this relatively inexpensive discovery technique prior to administering more expensive depositions. Unless limited by court order, rule, or statute, most supervising attorneys have their staffs prepare a massive amount of discovery. After the law office receives the answers to written discovery, the requesting party might then depose the other party in an effort to clarify responses and resolve questions.

Even though answers to both oral and written discovery are provided under oath, the deposition responses are spontaneous and may be more helpful. Some attorneys conduct depositions rather that written discovery at the close of pleadings in an effort to get the most accurate information possible. Written discovery may then follow the deposition testimony. A deposition is an out-of-court statement that a party to or witness of an action gives under oath. Under the statutes and rules in most states, either party in a civil action may take the deposition of the other party or of any witness. To be effective, a notice to take deposition must be served upon the deponent accompanied by a subpoena and a check for mileage and witness fees.

Attorneys frequently take depositions of important witnesses to preserve their testimony if they can't appear in court or if they reside in other states or countries. These witnesses may be friendly, neutral, or even hostile toward your office's client. Their deposition testimony assists in determining the nature of the evidence that they would testify to if subpoenaed as witnesses in the trial. The deposition may take the form of answers to written questions or of oral examination followed by cross-examination. A deposition isn't a public record and isn't available to the press unless it's made public by court order.

TIP

Depositions may also be professionally videotaped. The advantages of adding video to the discovery process include the ability of the court to view the demeanor of the testimony and the potential for greater access to busy expert witnesses. Video recording may be more expensive, however, than procedures that involve only a court reporter. It's very difficult for a state to compel a witness's presence at a civil trial if the witness resides outside the state. Therefore, often the witness's deposition suffices for trial testimony. When a party seeks the testimony of a long-distance witness, the witness applies to the court where the case is pending for the issuance of an out-of-state commission, commonly called *letters rogatory*. This document empowers an official or attorney in the jurisdiction where the witness is residing to take the witness's deposition and forward it to the court where the action is pending.

TIP

In some states, the issuance of an out-of-state commission is unnecessary; so you should always consult your local court rules.

If a witness is absent from the jurisdiction or is unable to attend the trial in person, her deposition may be viewed or read into evidence. If a person who has given a deposition also appears as a witness at the trial, the deposition may be used to attack the witness's credibility if oral testimony at the trial is inconsistent with that contained in the deposition.

Either party may submit written discovery questions (called *interrogatories*) to the other party. The receiving party must answer these questions under oath. Unlike depositions, parties do not routinely file written discovery unless the court orders it.

Other discovery documents include the following:

>> **Request for production of documents:** Requires adverse parties to produce books, records, and documents for inspection

>> **Request for admissions:** Requires the adverse party to admit to or deny the genuineness of statements and documents

>> **Request for a physical or mental examination:** Requires the adverse party to submit to a physical or mental examination

If the other party doesn't provide responses to discovery, a party may file a *motion to compel.* Because an underlying purpose of discovery is to uncover all relevant evidence and to promote settlement of the case, the courts liberally construe and apply discovery techniques. So, the court will more than likely force a party to provide the information required by the discovery process even though that same information may not necessarily be admissible at the ensuing trial.

REMEMBER

You can see sample discovery documents online.

Conducting the pre-trial conferences

After each of the parties finishes conducting discovery and the case is determined to be at issue, many courts set the case for a pre-trial hearing or *pre-trial conference.* Generally, the attorneys appear at this hearing without their clients. In the presence of a judge, the attorneys seek to agree on undisputed facts and issues called *stipulations.* These stipulations may include such matters as the time and location of an accident; the use of pictures, maps, or sketches at trial; and other matters, including points of law.

The objective of the pre-trial hearing is to shorten the actual trial time without infringing upon the rights of either party. Pre-trial procedure frequently results in the settlement of the case without a trial, and case settlement is actually a primary purpose of the pre-trial conference. If the case doesn't settle, the court assigns a specific trial date for the case.

Traveling through the trial

After the court assigns a date for trial, the case takes on a new light. The attorneys and their paralegals prepare trial notebooks containing pleadings, digested depositions and other discovery information, motions, exhibits, trial briefs, and any other information that may be pertinent to the trial. Organization of these trial notebooks differs with each attorney; your supervising attorney will provide you with careful instructions on how to prepare these devices. (You can find more information on preparing trial notebooks and other ways paralegals assist attorneys during trial in Chapter 14.)

On the first day of the trial, the parties engage in *voir dire*, which is the process of selecting the jury. During voir dire, the attorneys question potential jurors to determine whether there is any reason for the attorneys to exclude any of them. In most trials, the attorney has a certain number of exclusions that can be made for no reason. These are called *peremptory challenges.* Practically speaking, attorneys use the voir dire process to exclude any jurors who may appear to be harmful to a party's case. (For information on how you can help the supervising attorney during voir dire, turn to Chapter 14.)

After the parties select the jury, the attorneys make their opening statements. The plaintiff speaks first. In the opening statements, the attorneys lay out the facts and points of law regarding the case.

After the defendant's opening statement, the parties begin to introduce evidence. Again, the plaintiff goes first. Evidence consists of exhibits of information and the testimony of witnesses. The party that calls the witness asks the first set of questions, called *direct examination.* Then the opposing counsel has the opportunity to *cross-examine* the witness. After cross-examination, the first party is allowed to *redirect* the examination of the witness. When all the witnesses for one party have testified, the opposing counsel brings her witnesses to the stand and repeats the process.

After the parties have concluded their witness testimony, the attorneys make their closing arguments. The plaintiff presents the closing arguments first. The plaintiff's attorney may request an additional amount of time after the defendant's closing statement so he can speak last as well. It may seem inequitable for one party to speak first and last. However, the plaintiff almost always has the burden of proof, and is therefore allowed to initiate and finalize the closing arguments. The plaintiff's attorney may not bring up new arguments in rebuttal but may only address those points raised by the defense.

After the parties finish their closing arguments, the judge instructs the jury on the law of the case. The attorneys usually propose these instructions to the judge, and the parties have generally agreed to them ahead of time. After receiving the instructions, the jury recesses to deliberate. Deliberation may take as long as is necessary for the jury to reach a decision. When deliberations are finished, the court enters a verdict and renders the judgment.

Plodding along in the post-trial

After the judgment is rendered, two procedures remain. If the court awards monetary damages, the winning party must collect the judgment. The two means of collecting judgments from an uncooperative defendant are garnishment of wages and attachment of assets. Collection of the judgment in full finalizes the dispute.

As in criminal law, some civil cases go on to the appellate stage. A party who wants to appeal the original court's decision must file a motion for a new trial within the prescribed amount of time in order for the appeal to be heard. Procedural rules in the appellate stage differ from those in the trial stage. The losing party files a notice of appeal with the trial court and the appellate court. The appellant files an opening brief with the appellate court, and the appellee files a respondent's brief. The appellant may file a reply brief to address new issues raised by the appellee.

You can appeal a trial court decision only when it makes an error of law. Appellate courts don't consider new evidence except under very restrictive situations. If the appellate court decides to listen to the attorneys argue their points, it may allow them to present oral arguments. These arguments are short — usually 15 to 30 minutes in length. Based on each party's written briefs and oral argument, the appellate court renders its decision to affirm, modify, or dismiss the lower court's rulings. The ruling of the appellate court finalizes the case, unless one of the parties appeals the decision to the state supreme court or possibly the U.S. Supreme Court. The higher court doesn't necessarily have to hear the appeal. These discretionary appeals are rarely granted.

TIP

For more information on how you can help your supervising attorney with post-trial duties, check out Chapter 14.

Chapter **7**

How It's Done: Important Rules of Civil Procedure and Evidence

The cause of action may differ, but for every criminal case and every civil case, the system has specific procedural and evidence rules that must be followed. The rules are designed to make sure that court proceedings are fair and that evidence gets admitted in court that's relevant to the case and not unnecessarily prejudicial to either party. Without procedural rules, properly applying the substantive laws of society would be impossible. Because the majority of paralegals work in civil law, this chapter focuses on procedural law for civil cases. In researching either the rules of civil procedure or evidence, it's critical that you, as the paralegal, check for any amendments or modifications to these rules prior to relying upon them in research.

Distinguishing Between Procedural Law and Substantive Law

The United States judicial system has rules governing the actual laws and how those laws are litigated. The *what* is the substantive law, such as criminal law, real estate law, torts, and family law. The *how* is encompassed in the rules of criminal procedure, civil procedure, and evidence. To understand the difference between the two, think of each court case like a sporting event. Of course, there's usually much more at stake in the simplest court case than in the most-hyped sporting event, but the analogy helps to distinguish between substance and procedure in law. For example, every basketball game is different with different players, different plays, and different outcomes. The one thing that remains constant is the rules. Because the rules don't change, everyone knows what to expect and can concentrate on playing as well as possible for his team. If the rules were to change with every game, the focus of each player would be on the rules and not the game itself.

What is true on the court is also true in the courtroom. Both share the need for the participants' behavior to be governed by consistent rules. Rules keep the focus of the basketball game on the participants' play, and rules keep the focus of a trial on the evidence and the substantive law. Without consistent rules governing court proceedings, cases wouldn't be about arguments and facts, but instead would focus on procedural details, like which attorney was allowed to do what and when.

Substantive laws are the ones that actually regulate public behavior, like criminal laws, custody and child support statutes, and laws governing intellectual property and negligence. The substantive laws are the issues to be tried in court; the way parties present those issues is regulated by the rules of civil procedure and evidence. *Procedural law* occurs at all levels of government, but paralegals deal mostly with those on the federal and state levels.

Following the Federal Rules of Civil Procedure

When you work as a paralegal, you probably deal mostly with state civil procedural laws, but most states base their laws on the Federal Rules of Civil Procedure (FRCP), so the federal rules provide a good foundation for understanding how things are generally done in most states. Plus, you may find yourself working on a case that's heard in federal court. This section highlights the federal rules you'll deal with most as a paralegal.

Although the formal written abbreviation for the Federal Rules of Civil Procedure is Fed.R.Civ.P., this short form doesn't flow off your tongue when you talk about the rules. So, informally and in speaking, most legal professionals refer to the Federal Rules of Civil Procedure as the FRCP.

At www.dummies.com/go/paralegalcareer2e, we give you a link to the full set of federal civil procedure rules.

Beginning an action: Rule 3

Rule 3 may be the shortest of the FRCP. It simply states that a civil action is initiated by filing a complaint with the court. Although the rule contains few words, it gives you important information about these two issues:

>> A civil matter isn't an action until a plaintiff files a complaint.

>> A complaint has to be filed with the court.

Most people resolve civil matters without going to court. The process of settling a dispute over a business contract, for example, is usually mandated by the contract itself, which outlines the penalties for default. So, businesses often solve disputes through arbitration instead of filing a civil complaint. And insurance companies often take care of compensating injured parties in car collisions and other accidents without court involvement. Many potential civil suits get resolved by some other means and never approach the courthouse door. So, attorneys file complaints for cases they think can't be settled without the help of the judicial system or for cases that run the risk of exceeding the *statute of limitations*, which is the amount of time the law allows to file a lawsuit.

Federal and state statutes provide maximum periods of time within which civil (and criminal) actions can be filed with the court. These time periods usually start running from the time an injury occurs or is discovered and may be as short as one year. So, sometimes attorneys file complaints before they have thoroughly examined a matter just to make sure a client doesn't miss her chance to file a case due to the expiration of the statute of limitations. In these situations, the attorney often files the complaint without serving the defendant so that the attorney has more time to research the case before the defendant is brought into the matter.

When deciding when to file a civil complaint, attorneys must consider the statute of limitations, the availability of evidence and witnesses, the level of preparedness of the case, and the schedules of the attorneys, paralegals, and even the plaintiff, who must, after all, devote considerable time to the case.

Attorneys and their staffs have to file complaints with the proper court. Many cases fall under the jurisdiction of a single court, so determining the proper court is easy. In a surprising number of cases, however, several court jurisdictions may be possible. And some courts have advantages over other courts in substantive or procedural law, so you may help your supervising attorney determine the best court to file the complaint with.

Serving process: Rule 4

Rule 4 is a lot longer than Rule 3. It deals with serving a summons and complaint (known as *service of process*), which is something that paralegals commonly do. When your attorney files a complaint on behalf of a client, the legal team is responsible for properly serving a summons on the other party.

Rule 4 is lengthy because it spells out in detail what constitutes proper service. Serving a summons correctly can be crucial to a case. A party to a case who is served with a summons and doesn't answer the summons (by appearing in court) is said to have defaulted and loses the case without presenting a defense. So the rules regarding proper service are super specific to prevent a plaintiff from claiming to have served a defendant without actually doing it.

The usual method of serving process is by *personal service* (not to be confused with the kind of personal service you actually *want*, like your own private butler!). This kind of personal service is the physical delivery of a summons to the defendant or someone authorized to receive it. The rule gives specifications about who is authorized to accept service for another person. It also specifies the requirements for who is allowed to serve process (basically, someone who is at least 18 years old and not a party to the case, which usually means someone from the plaintiff's legal staff or a professional process server).

State rules regarding service of process get more detailed when it comes to who can serve process and how it can be done, especially in cases where the defendant is hard to find. Some states allow *substituted service*, where process may be served by mail or publication in a periodical.

Rule 4 also outlines the methods for proving that the summons was served (called *proof of service*) within the time limits for serving the summons. A sworn affidavit of the process server or a signed receipt from the person who was served is generally accepted as proof of service. If the summons isn't served within 90 days of filing the complaint, the court may choose to dismiss the case without prejudice (meaning that the plaintiff can file the complaint again).

Figuring out time limits: Rule 6

One of the more important things for legal professionals to do is keep track of deadlines for filing documents with the court. Rule 6 tells you how to compute time when a federal rule or statute presents you with a specific time limitation.

A deadline includes the last day of a time limit, and if the last day falls on a Saturday, Sunday, or legal holiday, the last day is the day that comes immediately *after* the weekend or holiday. To compute a time limit that's expressed in days (like 90 days), you don't count the day that the limit is issued, but you have to count Saturdays, Sundays, and legal holidays in the total amount of days. For limits expressed in hours, you begin counting hours from the day the limit issued. So, if you were told on Friday at 5:00 p.m. that you have 48 hours to file a document, you'd have to comply with the filing by 5:00 p.m. on Monday (the day following the Sunday ending time).

Time limits for filing by electronic means (eFiling) and other means are slightly different. For electronic service, you generally have until midnight of the due day. For other filing options, the deadline is by the time the clerk's office closes for the day on which service is due.

The rule lists the days that are considered to be legal holidays (New Year's Day; Birthday of Martin Luther King, Jr.; Washington's Birthday; Memorial Day; Independence Day; Labor Day; Columbus Day; Veterans Day; Thanksgiving Day; and Christmas Day) and allows for other holidays that the president may appoint and for state holidays. So, don't worry: You won't have to file a motion on Christmas!

TIP

For a list of federal holidays, along with the days of the year on which these holidays fall, go to www.opm.gov/policy-data-oversight/snow-dismissal-procedures/federal-holidays/.

WARNING

Missing a deadline can result in a client's automatically losing a case before the attorney ever presents the evidence and may be grounds for legal malpractice! If you're responsible for computing deadlines, make sure you follow the rules.

Drafting pleadings: Rules 8, 11, and 12

As a paralegal you'll get to know the rules for drafting legal documents well. Taken together, they give the basic forms and required elements of pleadings, defenses, and motions. The rules aren't particularly wordy, but each paragraph provides a requirement that must be met. Each state has its own rules regarding the elements of legal documents, so make sure you know the local rules as well as the federal ones.

Making a case: What goes into pleadings

As Rule 3 tells us, the initial pleading you file in a case is the complaint, which consists of a written statement of the plaintiff's claim against the defendant. Rule 8 of the FRCP requires that the claim contain three elements:

>> The plaintiff must state why the particular court has jurisdiction over the case.

>> The plaintiff must clearly state why he is entitled to relief and what relief he would like.

>> The plaintiff must *demand* (this is a legal term and not considered rude) that the court enter a judgment granting the relief requested.

The rule outlines the options the defense has in its answer to the complaint. If the defendant doesn't know anything about the matter, the defense may say so. The defendant may deny some of the plaintiff's claim and admit to others. The rules also list the kinds of affirmative defenses available to the defendant and state that any allegation that the defendant doesn't specifically deny will be considered admitted. (For more about pleadings, see Chapter 10.)

TIP

The federal courts don't encourage long-windedness. Allegations and defenses are supposed to be short and to the point. To comply with the FRCP, draft documents using clear, plain language. A clean writing style isn't just a good idea — it's the law!

Taking responsibility for filing a case

Rule 11 emphasizes the professional responsibility of lawyers (and, therefore, their paralegals) in submitting pleadings and motions. The attorney must sign each pleading or motion submitted to a court. In submitting the document, the attorney verifies that the pleading or motion isn't being used for an improper purpose, such as harassment in the case of an unmerited lawsuit, or to delay or increase the cost of litigation in the case of a motion. By submitting documents to the court, you, and the lawyers you work with, are verifying that you aren't merely wasting the court's time, but are genuinely arguing the law and the facts of the case in good faith.

WARNING

Rule 11 also contains specific *sanctions*, or penalties, imposed on law firms, attorneys, and parties to a case if they violate their duty to act in good faith.

Responding on time

Rule 12 deals specifically with defenses and objections made by parties who are the subject of a complaint. A defendant in a federal case has a limited time (currently 21 days from service of process) to respond to a complaint. Likewise, a plaintiff who is the subject of a cross-claim currently has 21 days to respond. (According to Rule 6, you have to include weekends and holidays in the 21 days.)

But the U.S. government has 60 days to respond if it's the defendant. Apparently, the government really *does* take more time to accomplish things!

Uncovering the facts: Rules 26, 27, 30, 33, 36, and 37

One of your most important tasks will be to participate in the discovery process, especially if you work in a firm that specializes in litigation or areas that frequently lead to litigation, like personal injury, product liability, medical malpractice, or family law. *Discovery* is the term used for a variety of means of gathering information, like interrogatories, requests for admissions, requests for production, and depositions. The FRCP sets up rules for performing discovery, too.

Disclosing information

Rule 26 covers the general rules about the discovery process. It's especially concerned with the duty each party has to disclose information to the other. In most cases, both parties to a lawsuit must initially disclose important information, like the names of and contact information for individuals who are likely to provide relevant testimony. The parties must also provide copies of all "documents, data compilations, and tangible things" that they expect to use in their case.

The purpose of the initial disclosure is to make sure that both parties have knowledge of important information before the trial so that they can investigate the opposing side's witnesses and evidence. This allows each trial to be about the relevant facts and related law instead of which lawyer can pull off the biggest surprise. As a paralegal, you may be the one who gathers the materials for the client's initial disclosure and the one who reviews the materials provided by the other side.

The rule governs the use of expert witnesses by mandating that the parties reveal the names and testimony details of all their expert witnesses at least 90 days before trial. The disclosure includes

>> The expert's qualifications

>> A statement of the expert witness's opinions and rationale behind them

>> The fact behind the witness's opinions and the exhibits that will be used to support them

>> The trials the expert has testified in during the last four years

>> The amount of money the expert is being paid to testify

You may be responsible for gathering this information on behalf of your supervising attorney.

After the initial disclosure, parties may obtain additional information through discovery by requesting information from the opposing party about any of her relevant evidence. As a paralegal, you may be the one drafting these formal requests for information.

There are few limits to what information is discoverable. The court may order a party to turn over evidence in discovery even if it isn't admissible in court, so long as it may lead to other admissible evidence. Limitations on discovery are based on the relevancy of the information sought and the burden to the party providing the information. If the information isn't relevant to the case, the party doesn't have to share it. If information is available from another, more convenient source, or if the cost of preparing the information outweighs its value, a party doesn't need to provide it.

Conducting depositions

One of the most important ways of gathering information is through depositions of the parties to the case and any potential witnesses. *Depositions* are formal question-and-answer sessions conducted orally in person or remotely and under oath, and rules 27 and 30 govern their proceedings.

In a deposition, the lawyers for both sides ask questions of the party or witness being deposed (called the *deponent*), and a court reporter transcribes the oral answers into a written document (called a *transcript*). Depositions may also be video and audio recorded. Because depositions are conducted under oath, they may provide valuable evidence in trial, especially when a witness's testimony significantly differs from what he stated in the deposition. Consult Chapter 14 for more information.

Depositions are crucial to the trial process and paralegals play an integral role in most of them. You may do any or all of the following:

» Gather background information on deponents

» Draft questions to ask during the deposition

» Prepare your side's witnesses for the deposition

» Arrange for the court reporter

» Summarize the transcript for your supervising attorney

» Follow up on any new information gained from the deposition

The examination and cross-examination of deponents is very similar to what goes on at trial. No judge is present for standard depositions, but parties can make objections to certain questions and can stop the deposition to make motions. The deposition is an official court proceeding and falls under the jurisdiction of the judge assigned to the case.

Each witness deposition is usually limited to one seven-hour day of questioning. The court can extend this time, if necessary, and deponents aren't allowed to stall in order to avoid answering questions within the one-day time limit.

After a deposition, the lawyer, or often the paralegal, will go over the transcript or recording with the deponent to see if it contains any error. Changes appear in signed statement in an appendix to the deposition transcript or recording.

Asking questions

Discovery takes written forms, too. As a paralegal involved in litigation, you'll find yourself asking and answering questions. You create good questions to ask the opposing party during the discovery process, and with the attorney's supervision you help the client provide answers to the questions the opposition provides. Rule 33 covers the way you ask and answer the written discovery mechanism called *interrogatories*.

Written interrogatories may be addressed only to a party — not witnesses — and the answers won't be as spontaneous as in a deposition, but interrogatories are cheaper than depositions and allow for more thorough responses. Like depositions, interrogatories are answered under oath. Federal rules limit each party to 25 written interrogatories, so it's important to ask meaningful questions designed to produce information that can't be gathered any other way. Most state rules allow for many more questions, and some states don't pose limitations. You can find out more about drafting interrogatories and see a sample document in Chapter 10.

Requesting admissions

A trial should concern only *disputed* facts; producing arguments about facts that both parties agree on wastes time. A *request for admissions* requires the other party to either admit to or deny alleged facts in a case so that parties can determine exactly which facts are in dispute and must be decided at trial. Rule 36 governs the scope of and time limits for requests for admissions.

For example, in a medical malpractice case your supervising attorney may ask you to draft a request for admissions asking the defendant doctor to admit that he had not slept for 36 hours prior to performing surgery on your client. The doctor then has 30 days to either admit to the statement or deny it. If he denies the statement, he must do so by addressing the facts cited in the request for admission. So, he might deny the statement and say that he had slept for four hours on the previous night. If he fails to answer within 30 days, he is considered to have admitted to the statement by not denying it. (For more on drafting requests for admissions and other discovery documents, consult Chapter 10.)

You can view a sample request for admissions online at www.dummies.com/go/paralegalcareer2e.

Failing to discover

The FRCP sees the discovery process as serious business. On the small screen and in the movies, lawyers hold back evidence to surprise the witness on the stand for drama. But these surprises shouldn't happen in a real civil trial. The rules of civil procedure allow for the revelation of the disputed facts and law, and prevent attorneys from playing games with witnesses and evidence. To make sure everyone stays on the right track, Rule 37 provides penalties for parties that don't fully adhere to the rules of discovery.

If one party to a case fails to make an initial disclosure, fails to answer a written interrogatory, fails to make an admission, or doesn't participate in a deposition, the other party may file a motion in court. The offending party will be required to make full disclosure and will probably owe for legal fees incurred because of the extra work.

If a party participates in a deposition or answers written questions but the responses appear to be evasive or incomplete, the FRCP may treat the responses as though they were nondisclosure. If a party fails to admit to a fact that's later proved to be true, that party may owe for what it cost the opposition to gather evidence to prove the fact. And if a party fails to disclose a witness or evidence, the witness or evidence is likely to be excluded from trial.

Courts expect attorneys to comply with the rules of discovery. Encourage clients to answer questions truthfully and provide reasonable disclosure of the requested information.

Requesting a summary judgment: Rule 56

Before the trial begins, before the attorneys even select a jury, the attorney may submit a motion requesting the judge to decide the case in the client's favor (called a *summary judgment*). After the discovery process has ended and before the trial commences, a party may believe that all the important issues should be decided in its favor. That party may move for a summary judgment. Rule 56 concerns the time limits and procedures for these types of motions.

When considering a motion for summary judgment, a judge looks at the other party's case in the most favorable light. For example, if a defendant moves for summary judgment, the judge looks at the evidence in the way most favorable to the plaintiff. The judge acts as though the jury will believe all of the plaintiff's witnesses and none of the defendant's and construes the facts in a way that favors the plaintiff. If, even under these circumstances, the judge feels that the plaintiff couldn't win the case, she issues a summary judgment and the case ends before trial begins.

REMEMBER

As you might imagine, earning a summary judgment is difficult. Judges are reluctant to grant a summary judgment if there's any possibility that the other party can win the case.

Sticking to State Procedural Rules

Each of the Federal Rules of Civil Procedure has a state counterpart. You'll likely deal more in state judicial proceeding and with state rules than federal ones, so you need to find out the specific details for your state.

It may help to think of civil procedure as you would traffic laws. Traffic laws also govern behavior and differ slightly from state to state. In some states, you can turn right at a red light; in others, you can't. Some states allow U-turns and some have speed limits of 75 miles per hour. But certain fundamental things are the same in each state. In the United States, you always drive on the right-hand side of the road and red traffic lights and stop signs always mean you have to stop.

REMEMBER

Different states may have different document formats or different time limits for responses, but the fundamentals, like what constitutes process, will be the same. In every state, you file complaints (some states call them *petitions*) and motions, take depositions, answer interrogatories and requests for admissions, and disclose evidence in relatively the same manner that you do in federal cases. (The exception is Louisiana, which operates under a different system from other states, but even Louisiana has federal courts.)

REMEMBER

So that you can find out the deadlines and specific procedures for your state, we provide links to the individual state rules of court online.

Figuring Out Federal Rules of Evidence

Knowing the rules of civil procedure may keep a party from losing a case, but introducing convincing evidence is integral to winning one! Presenting evidence is the heart of the litigation process. In preparing for the trial, you may gather evidence (see Chapter 11). But evidence is only useful if the judge allows the attorney to present it at trial. So, you have to make sure the evidence follows the rules. At the same time, you assist your supervising attorney to limit the impact of the evidence presented by the other side.

From your exposure to popular culture you've probably already figured out that some evidence gets admitted in court and some doesn't. You probably know that the exclusion of certain key evidence can be the difference between winning and losing a case. But you may not know why some evidence makes it in and other evidence doesn't. It's not just a snap judgment on the part of the judge; it's based on some very important rules, which, for the most part, apply to both civil and criminal cases.

Jurors are the primary finders of fact in the U.S. legal system. Some trials are conducted in front of judges only, but a jury decides most important litigation. The rules of evidence reflect the extent to which we as a nation feel we can trust juries. Certainly, juries aren't considered entirely trustworthy because one of the purposes of the rules regarding evidence is to limit what jurors are exposed to, beginning with the jury selection process and continuing through open statements and the trial itself.

REMEMBER

When only a judge hears a trial, the evidence rules are more relaxed because the judge is thought to be capable of giving the evidence the weight it deserves. When a jury hears a case, the judge must decide if the illumination that the evidence provides is greater than its possible prejudicial effect on the jury. Juries are thought to overreact to certain kinds of evidence and misunderstand others. In the end, the judge must decide if the jury should hear the evidence.

The main event: General provisions

We focus our discussion on the Federal Rules of Evidence (FRE), not only because they govern federal cases but also because so many state rules are modeled on them. The federal rules and most of their state counterparts begin with general provisions that set the foundation for the remaining more specific rules that deal with the admissibility of evidence.

TECHNICAL STUFF

The formal written abbreviation for the Federal Rules of Evidence is Fed.R.Evid., but most people refer to these federal rules as the FRE because it's much easier to say this abbreviation than the formal one. So, informally and in speaking, most legal professionals refer to the Federal Rules of Evidence as the FRE.

REMEMBER

We limit our discussion of the FRE to those rules we think are most pertinent to paralegals, but you can find a link to the entire text of the FRE online.

Article I of the FRE states that the purpose of the rules is to promote fairness and gives general procedural standards for admitting evidence. The rules clearly protect the jury from hearing anything that might prejudice its deliberations.

The court has to conduct rulings on the admissibility of evidence so that inadmissible evidence isn't suggested to the jury by any means. The court must conduct hearings on the admissibility of confessions out of the hearing of the jury. The general provisions also address the partial admission of evidence and the admission of evidence based on the condition of certain facts being proved later.

What matters: Relevancy

The first consideration for any evidence is *relevancy*, which is the focus of Article IV of the FRE. If a piece of evidence has no bearing on the matter at hand, it can't be admitted in court, but sometimes determining whether evidence is relevant isn't clear-cut. Direct evidence of a fact is certainly relevant, but evidence that just provides context may not be.

For example, a defendant in a personal injury case may argue that accounts of the plaintiff's personal life relate to the matter at hand. Sordid details the defense reveals about the plaintiff may influence the jury to disengage from the plaintiff and decide for the defense. The plaintiff argues that such details have nothing to do with the case at trial. It's up to the judge to decide whether the private life of the plaintiff is, in fact, relevant and, therefore, admissible.

To determine the relevancy of a piece of evidence, the judge weighs the answers to two questions:

>> Does the evidence help to prove or disprove a disputed fact?

>> Is the fact in dispute *material* (or integral) to the case at hand?

If the evidence isn't relevant to a fact or if the fact isn't relevant to the case, the judge probably won't allow the jury to hear it.

Sometimes even relevant evidence doesn't make it to the jury. Under the FRE, the only way that relevant evidence may be excluded is if its importance to a party's case is significantly offset by the danger that the evidence may unfairly prejudice or mislead the jury, confuse the issues, or cause an excessive delay in the proceedings. So, relevant evidence that's repetitive may be excluded from a trial, as may evidence that excites the emotions of the jury in a way that gives the evidence more weight than it logically deserves.

Something special: Privilege

Article V of the FRE regarding privileged communications is very general. It maintains that the law considers communications in certain relationships to be privileged. This means that communications conducted within these relationships may not be revealed in court testimony unless both members of the relationship agree to the disclosure.

It's up to the states to determine which relationships are privileged, but in most cases communications made in the following relationships are privileged and, therefore, inadmissible:

>> Attorney and client

>> Doctor and patient

>> Husband and wife

>> Psychotherapist and patient

>> Clergy and penitent

These privileges protect confidential communications, limit government invasion into people's lives, and avoid likely perjury as a result of coerced testimony.

REMEMBER

Privileged communications aren't boundless. For example, attorney-client privilege doesn't apply when the confidential communications concern the client's plans to commit a crime or cause harm to others.

All there?: Competency to testify

Article VI concerns testimonial evidence, too. The general rule is that people are competent to testify unless they meet specific provisions. The judge and jury are, or course, free to weigh the value of the testimony based on their own consideration of the witnesses' fitness.

The FRE does provide some guidelines for determining competency, however. A witness may be disqualified from providing testimony if it's proved that the witness lacks personal knowledge of the event at trial. An expert witness can review the case and testify, but other witnesses can only address issues that they have personal knowledge of. The presiding judge and members of the jury can't be called as witnesses.

The rules also outline circumstances that don't affect competency to testify. For instance, requiring an interpreter doesn't make a witness incompetent to testify. And children and the mentally challenged may be called to testify, but they may have to answer a series of questions designed to determine their competency. These question-and-answer sessions usually occur outside the presence of the jury to determine whether the witness understands the need to tell the truth, can distinguish fact from fantasy, and has the ability to communicate with the judge and jury in a meaningful way. If a witness can demonstrate these qualities, under the federal rules she's competent to testify.

Thinking logically: Reasonableness of opinion

In a court of law, there are opinions and there are *expert opinions.* Article VII addresses opinion testimony. The FRE refers to non-experts as *lay witnesses.* The rules limit the opinions that lay witnesses may present. They can only give opinions that are rationally based on their own knowledge and helpful to the jury's understanding of their testimony, which means their testimonies may consist only of recitations of the facts and not their interpretation of those facts.

Expert witnesses, on the other hand, aren't limited by either the rule requiring firsthand knowledge or the rule against opinions. If an expert's knowledge can assist the judge or jury in their understanding of a case, that expert is allowed to testify and give opinions on areas of the case that fall within his expertise. A common example is a doctor who provided testimony as to the severity of an injury in a personal injury case or about the cause of an injury in a medical malpractice case.

A judge may determine the reasonableness of an expert's opinion or whether the expert witness has strayed beyond his area of expertise. If the judge believes the expert opinion is unreasonable or beyond the scope of expertise, the testimony may be stricken from the record.

TIP

You may assist in finding individuals to provide expert testimony on important matters at trial. Make sure you let the witnesses know that they must stick to their areas of expertise.

The telephone game: Hearsay

Generally, only those who have firsthand knowledge of the circumstances can present testimony about the truth of certain facts in a case. Article VIII of the FRE broadly states that the persons who may testify to a statement or event are those who actually made the statement or witnessed the event. Testimony to a statement by someone other than the one who made the statement (unless the one who made the statement is a party in the case) is called *hearsay.* As the word implies, this type of testimony involves a witness who *hears* something and then *says* it on the witness stand.

Anyone who has ever played the telephone game at parties knows the problems that occur when someone repeats what he has heard from someone else. The person overhearing the testimony may be wrong in what he hears or reports. The person telling the story may embellish or assume facts that he doesn't have firsthand knowledge of. For these reasons, and because hearsay evidence doesn't allow the other side to cross-examine the one who actually made the statement, federal and state courts usually don't allow for the admission of hearsay evidence. If you want eyewitness testimony allowed in a case, you have to bring in the actual eye-witness and not that witness's best friend to whom she related the whole story.

The rules don't consider testimony about statements made by a party to a case to be hearsay when the testimony is used to prove whether that party is telling the truth. Nor is it hearsay to provide testimony that contradicts statements made by a prior witness.

The rules of evidence provide for some exceptions to the hearsay rule. In these cases, testimony may be admitted as evidence even though it's hearsay. The exception rules are too numerous to list here, but one example is testimony regarding comments someone overheard another person say in an excited state immediately after the relevant event (called the *exited utterance exception*).

TIP

The rules regarding hearsay and its exceptions are voluminous and complex, so make sure you familiarize yourself with the complete text of Article VIII of the FRE, as well as with your state's rules regarding hearsay, so you have an under-standing about what kinds of testimony may or may not be allowed.

The real deal: Authenticity and originality

Most of the rules we've discussed concern testimonial evidence, but articles IX and X primarily concern tangible evidence. (For more about the difference between testimonial and tangible evidence, turn to Chapter 11.) Documents or tangible objects used at trial have to be *authenticated* so that the court knows the objects really are what they're purported to be. You should only present originals so that no controversy arises over the item's legitimacy. For example, a document said to be written by the deceased in a controversy over a will needs to be authenticated because it's only relevant to the proceedings if the deceased actually wrote it. A gun said to be found at the scene of a crime and belonging to the defendant is only relevant if it's *proved* that it was found at the scene and belonged to the defendant.

Methods of authentication vary based on the type of evidence. Handwriting experts may provide testimony about signed documents. In other cases, serial numbers, fingerprints, and eyewitness testimony may help authenticate whether an item belonged to a particular individual. It may be your job to provide proof of the authentication of evidence in court. This could require testing at labs or the use of expert testimony to prove that a piece of evidence is what your attorney claims it is.

Chapter **8**

Because I Said So: The Categories of Legal Authority

egal authority consists of any recorded source of material that states the law. According to the concept of stare decisis, legal authority is something the court may or must use in reaching its decision. There are two main categories of legal authority: primary and secondary. And, legal authority is further divided into mandatory and persuasive authority. Even nonauthority serves its purpose for the paralegal, legal researcher, and attorney as a case and statute finder.

Legal authority forms the foundation of legal research, which is the bread and butter of any quality law office. You can read about researching legal authority in a lot more detail in Chapter 13. In this chapter, we let you know what you'll be looking for.

Déjà Vu All Over Again: Review of Stare Decisis

Contrary to some popular opinions and those of a few radio talk show hosts, courts don't simply grasp for decisions out of the blue without giving thought to their legal implications. As bizarre as some court decisions might seem, tribunals must rely on past case decisions when they arrive at any new decisions. The popular press doesn't always give you the whole story. (That's why you snagged this book, isn't it?)

Courts make thousands of decisions every day. The one strand in the arsenal of legal tools that holds all court decisions together is the doctrine of *stare decisis*, the concept that courts must follow the rules laid down by higher courts in prior cases. Without this doctrine, the legal system would break down into something akin to anarchy. Stare decisis provides paralegals, attorneys, and judges with security, certainty, and predictability in researching the law. Without it, there would be no basis for legal decisions and lawlessness would prevail. (Okay, that may be a little melodramatic, but you get the idea!)

As long as the facts and issues of a precedent case are sufficiently similar to those of the present case under review, and as long as the court that rendered the decision in the precedent case is within the same system as and higher than the present court, the present court is bound to use the decision of the precedent case as authority in rendering its decision.

The one valid exception to following stare decisis occurs when the court finds that the reason for the rule or past precedent no longer exists. Courts can break with past tradition in order to remedy an unjust situation or change the law when the original logic or rationale for the prior rule ceases to exist. An example is the evolution of the law of racial desegregation in public schools. The U.S. Supreme Court overruled its prior precedent when it declared that segregated public schools violate the equal protection clause of the U.S. Constitution.

Sometimes courts don't have a firm rule of law from past precedents, so they have to fashion a decision that's not only just but also fills in empty spaces in the law. A *case of first impression* is one in which the court has no prior precedent or stare decisis to guide its decision making. A case of first impression is very often resolved on the basis of nonlegal traditions and, consequently, forms the foundation for future precedent.

TIP

Stare decisis is the name given to the courts' requirement to follow prior precedent. In simple terms, a court must follow prior court decisions involving similar facts and legal issues unless there is a very good reason to break with past tradition.

Who's the Boss? The Premises of Primary and Secondary Authority

Courts rely on two types of authority under the doctrine of stare decisis: primary authority and secondary authority. *Primary* sources of authority include cases, statutes, constitutional provisions, and administrative regulations. *Secondary* sources of authority aren't written by the courts, legislatures, or administrative agencies; instead, they're presentations of legal definitions or opinions on how the law ought to be interpreted. Table 8-1 defines the types of materials that fit into each of the two categories.

REMEMBER

Check online at www.dummies.com/go/paralegalcareer2e to see a list of the specific law texts that contain the primary and secondary authority listed in Table 8-1.

TABLE 8-1 ## Primary and Secondary Authority

Sources of Primary Authority	Sources of Secondary Authority
Any on-point case from the following sources:	Any on-point authority from the following sources:
U.S. Supreme Court	Legal dictionaries
U.S. Courts of Appeals	Legal encyclopedias (such as *American Jurisprudence 2d* and *Corpus Juris Secundum*)
U.S. District Courts	Annotated Reporters (such as *American Law Reports*)
State supreme courts	Law reviews
State appellate courts	Treatises
U.S. Constitution	Formbooks
U.S. Code	Live or pre-recorded seminars
State constitutions	Legal blogs or podcasts
State statutes	
Court rules	
Treaties	
Executive orders	
Administrative agency rules and regulations	
Municipal ordinances	

First chair: Primary authority

Primary authority is the most important source and type of law. It consists of the *actual written law* as opposed to something written *about* the law. Primary authority is either *judge-made* (laws created by judicial decisions — also known as common law) or *enacted* (rules and statues created by legislatures — also known as civil law).

Handing down the judge-made law

Judge-made law passes down through written court decisions, which are also called *opinions.* Opinions explain how a court has ruled on an issue and why it ruled in that manner. So, if a court rules that Jim, a dog owner, isn't responsible for the first injury caused by his pet, Rover, lower courts within the same jurisdiction that decide cases with similar facts are obliged to rule in the same way. Written opinions almost exclusively regard state and federal appellate court decisions because trial court opinions (with the exception of district court cases) aren't usually reported in law books.

Following the rules of enacted law

In addition to relying on court decisions, courts are also subject to the rules and regulations enacted by legislatures. The U.S. Constitution is the highest form of enacted law in the United States. So, it's considered the blueprint for all other laws. If a provision of the U.S. Constitution applies to a particular legal matter, the provision supersedes any federal or state laws to the contrary. Federal statutes and the regulations of federal administrative agencies also supersede state laws in those areas, like interstate commerce, patents, bankruptcy, or foreign affairs, that are entrusted to the federal government by the Constitution.

Enacted law also includes statutes. Congress and state legislatures create laws, called *statutes,* that citizens of their jurisdictions must follow. (If you want to know more about the nuts and bolts of how a bill becomes law, check out Chapter 4.) When a local legislative body such as a city council or board of county commissioners creates laws, they're called *ordinances.* Because an ordinance is a primary source of authority, it comprises the force of law for the local jurisdiction. Courts must enforce ordinances to the letter as long as these local laws don't conflict with the U.S. Constitution or state and federal statutes.

A third type of enacted primary authority, *regulations,* are every bit as much a part of the law as statutes passed by the legislature. Administrative agencies write regulations as part of their legislative capacity delegated by the legislature. Unless they conflict with statutes, court decisions, or the U.S. Constitution, regulations govern the conduct of the administrative agencies themselves, as well as the general public.

Second fiddle: Secondary authority

Secondary sources of authority include legal dictionaries, legal encyclopedias, annotated reporters, law reviews, treatises, formbooks, and even seminars. They're secondary because they offer explanations of primary authority but don't make up the actual laws written by the legislature, the courts, or agencies. In terms of its importance in legal research, secondary authority is a second-class citizen. So, although a court may consider the legal opinion of a law professor as written in the *Harvard Law Review,* the court isn't obligated to rely on that opinion in the way it must rely on an on-point federal statute.

TECHNICAL STUFF

A precedent case is *on-point,* or *on all fours,* when it involves an identical issue of law and the same or a substantially similar set of facts as the law and facts of the case that a court is currently considering. When a case is on all fours or on-point, the current court must rely on it as mandatory authority if the precedent case is primary authority.

Applying the Law: Mandatory and Persuasive Authority

In addition to the distinction made between primary and secondary authority, you can make a further distinction between the way courts have to use authority. Authority may be mandatory or persuasive.

Counting on cases and statues: Mandatory authority

Mandatory authority is anything a court *must* use in reaching its decision, and includes on-point enacted law and judge-made law from a higher court in the same jurisdiction. So, mandatory authority includes relevant statutes and rulings from a higher court. This means that all mandatory authority is primary authority, but primary authority isn't necessarily mandatory unless it's on-point from a higher court.

In following the doctrine of stare decisis, a lower court must use applicable statutes as written and relevant mandatory higher court rulings in deciding its cases. For example, the Circuit Court of Appeals must use analogous U.S. Supreme Court cases to decide its cases. Therefore, when you conduct legal research for a client's case, your objective is to find as much mandatory, primary authority to a research problem as possible.

WARNING

A higher court's decision isn't always mandatory on a lower court even if it's on-point. The higher court must be within the same system as the lower court. For example, a decision from the Supreme Court of Arizona is not binding on the lower courts in neighboring California.

Enacted laws (constitutional provisions, statutes, ordinances, or administrative regulations) are mandatory authority and must be used to decide a case in the following circumstances:

>> When they're used in the geographic area over which they have jurisdiction

>> When they apply to the facts of the case

>> When they don't violate another law that supersedes them

For these reasons, state enacted law (such as a state statute or a state administrative regulation) is usually only mandatory in the state that enacted that law. Federal enacted law (like the U.S. Constitution, a federal statute, or a federal administrative regulation) can sometimes be mandatory authority in state courts. And on-point U.S. Supreme Court decisions are mandatory authority in federal courts and state courts.

A court is required to follow a case opinion, or precedent, in these instances:

>> When the case precedent is sufficiently similar in fact to the case at hand

>> When the case precedent comes from a court in the same jurisdiction that's higher than the one deciding the case at hand

TIP

So, to be mandatory authority, an opinion must be on-point and must have been written by a court that's superior to the court currently considering that opinion. If the opinion doesn't meet one of these tests, it's either persuasive authority or nonauthority. The concept of on-point is susceptible to various interpretations, and what is considered to be on-point by one court may not be by another. The concept of on-point, then, serves as a basis for appeal, because facts or issues that may be on-point to one court may be irrelevant to another.

WARNING

Beware of dicta or *obiter dicta* in a court decision that appears to be on-point mandatory authority. *Dicta* (or it's singular *dictum*) consist of additional language in a court's opinion that's irrelevant to the court's decision. They appear primarily in appellate court decisions because these opinions are traditionally written and compiled in law books. This unnecessary language can masquerade as mandatory authority, but don't quote it as mandatory authority in your legal memos.

For example, a court might rule that Jim is not responsible for his dog Rover's first attack on a neighbor because of provocation, but the written opinion may provide the judge's dissertation regarding how Rover's breed is a nuisance to society and that the town council ought to pass an ordinance outlawing ownership of this breed within the city limits. With dictum, the judge goes off on a tangent and states things that aren't relevant to that particular decision. The additional language might be interpreted as a signal to anyone researching the case that the court may decide future cases using that information, but that isn't always the case. For instance, a court can't use the judge's opinion to ban Rover's breed. So, you need to be particularly cautious if you decide to use dicta in your legal analysis. At most, it can be persuasive authority for a future case with similar facts.

Getting creative with sources: Persuasive authority

Persuasive authority is legal authority, generally case law or a piece of secondary authority, that a court *may* use in deciding cases (but doesn't have to). Persuasive authority includes rulings from other courts, rulings from the same court, or non-binding statutes from other jurisdictions. For instance, the New Mexico Supreme Court may consider an on-point ruling from the Ohio Supreme Court, but the Ohio ruling would only be persuasive, not mandatory, authority.

A court opinion isn't mandatory if it's written by an inferior court and is being considered by a higher court within the same judicial system or if it's written by a court from a judicial system other than the one of the court that's considering that opinion. In either of these two situations, the court doesn't have to follow the opinion. However, if the opinion is on-point, the court may adopt it as persuasive authority.

A court considers several factors to determine whether an opinion is substantially persuasive, including the following:

- » How many other courts throughout the country have adopted the opinion?
- » Has the opinion been frequently cited with approval?
- » Is the opinion well-reasoned and compatible with the opinion of the court?

The U.S. Constitution is the only mandatory authority for the U.S. Supreme Court. There's no mandatory case authority for the U.S. Supreme Court, because its own rulings are the highest rulings in the United States. Although the U.S. Supreme Court isn't necessarily bound by any of its prior decisions, these decisions constitute persuasive authority upon the Supreme Court, which means that in future rulings the Court may either consider or disregard its prior rulings. On-point cases from the federal trial court and federal court of appeals are at most persuasive authority upon state supreme and appellate courts.

Secondary authority can never be mandatory authority; it can only be persuasive authority. Although secondary sources of authority often make for good reading, a court is never required to decide an issue according to the way secondary authority treats the law.

WARNING

In compiling legal authority for your case, don't rely solely on secondary authority. Your argument will be much stronger with the support of primary authority. Sometimes secondary authority leads you to primary authority. If you're so fortunate, quote the primary authority rather than the secondary authority in your legal argument. (We talk more about quoting sources in Chapter 13.)

Helpful But You Can't Rely On It: Nonauthority

Nonauthority is anything the court may *not* rely on in making its decision. So, if a case isn't on-point, it's considered to be nonauthority rather than mandatory authority. Other examples of nonauthority are *Shepard's Citations*, digests, *A Uniform System of Citation*, and any authority that's no longer valid because it's been overturned by a later case. (You can find out more about these other sources in Chapter 13.) Just because a resource is considered nonauthority doesn't mean it's useless. It can be extremely valuable to the paralegal, legal researcher, or attorney in terms of finding case law that *is* on-point.

» Bouncing with the boom and bust: Business law and bankruptcy law

» Easing the pain and suffering: Personal injury and medical malpractice

» Cutting through the contracts: Real estate and entertainment law

Chapter **9**

The Substantive Law Areas Most Commonly Practiced by Paralegals

You may choose to specialize in a particular area of law in your paralegal career. In this chapter, we take a look at some of the areas of law available to paralegals and the specific duties paralegals perform in these areas.

Facing the Family: Domestic Law and Estate Planning

Domestic law and estate planning may touch more average American lives than any of the other areas of law. Domestic law includes the important legal considerations affecting families; adoption, divorce, custody battles, prenuptial agreements, paternity, and child support are just some of the subjects covered by domestic law. Estate planning focuses on wills and the distribution of assets at the time of death.

Settling the family affair: Domestic law

In most jurisdictions, the family law courts have the most crowded dockets, which means that employment opportunities for paralegals in family law firms abound.

Here are some of the common types of cases handled by a family law practice:

>> Name changes

>> Prenuptial and antenuptial agreements

>> Common law and ceremonial marriages

>> Contract cohabitation

>> Annulments

>> Separation agreements

>> Divorce settlements

>> Restraining orders

>> Paternity and illegitimacy

>> Parental liability and torts

>> Child custody matters, including visitation and support

>> Collection of delinquent support payments

>> Adoption

>> Emancipation of minors

>> In vitro fertilization and surrogacy

As a paralegal working in the field of domestic law, you often deal with people who are quite desperate for help, which requires empathy, understanding, and objectivity on your part. Having a sociology, psychology, or related background helps when you work in a family law environment; those who've experienced divorce or other domestic issues are excellent candidates for paralegal work in a family law practice because they have the compassion that comes from having been there.

In family law practice, your office's client may be trying to win visitation rights to see her children. Another client may be struggling through a divorce and trying to get the child support he needs to survive. A couple may be desperately trying to adopt a child. The nature of the cases can make domestic law an emotionally challenging yet rewarding area in which to work.

Because of the sensitive nature of domestic law issues, maintaining discretion and impeccable ethical standards is absolutely crucial.

However emotionally charged domestic law cases may be, they're still decided in the court system. These cases often go to trial so, as in all civil litigation, your paralegal assignments may include several different duties. You may interview clients to secure information about the case and interview the client's friends, family, and others to obtain eyewitness or expert testimony or character witnesses (we get into more detail about interviewing techniques in Chapter 12). Your supervising attorney will likely ask for your assistance in drafting discovery, pleadings, and motions (see Chapter 10 for document drafting techniques), and you'll be instrumental in insuring compliance with discovery requests, serving subpoenas, and assisting at trial.

You may have to do a little investigative work as well. Ascertaining parties' assets is important in drafting prenuptial agreements and determining spousal and child support in divorce cases, so you may have to collect information on somebody's sources of income, assets, and expenses. Investigative work can get complicated in some cases, so you may need to enlist the services of a private investigator to gather evidence of wrongdoing on the part of a spouse or of abuse committed by a parent.

Domestic law contains a little of everything and most cases involve issues of immediate importance to the client. Most domestic law offices don't even shut down fully on weekends. So, if you're no stranger to hard work, long hours, and multitasking, and you have a compassionate shoulder to cry on, family law may be a good fit for you.

You can find out more about some of the elements of domestic law in the latest editions of *Divorce For Dummies* by John Ventura and Mary Reed and *Law For Dummies* by John Ventura, JD (both published by John Wiley & Sons, Inc.).

Looking to the future: Estate planning

Estate planning and probate are areas of law that are surprisingly interesting for both attorneys and paralegals. Wills and trusts can be complex documents specifically tailored to match the wishes of clients. Family members often go to court over the validity of wills and the distribution of assets. Planning for the future allows you to use all your skills and intellect on behalf of the client.

As a paralegal, you can take part in most aspects of estate planning. You can assist your supervising attorney with the initial client meeting. Later in the process, you can draft wills and trusts. And, when the time comes, you can act as the liaison with the probate court. Paralegals are integral to the entire estate planning process. Although you can't represent clients in court, there are very few aspects of estate law that you *won't* be involved in. Here's a quick look at some of the elements of estate planning:

>> **Creating a will:** A will allows a person to decide what will happen to his assets and property when he dies. He wants to know that his will is carefully written and can stand up to legal challenges. As a paralegal, you may participate in discussions with clients and assist in plans to distribute their assets. You may be asked to assist your supervising attorney with drafting wills according to the wishes of clients.

>> **Acknowledging nonprobate instruments:** When a client comes in to discuss a will, that client may not be thinking of other means of wealth transfer. As part of the legal team, you may help clients consider all the ways they can pass assets to their beneficiaries, and not just those included in their wills. As you become familiar with nonprobate instruments, you'll be better able to help your office's clients fulfill their wishes.

>> **Helping out after the client dies:** When a client dies, all assets that pass through a will to beneficiaries or assets that pass *intestate* (those who die without a will) pass through the probate court system. If a client dies intestate, the court awards portions of the estate to the deceased's relatives based on how closely they were related. As a paralegal, you may be asked to help one of the deceased's family members obtain the share of the estate she's entitled to. At this point, the issue moves from one of family planning to one of civil litigation. Of course, you can avoid lawsuits among relatives and the threat of Uncle Sam's inheriting someone's hard-earned dollars by some forward thinking and professional estate planning. That's why estate planning is so important.

>> **Litigating a will:** Just because someone dies with a will doesn't mean everything's peachy keen. All sorts of unresolved family issues crop up when a will is involved. When someone dies, there's the potential for a lot of money to change hands. Those who are excluded from a will, especially if they're close family members, often challenge the validity of the will. If the will is broken (found to be invalid), an earlier will may become valid, or the assets may pass as though the deceased had no will. Those who challenge wills are usually the family members who have the most to gain from breaking the will.

In estate planning practices, the client authors the will and has reasons for distributing assets a certain way. Even after the client has died, your office still acts on his behalf to see that the will is enforced. It'll be your job as a member of the legal team to be so good at estate planning that you avoid will contests due to alleged fraud or undue influence.

>> **Frauds and forgeries:** Sometimes it's questionable whether the deceased actually wrote the will, so descendants may challenge wills because they think they're fraudulent. If your supervising attorney specializes in estate planning, you may be asked to investigate the legitimacy of wills for the descendants of the deceased. Or if a will suddenly appears that's different from the one your office has on file for a client, you may have to investigate the authenticity of the surprise document. *Note:* To prevent challenges to your office's clients' wills based on fraud allegations, your and your supervising attorney should make sure that several competent adults sign a client's will as witnesses to its validity.

>> **Undue influence:** Heirs may challenge a will with allegations that the author of the will was under undue influence or coercion when he signed the will. Examples of exerting undue influence on a will maker include making physical threats, overmedicating the author during the process, applying mental manipulation, and providing gratuitous favors in exchange for consideration. Assisting with cases of undue influence requires keen investigation skills.

>> **Lack of capacity to make a will:** Heirs may challenge a will with allegations that the author of the will lacked the necessary mental capacity when she signed the will. This may require medical professionals and other witnesses to testify as to the mental state of the will's author.

Estate planning law may be for you if you're organized and like working with forms, numbers, financial issues, and people. When you work in estate planning, you can expect to play an important role in the process. Your focus may include any or all of the following:

>> Drafting documents, like wills and trusts

>> Researching pertinent inheritance and tax laws

>> Gathering and filing client asset information

>> Communicating with clients and their beneficiaries

>> Locating heirs

>> Maintaining bank accounts

>> Drafting tax returns

>> Preparing settlements

TIP

You can find out more about estate planning in the latest edition of *Law For Dummies* by John Ventura, JD (John Wiley & Sons, Inc.).

RIPE FOR A CONTEST: SUSPICIOUS WILLS

In one unusual case, a will appeared to be genuine but was actually a fake. It was neatly typed on notebook paper and was signed with the authentic signature of the deceased. It left everything to the husband of the deceased and declared that the deceased's children should have no part of the estate. The children challenged the will and a document expert tested its authenticity. Under ultraviolet light, it turned out that the husband had erased a handwritten note asking for laundry money and typed the will over the erased note, leaving the wife's valid signature at the bottom.

In another interesting case, a will wasn't forged, but the basis for the will was fraudulent. A woman left most of her estate to her husband, but it turned out that the man was actually still married to someone else. Her children contested the will, and the court ruled that the woman's intent had been to leave her estate to her husband. Because the man had fraudulently led the deceased to believe they were legally married, the court found that the provision of her will that left the assets to the fraudulent spouse was invalid.

The court, in a relatively unique case, found that a sole beneficiary of a will exerted undue influence because she had her own attorney draft a new will for her ill stepmother at the stepmother's bedside immediately before her death. The stepmother spoke little English, so the stepdaughter served as the translator during the drafting of the new will. The beneficiaries of the stepmother's previous will — her nieces, nephews, and a charity — contested the new will, and the court found that there was no valid reason other than duress for the deceased to make drastic changes to the will so near the time of her death. It invalidated the new will and enforced the previous one.

Building the Boom and Blanketing the Bust: Business and Bankruptcy Law

Both business law and bankruptcy law deal with money issues. Law firms can assist large corporations and one-person operations with the legal ramifications of getting started, making contracts, defending litigation, and other legal matters. In fact, most large corporations have their own legal staffs. Attorneys and their staffs are also there when companies and individuals face financial problems that may result in bankruptcy. Paralegals provide vital assistance to attorneys in all legal matters relating to business law and bankruptcy.

Keeping up with capitalism: Business law

Business law represents another high-growth area for paralegals. In addition to private law firms that specialize in corporate law and have long used paralegals, corporate legal departments, banks, real estate companies, and insurance companies have increasingly hired paralegals and continue to do so. Currently, paralegals in the business law area take on duties that, in the past, were performed primarily by attorneys.

Attorneys usually advise business clients on which business organization (sole proprietorship, partnership, corporation, or limited liability company) is best for them to adopt. And their paralegals often draft the initial startup documents and documents necessary for the subsequent smooth flow of the business structure.

Some of the things you may be responsible for when you help your attorney's client initiate a new business include

>> Registering the corporate name

>> Drafting the articles of incorporation and by-laws

>> Preparing to issue stock

>> Completing the documents necessary for a corporate bank account

>> Drafting employment contracts

>> Filing paperwork with the IRS

>> Preparing documents to obtain business licenses

After the business is up and running, your tasks may include preparing documents for shareholder meetings, writing the minutes of completed meetings, drafting stock-option plans, reviewing lease agreements, drafting articles of a merger or consolidation, preparing reports for regulatory agencies, and obtaining the necessary authorizations to do business overseas.

Business law doesn't usually focus on litigation because businesses want to avoid litigation if at all possible. The legal staff perpetuates this goal by helping businesses plan well and avoid disputes that might lead to unnecessary government regulation or defending a lawsuit. So, corporate legal professionals plan for possible difficulties in advance. They structure deals and documents with great care so litigation isn't necessary if partnerships split up, employees need to be fired, or the business dissolves. Registering business names, logos, or slogans avoids the possibility of conflict with another business that may already use the same name, logo, or slogan. Drafting employment contracts, working with state and federal regulators, obtaining the proper licenses and insurance, checking lease agreements, and carefully recording stock transactions keep businesses, and the legal professionals who represent them, out of court. You'll know that you have been part of successful legal team for a business if after many years that business hasn't been involved in litigation.

Because business law deals more with documents than litigation, you may not face as many long hours and stressful deadlines as litigation paralegals do. But job pressures do exist in business law, especially when one corporation acquires or merges with another, when a privately owned company issues stock for the first time, or when a company begins to do business overseas. These events require precise legal documentation and may lead to tremendous workloads for a period of time.

Business law can be very interesting and challenging, especially if you have a business background. You'll have the opportunity to work on important assignments that affect the future of companies of all sizes. And if you decide to work as a freelance paralegal, that company could be your own!

TIP

You can read more about the law pertinent to business in the latest edition of *Law For Dummies* by John Ventura, JD (John Wiley & Sons, Inc.).

Providing debt relief: Bankruptcy law

When an individual or business carries more debt than can possibly be paid off, the solution may be bankruptcy. Legal representation is almost always necessary during a bankruptcy, and attorneys who specialize in this technical and rapidly changing area of law rarely take on other types of cases.

Special courts hear bankruptcy cases. The U.S. Bankruptcy Courts are a part of the U.S. District Courts. States aren't allowed to regulate bankruptcy law and state courts may not hear bankruptcy cases.

As a paralegal working in the area of bankruptcy law, your duties won't vary greatly from case to case. You can work for bankruptcy attorneys who specialize in representing debtors or for attorneys who represent creditors.

On the debtor side, the legal team interviews the client to gain an initial summary of the financial situation and proposed dates for the bankruptcy filing. Based on the information that the client supplies and that you collect, your supervising attorney advises the client on the appropriate type of bankruptcy for him (Chapter 7, Chapter 11, Chapter 12, or Chapter 13), or the attorney may advise the client to pursue a course other than bankruptcy. (Bankruptcy has very serious implications for an individual's credit rating, so it should be implemented only as a last resort.)

If the client decides to pursue bankruptcy, you draft and file the necessary petitions with the bankruptcy court. You may attend court hearings with the client and the attorneys. Depending on the client's repayment plan, you may need to file monthly reports with the creditors and maintain a log of debts that your client owes.

If you work on the legal staff that represents the creditor, your job is to make sure your client receives its fair share of the debtor's nonexempt assets. The creditor side requires keeping track of filing deadlines and drafting legal documents as well.

Bankruptcy may not seem as exciting as a high profile personal injury litigation practice because procedures remain pretty much the same for each case, but some cases involve other areas of law, like family law, probate, business law, real estate law, and criminal law — so bankruptcy practices may be more diverse than you think. And bankruptcy law practices tend to keep more normal work hours than other litigation practices. On the debtor side, providing relief to those who are in serious financial difficulty makes bankruptcy law a rewarding area to work in.

TIP

You can find out more about bankruptcy law in the latest edition of *Personal Bankruptcy Laws For Dummies* by James P. Caher and John M. Caher (John Wiley & Sons, Inc.).

Compensating for Pain and Suffering: Personal Injury and Medical Malpractice

Personal injury and medical malpractice law usually result in civil litigation. As a paralegal working in these fields, you help prepare cases for trial. Even those cases that are eventually settled out of court typically involve a discovery process that includes assessing injuries and damages, investigating facts, researching applicable laws, deposing witness, and seeking expert testimony. Cases that go to trial usually require drafting briefs and motions, selecting a jury, preparing witnesses for testimony, and composing opening and closing statements. (You can find out more about the trial process in Chapters 6 and 14.)

Attorneys almost always handle personal injury and medical malpractice cases on a contingency fee basis, which means plaintiffs with clear-cut liability actions can count on the contingency system to attempt to restore them to their former lives without spending much money up front. Under this agreement, an attorney receives a percentage of what the client receives from the defendant, so the attorney gets paid only if the attorney recovers for the client. When you work as a personal injury or medical malpractice paralegal for a plaintiff's attorney, you know that your supervising attorney won't collect fees unless you help the plaintiff win the case.

As a paralegal working in the fields of personal injury and medical malpractice, you'll have some very important duties. These duties may include

>> Drafting the complaint on behalf of the plaintiff or the response on behalf of the defendant

>> Reviewing client files and gathering factual information

>> Examining locations and objects

>> Taking notes and photographs

>> Preparing and serving subpoenas and summons

>> Drafting questions for witnesses' depositions

>> Doing research into medical matters

>> Calculating damages

>> Obtaining biographical information on jurors

>> Preparing exhibits

>> Attending trials to take notes of nuances the attorneys may miss

Personal injury and medical malpractice cases require a tremendous effort from the legal teams of both the plaintiff and the defendant. If you want to be close to the courtroom in your paralegal career and you don't mind working long hours, these areas may be the ones for you.

Placing the blame: Personal injury law

Although some high-profile personal injury scams make it seem that people file injury suits just to cash in at the expense of a deep-pocket corporation, most cases are serious and involve permanent injuries, substantial pain and suffering, and even death.

To understand personal injury cases, you need to know about tort law. Chapter 5 provides a much more detailed explanation of the key elements of this area of law. Essentially, the two defining features of personal injury claims are *harm* and *negligence.* As a paralegal working in this area, you may be responsible for gathering proof of the harm done, including medical records, police reports, and insurance estimates. If you work with the defense, you may be seeking these documents in order to show that the harm doesn't exist or is minimal. If you work with the plaintiff, you need to establish the full extent of the client's injuries.

REMEMBER

The harm done must be caused by another's negligence. Persons are said to be negligent if they fail to use the ordinary care that a reasonable person would use and this failure results in another person's injuries. Under the reasonable person standard, the defendant is not liable for the injury to another if the injury was purely accidental. However, if the injury is foreseeable, and the defendant does nothing to prevent it, the defendant is likely negligent and liable for the harm she causes.

Ideally, cases for personal injury accomplish two things:

>> They provide compensation for someone who has suffered harm.

>> They modify the behaviors of individuals and businesses that may harm others.

As a paralegal working in the field of personal injury, you play a part in helping the system work properly. By working vigorously for the client, either as a plaintiff or defendant, you'll help ensure that people who are truly injured by the negligence of others are compensated and that those cases involving no harm or pure accident are dismissed.

In personal injury law there are a wide range of assignments for paralegals:

>> You may be asked to do investigative work — such as taking notes and photographs — at the scene of the injury.

>> You may do research into previous cases with similar fact patterns or into laws that apply to the client's case.

>> Under your employer's supervision, you may draft motions, complaints, settlement offers, and appeals.

>> You may search for and interview witnesses and arrange for experts to testify at trial.

>> You may prepare the exhibits, maps, and charts the attorney uses during trial to make the client's case.

Questioning the bedside manner: Medical malpractice

Medical malpractice is a specialized area of personal injury law that involves complicated issues and lots of expert testimony. Medical malpractice is unlike any other area of personal injury law because of the complex scientific and ethical issues raised.

The standard of negligence in a common personal injury suit is the reasonable person standard, but in medical malpractice this standard doesn't fit. A reasonably prudent person who's not a medical professional probably wouldn't know what to do when confronted with a compound fracture, for example. So, in medical malpractice, the standard takes into account the specialized knowledge and skill of the medical professionals, which leads to a much higher standard of conduct.

Although the law imposes this high standard of conduct, it also allows the medical profession to determine what reasonable conduct is for doctors, nurses, dentists, pharmacists, and other medical workers. At the heart of a medical malpractice claim is the question of whether the defendant acted within the bounds of common practice of the medical profession. This standard, in turn, places a heavy burden on the plaintiff to prove to the jury what the appropriate standard of care should be. This almost always means that the jury will hear testimony from expert witnesses who are also medical professionals. Your job may be to secure the testimonies of the experts that best support the client's case.

Being a paralegal in the field of medical malpractice may be one of the most challenging careers to pursue. A background in science and medicine is sometimes required. Here are just some of the challenges facing a paralegal in this field:

>> Investigating complex procedures

>> Deciphering medical and legal jargon

>> Taking testimony from expert witnesses

>> Trying to create a case that is clear to the average juror

This area of law is not for everyone, but if you can become an expert medical malpractice paralegal, you'll be in high demand.

TIP

A new career is emerging in the legal field, and it's called *legal nurse consultant.* Attorneys have long recognized that they have too little medical knowledge to assess medical malpractice cases on their own. So, they rely on seasoned registered nurses (RNs) who know about the law to help them out. If you're an RN with an interest in the law, you may enjoy this very lucrative option. Many nurses have found second careers in legal nurse consulting by combining a paralegal education with their medical experience.

Getting It in Writing: Entertainment and Real Estate Law

Although entertainment and real estate law concern very different topics, they are similar in that both deal heavily with contract law. (For more about the nature of contract law, check out Chapter 5.) Both areas concern other types of law as well. For instance, entertainment is greatly impacted by copyright law, and real estate attorneys may assist their clients with zoning issues.

All that glitters: Entertainment law

The types of cases available to an entertainment law paralegal vary considerably. In the period of only a few months, all the following lawsuits were filed:

>> The original creator of a popular television show sued the movie studio that two decades later released a movie based on that TV show.

>> A famous guitar manufacturer sued another company with similar-looking guitars.

>> The author of a book distributed via late-night infomercials sued the state of New York because that state's Consumer Protection Board allegedly interfered with the sale of his text on natural cures.

>> A restaurant owner sued the publisher of a guide to restaurants for writing a review indicating that people didn't go to the restaurant for the food.

>> The author of a previously published book sued the author of a new book, alleging the new book was just a reworked version of the earlier work.

Despite the variety in these cases, much entertainment law boils down to two issues: copyright infringement and breach of contract. Entertainers hire attorneys to protect the ownership of their craft, negotiate and litigate their contracts, and protect their reputations.

WARNING

Although all clients deserve their privacy and are protected by attorney/client privilege, being a paralegal in the entertainment industry may require more discretion than any other area of law. The tabloid papers as well as the mainstream news are always hungry for more information about celebrities. You may have access to information that must be kept secret. If you can't show the proper amount of discretion, your career in entertainment law will be very short indeed.

The job of an entertainment law paralegal encompasses many types of law. You may be involved in drafting sound contracts or securing copyright protection, and your entertainment law firm will inevitably enter litigation when the contracts are breached or the copyright is infringed upon. So, if you have experience in the entertainment business and feel confident about your skill level, you may feel at home in entertainment law.

Preserving the American dream: Real estate law

Real estate law can seem fairly routine when all goes according to plan. As a real estate paralegal, you may be involved in preparing all the documentation necessary for a real estate deal to close. You may be assigned to

>> Conduct the title search of the property to be closed

>> Prepare a preliminary abstract of title and opinion of title

>> Negotiate for title insurance coverage

>> Review the mortgage contract and application for mortgage

>> Prepare quitclaim deeds for any third parties who may have easement rights to the property

>> Appear at closing

>> Notarize documents at closing

Another aspect of a real estate practice is landlord/tenant law. When a person signs a lease for property with another person, potentially volatile legal issues may result. Because a lease is a contract, breach-of-contract cases are common in landlord/tenant law. General terms of leased property follow the dictates of state law, and generally landlords and tenants can't break a lease without legal justification. (For more information, check out the latest edition of *Law For Dummies* by John Ventura, JD [John Wiley & Sons, Inc.], which contains a section on buying and selling real estate.)

As a real estate paralegal, landlord/tenant relations may provide you with some of your most interesting and challenging work. You assist your supervising attorney in keeping on top of state laws governing leases and help craft leases that address all possible renting nightmares. In case of a dispute, you'll need to assist with drafting and filing the necessary paperwork on behalf of your office's client, either the tenant or owner in a lease arrangement. Real estate legal professionals provide their clients with advice that preserves the clients' rights.

Another interesting area of real estate law involves zoning questions. Zoning laws regulate what kinds of uses can be made of land in a specific area. When businesses and individuals seek a variance in the standard zoning, they often employ the help of real estate law professionals. For example, a business may want to operate in a residential area. The first step in the process is consulting with local officials to obtain the variance. If the request is denied, the landowner may have to go to court to try to get the desired permission.

The types of things you'll be doing if you become a real estate paralegal really depends on the type of real estate law you choose to work in. You can work with a firm that does mainly title searches and closings, which results in fairly steady and predictable work.

If you work with commercial or residential leases, you learn to expect the unexpected. The entire relationship between landlord and tenant is based on one person using another person's property. Although this situation usually works out well for both parties, when things go wrong it can be a race for the courthouse door. The only acceptable place for landlords and tenants to settle their disputes is in the courtroom. As a paralegal working with leased real estate, you can expect to perform many of the duties associated with various other areas of law. For example, you'll need to write contracts as carefully as you would in business law. And landlord/tenant issues may go to trial and produce the work commensurate with other civil litigation cases.

You may also choose to work for a firm that takes on real estate cases involving government taking of property, zoning issues, covenants and restrictions used by homeowners associations, easements, and adverse possession of property. Many of these unusual cases also involve civil litigation, while others require filings with local, state, and federal regulatory bodies. Some issues, like the government's taking of land, may even involve constitutional law.

If you enjoy a little variety and have a real estate background, you may fit right in with a real estate law practice.

Protecting Assets: Tax and Intellectual Property Law

Providing assistance to those who have tax issues or need to protect their ideas and inventions may not seem as exciting as prepping for a high-profile criminal case, but paralegals who work in law firms that specialize in these areas are rewarded with relatively predictable work schedules and the opportunity to help clients hang on to and maintain the fruits of their hard work. If you work for tax or intellectual property attorneys, expect to handle a large number of documents. This section gives you an overview of what you may encounter.

Dealing with the IRS: Tax law

As a tax law paralegal, you may assist the IRS attorneys who attempt to collect taxes from citizens or the private attorneys who represent individuals and corporations that the IRS pursues. Cases involving the IRS may be criminal or civil. The majority of tax issues are civil, but if the IRS can prove that an individual or business has committed *tax evasion* (deliberately falsifying records and engaging in other activities to fraudulently reduce tax liability), the government may impose criminal charges. In those cases, a criminal attorney would likely represent the defendant, and the duties and procedures would follow those specified for criminal cases (see Chapter 5).

Although it's possible to work as an IRS paralegal with both the benefits and liabilities of working for the federal government, the majority of positions for tax paralegals are in firms providing private defense for civil tax matters.

For tax matters, presumption of innocence doesn't exist. If the IRS determines that someone owes $100,000 in taxes, that individual must pay the amount or provide proof that the government is wrong. Otherwise, that unfortunate soul is likely to face huge penalties and interest and may even be charged criminally. However, IRS's computations are often incorrect. The combination of complex tax laws and dealing with a federal agency makes handling tax matters without the help of an attorney undesirable, which is where tax paralegals come in handy.

REMEMBER

As a paralegal working for an attorney who helps individuals and businesses stare down the government, your tasks will likely include the following:

>> Communicate with clients regarding securing records and documents to support a challenge of the IRS's tax determination

>> Provide documentation and research results to IRS agents and attorneys

>> Draft and finalize letters on behalf of your supervising attorney to clients and the IRS

>> Work with accountants to obtain records and documentation

>> Prepare IRS forms and documents (such as Forms 433A, 433B, 4868, FBARS, and voluntary disclosure letters)

>> Conduct legal and factual research

>> Advise the supervising tax attorney on legal and tax strategies

>> Analyze a client's tax liability

>> Enter clients' financial data into tax software

>> File tax returns on behalf of a client

>> Collect, organize, and manage tax documents from clients

>> Maintain a client activity and task log

>> Draft Installment Agreements and Offers in Compromise

>> Create finished case files for supervising tax attorney

If you enjoy working with data, are good with numbers, and are equally comfortable communicating with clients and government representatives, you may enjoy working as a tax paralegal.

Clarifying the rightful owner: Intellectual property law

Intellectual property (IP) law involves protecting intangible assets. These assets may be in the form of artistic endeavors and copyrights, and in this area, the duties of an intellectual property paralegal may be very similar to those of a paralegal who works in entertainment law (see "All that glitters: Entertainment law" earlier in this chapter). Additionally, IP may include inventions, designs, certain phrasings, trademarks, service marks, patents, and trade secrets. Your work environment may be a government agency or in-house as a paralegal of a company who needs to protect its intangible assets, or you may work for the IP attorneys whom individuals and businesses hire to help them protect their ideas and inventions. Regardless of the workplace, an IP paralegal may be called upon to work in these aspects of IP law:

>> Research existing trademarks, service marks, and patents to determine the originality of a client's product or service

>> Work with clients to create online patent and trademark applications with the U.S. Patent and Trademark Office

>> If necessary, file requests for reconsideration when an application is denied or the patent office requires additional information

>> Register a copyright with the U.S. Copyright Office

>> Record copyright transfers or terminations for clients and otherwise manage existing trademarks, service marks, and patents

>> Draft and review licensing agreements

>> Assist with litigation associated with copyright or patent infringement

Because inventions often concern products and services related to technology, many IP attorneys have expertise in science and engineering. So, having a background in the sciences may help you communicate with clients better and understand the mechanics behind certain inventions. If you have an interest in technology and enjoy working with documents, working as an IP paralegal may be right up your alley.

3

Putting It into Practice: The Paralegal in the Civil Litigation Process

Prepare clear, convincing, and properly formatted legal documents.

Uncover evidence and build a case through effective legal investigation and interviewing techniques.

Scour the literal and virtual shelves of cyber and brick-and-mortar law libraries to discover applicable case law and statutes.

Organize the components of a prepared case and follow it through the trial process.

Maintain a standard of ethical responsibility to your supervising attorney, office clients, and the legal profession.

Chapter **10**

The Paper Chase: Preparing Documents

As a paralegal, you need to familiarize yourself with all the types of documents that are relevant to the practice of law. This chapter covers the most important civil law legal documents in rough chronological order as they show up in the course of litigation. We focus on civil law rather than criminal law because paralegals are most apt to prepare documents for civil litigation. These documents range from the demand letter that tells the opponent to "cough up" prior to filing a lawsuit all the way to the appellate brief that seeks to either overturn a losing decision or uphold a winning verdict. After we explain what each document is used for and what it contains, we show you what they look like and give you tips on how to draft each one.

Communicating in Writing: Types of Legal Documents

We think that the best way to introduce you to the multitude of legal documents involved in a common civil law action is by taking you through a hypothetical case. In order to highlight the important types of legal documents, assume that a prospective client, Kelley Klutz, has just slipped and fallen on the vinyl tile surface of Worst Deal electronics store while comparing the prices and features of karaoke machines. As a result of the fall, Mr. Klutz suffers a broken hip. Mr. Klutz knows of a particular law office's reputation for integrity, competency, and great paralegals, so he calls and briefly discusses his case with the attorney, Ima Gogetter.

Getting started: Preliminary documents

Ms. Gogetter suggests that Mr. Klutz arrange an appointment with her paralegal and asks the paralegal to prepare an intake memorandum based on the initial client interview. The *intake memo* summarizes background information about Mr. Klutz, details the facts of the slip and fall, and proposes the action that Mr. Klutz would like the law office to take on his behalf. An intake memorandum is just one of the many types of memoranda of law that paralegals often prepare. After submitting this intake memo to Ms. Gogetter, Pat Paralegal calls Mr. Klutz to tell him that Ms. Gogetter has offered to represent him in a slip-and-fall action against the electronics store under a contingent fee agreement.

A *contingent fee agreement* is one where the attorney gets paid only if the client wins the lawsuit. In other words, the attorney's fees are *contingent* on a favorable outcome of the case. A *retainer agreement,* on the other hand, provides that the client pays the attorney an hourly fee for services no matter what the outcome. In either case, although the attorney might make advance payments for necessary costs associated with litigation, the client is ultimately responsible for repaying those costs regardless of whether the case is won or lost.

After reading and agreeing to the terms of representation, Mr. Klutz and Ms. Gogetter execute the contingent fee agreement and the attorney/client relationship begins. A typical contingent fee agreement stipulates that if the case is settled before trial, the client will keep 67 percent of the settlement proceeds after costs are deducted, and the attorney will keep the remaining 33 percent. If the case doesn't settle before trial, a typical contingent fee agreement provides that the attorney will retain 40 percent, or even 50 percent, of the award as a result of a favorable trial court decision. The contingency percentages are negotiable so that given a strong case with clear-cut liability, the attorney may agree to keep less than 33 percent because strong cases don't usually require lengthy settlement negotiations or trials.

Defendants in *tort cases* (cases that concern non-contractually-based civil wrongs) and both parties in *non-tort cases* (civil cases that don't involve a tort, such as contracts and divorces), usually execute retainer agreements with their attorneys. Retainer agreements provide for a certain sum of money to be paid up front as a retainer and specify an hourly fee for services, which are usually billed monthly.

The monthly bill will draw down the retainer fee until it's depleted, and the lawyer might request the client to pay an additional retainer amount as security for continued billings.

WARNING

If the law firm decides not to represent the client, communicating that fact *in writing* to the potential client as soon as possible is extremely important. Although the attorney decides whether to take on a case, the paralegal is often responsible for making sure the law firm notifies potential clients about the attorney's decision. So, you need to keep track of the status of cases after the initial client interview and gently remind your supervising attorney if he hasn't made a decision about a client within a reasonable period of time.

After the attorney/client relationship has been established, Ms. Gogetter attempts to resolve the dispute without litigation. In fact, even though the number of lawsuits increases every year, civil litigation should be the last resort for the resolution of disputes. Attorneys, with the help of their paralegals, should explore all efforts at settling cases without litigation, including mediation and arbitration.

The initial effort to resolve litigation involves making Worst Deal aware of the damages Mr. Klutz has sustained as a result of Worst Deal's negligence, so the paralegal prepares a demand letter. This *demand letter* notifies Worst Deal of the circumstances underlying the damages that Mr. Klutz has sustained and provides Worst Deal the opportunity to settle the dispute for a specific amount of money to avoid litigation. Demand letters usually allow the defendant 30 days to respond before the plaintiff initiates litigation. After Ms. Gogetter proofs and signs the letter, Pat Paralegal sends it to Worst Deal or its insurance company. (See "Commanding attention: Format of a demand letter," later in this chapter, for an example of a demand letter.)

Begging for attention: Pleadings

Not surprisingly, demand letters seldom end disputes. What self-respecting defendant wants to part with cold hard cash without making the plaintiff work for it, right? As soon as the response time period provided in the demand letter expires and it appears to Ms. Gogetter that the matter will not be resolved without litigation, the paralegal drafts a complaint to be served on Worst Deal and filed with the court. The defendant, Worst Deal, then responds with an answer to this complaint. It's up to Chris (the paralegal for Worst Deal) to make sure that the attorney responds to the complaint within the specified deadline. In fact, Pat and Chris are responsible for maintaining a tickler system throughout the litigation process to make sure no deadlines get missed. (For more about tickler systems, see Chapter 17.)

A PLEA FOR HELP: COMPLAINTS

The complaint presents the prima facie case against Worst Deal and requests damages or other relief. (You can see what a complaint looks like in the "Making your case: The complaint" section, later in this chapter.) The complaint should be served with a summons, which is a document issued by the court explaining that Worst Deal has been sued and that it has a certain time limit in which to respond to Mr. Klutz's allegations. Pat Paralegal merely fills in the blanks in the summons with the necessary information.

REMEMBER

An example of a federal court summons appears online at www.dummies.com/go/ paralegalcareer2e.

TIP

The summons and complaint together are known as *process.* The complaint shows a prima facie case against the defendant, meaning the document on its face contains enough allegations that, if believed, would cause the court to order the defendant to pay damages or some other form of relief to the plaintiff.

In Mr. Klutz's case, Pat Paralegal prepares a complaint that says the electronics store was negligent and requests damages to compensate for Mr. Klutz's medical bills, lost wages, and pain and suffering. Pat also prepares the summons and submits it with the complaint to Ms. Gogetter for her review and signature. With Ms. Gogetter's approval, Pat arranges that both the summons and complaint be served upon the electronics store or its designated agent.

A LITTLE GIVE AND TAKE: ANSWERS AND REPLIES

Within about 20 to 30 days of service of process, depending on your state's rules of civil procedure, Worst Deal prepares an answer to the complaint. The answer either admits or denies each of Mr. Klutz's allegations. The answer may also include affirmative defenses. For instance, Worst Deal might allege that Mr. Klutz was contributorily negligent because he was running at the time of the slip and fall. (You can find out more about affirmative defenses in Chapter 5.)

Worst Deal may also assert a counterclaim against Mr. Klutz for damages that the electronics store sustained because Mr. Klutz knocked over four of the store's karaoke machines as he was falling. Talk about adding insult to injury! If there are multiple defendants, Worst Deal may file a *cross claim.* For instance, Mr. Klutz may sue the independent cleaning company that maintains the floors at Worst Deal or the manufacturer of the floor tiles.

In many states, after the defendant files the answer to the complaint, the plaintiff may then file a reply to the answer. A reply responds to the new matters or allegations that may have been brought up in defendant's answer. (You'll find a sample answer in "Striking back: The answer," later in this chapter.)

BLAMING OTHERS: THIRD-PARTY COMPLAINTS

Another pleading that may be served and filed is the third-party complaint. Through a third-party complaint, the defendant may bring a new party, or parties, into the litigation who wasn't listed in the original complaint and who may be liable to the plaintiff for some or all of the damages alleged by plaintiff. So, Worst Deal could file a third-party complaint against the manufacturer of the vinyl floor tile alleging that this tile should have prevented slips and falls and was, therefore, defectively designed and manufactured. The tile manufacturer would become a third-party defendant and would have to file an answer to the third-party complaint filed by the electronics store.

Making your move: Motions

A *motion* is a legal document that requests the court to take specific action or else order that one or more of the parties takes some action. Think of a court as having a whole lot of inertia, and in order to get it to do anything, you have to *move* it. When you bring a motion, you are "moving the court" to take action. Although the defendant may file a motion to dismiss in response to a complaint, most motions occur during and after discovery. (You can read more on discovery in "Playing detective: Discovery," later in this chapter.)

REMEMBER

A motion is merely a document you file with court to ask the court to do something or to get the court to make the other party do something.

All sorts of pretrial motions exist:

>> **Motion to quash:** If a party receives improper service of process, that party may file a motion to quash service of summons or a motion to quash the return of the service of summons.

>> **Motion for change of venue:** A defendant could file a motion for change of venue if he feels that a fair trial can't be had in the court or county where the suit was filed.

>> **Motion to recuse:** Either side could file a motion to recuse if it feels the appointed judge is biased and should be disqualified from presiding over the case.

>> **Motion for more definite statement:** A defendant can file a motion for more definite statement in response to a complaint that lacks enough clarity or specific detail for the defendant to answer the allegations in the complaint.

>> **Motion to strike:** If a party doesn't like the language in the pleading, it can file a motion to strike. This doesn't mean that the party is asking the court to hit the opponent (even though the thought may appeal to him). The motion to strike asks the court to delete part or all of the allegations in a pleading, especially if those allegations are scandalous or indecent.

>> **Motion to file an amended pleading:** If a party wants to add some information or name an additional party defendant or just fix a mistake in the initial pleading, she can file a motion to file an amended pleading to add or subtract a party to the litigation or otherwise change some aspect of a pleading on file.

>> **Motion for enlargement of time:** This motion is a commonly filed request that the court grant additional time for one of the parties to take some action or file a notice, motion, or brief.

>> **Motion for protective order:** The party who feels a discovery document contains irrelevant questions or feels like the other side is abusing the discovery process may file a motion for a protective order, in which she asks the court to rule on whether she has to respond to all or some of the discovery.

>> **Motion to compel:** Conversely, if a party doesn't respond on time to a discovery or provides incomplete or evasive answers, the opposing party may file a motion to compel the answers to the discovery.

>> **Motion *in limine*:** Another pretrial motion is a motion *in limine* in which either party requests that the court limit what the jury hears about a specified piece of evidence, usually because that evidence is irrelevant or too gruesome or in some way unduly prejudicial.

>> **Motion for judgment on the pleadings:** Either party can make this motion, which merely asks the court to review all the pleadings (that is, the complaint, answer, and reply) and make a decision on those documents alone.

>> **Motion for summary judgment:** Similar to a motion for judgment on the pleadings, this motion claims that the parties don't dispute the material facts in the case and, therefore, requests that the court reach a decision on all or a portion of the case on the basis of the pleadings and any affidavits of facts without conducting an entire trial. If the court grants the summary judgment motion, it saves the moving party lots of time and money in litigation costs. (You can see an example of a motion for summary judgment in "Exerting your will: Motions," later in this chapter.)

TIP

When you file a motion, it's always a good idea to make an extra copy (a working copy) for the judge who hears the case. Doing so is a mark of professionalism and shows respect for the court.

More motions can appear during the trial and post-trial phases of the proceedings:

>> **Motion for directed verdict:** During trial, either party may file a motion for directed verdict requesting the court to enter a verdict in favor of the party making the motion. The defendant may request a directed verdict after the

plaintiff has rested her case, and the plaintiff may request a directed verdict after the defendant has completed his defense.

>> **Motion for a new trial:** After the court or jury has rendered a decision, either side may request a motion for new trial asking the judge to set aside the verdict or judgment and grant a new trial to the parties.

>> **Motion to amend judgment:** Similarly, a motion to alter or amend judgment requests that the judge change, modify, or otherwise vary the judgment rendered.

>> **Motion for a judgment notwithstanding the verdict:** Another way a party can get post-trial relief from the trial judge is to ask for a motion for a judgment notwithstanding the verdict, otherwise known as a JNOV (an acronym for the phrase "judgment *non obstante veredicto*," or judgment notwithstanding the verdict). This motion asks the court to set aside the jury's verdict that was, as a matter of law, allegedly rendered incorrectly.

TIP

When you file each motion for your supervising attorney, consult the pertinent local court rules to find out the nuts and bolts of when and how to file a notice to set the hearing on the motion, a notice of hearing on the motion, a memorandum of law or brief in support of the motion, and a proposed order. Prior to filing these documents with the court and sending them to the opposing party, have your supervising attorney review and sign each document.

The great paper waste: Discovery

Generally, after the last pleading is filed, the discovery stage of litigation commences. During discovery, each party seeks information from the other in an effort to learn as much about the other party's position as possible, prevent surprises at trial, and settle the case prior to trial. Discovery can be either written or oral.

THE WRITTEN RECORD

Each side can serve the following discovery documents upon the other side:

>> *Interrogatories* are written questions that require a response with written answers that are provided under oath. (You can see an example of written interrogatories in "Playing detective: Discovery," later in this chapter.)

REMEMBER

>> *A request for admissions* asks a party to admit to the truthfulness of facts or opinions or verify the genuineness of documents. (You can find a sample request for admissions online.)

>> A *request for production of documents* asks that one party be allowed to inspect or duplicate documents or other materials that are relevant to the subject matter of the litigation. Parties may also request permission to enter land for the purpose of inspecting it.

>> A *request for a physical or mental examination* asks a party to submit to a physical or mental examination to determine the legitimacy and extent of the physical or mental injuries claimed by that party. Examinations usually require a court order.

THE SPOKEN WORD

A *deposition* is another common form of discovery where a witness or party provides oral testimony under oath in a location outside of a courtroom, often the conference room of the opposing attorney. A deposition requires the presence of a court reporter to swear in the witness and to create a *verbatim* (word-for-word) transcript of witness testimony. Parties usually undertake other written forms of discovery before launching into a deposition because holding a deposition is expensive. The key is to find out information ahead of time so the deposition yields more useful information. Depositions generally allow the parties to find out a whole lot more information than the interrogatories or requests for admission or production. At the very least, depositions draw on the knowledge gained from the other written forms of discovery before the parties spend the big bucks on the deposition.

TIP

Attorneys often ask their paralegals to summarize depositions for them using the transcribed document. Your job in this case would be to determine the important testimony, and outline it so that the attorney could skim through the deposition in much less time than it would take to read through the entire deposition. Some depositions last all day!

In the electronics store slip-and-fall scenario, both parties submit interrogatories and requests for admissions to each other in an effort to determine background information, insurance coverage, and facts underlying the incident. A request for production of documents would also be appropriate to gather documentation regarding the earnings of both parties, possible existing insurance policies, and other information relevant to the action. Finally, Worst Deal could serve a request for physical examination upon Mr. Klutz, requiring him to be examined by the electronics store's physician to assess the severity of his broken hip.

Discovery is that part of the litigation process where you find out about the other side's case. The cheaper methods include written documents, like interrogatories, requests for admissions, requests for production, and requests for physical or mental examination. The more expensive method is oral deposition.

Taking it to the judge: Trial and post-trial documents

As the trial nears, paralegals really earn their keep when they help prepare and file pre-trial statements. A *pre-trial statement* is a lengthy document outlining the manner in which each party plans to proceed up to and during trial. The contents of the pre-trial statement are products of the pre-trial conference. When it becomes likely that the case will go to trial, the paralegal assists in the preparation of the *trial brief*, a document that states the legal issues of the case and establishes the validity of the party's position on each issue.

The paralegal will also assist in the selection and preparation of *jury instructions,* which the judge reads to the jury after closing statements and before deliberation. You can see some sample jury instructions online.

After the trial, paralegals assist in the preparation of documents that assist in the collection of judgment, such as writs of execution, garnishment, and attachment. If a party loses the case, the paralegal may prepare and file a notice of appeal, a designation of record on appeal, and an appellate brief (which presents the reasons that the party thinks the trial court erred). The party that was victorious in the trial court responds to the appellate brief with an answer brief, to which the other party may respond with a reply brief.

Making the Case: Effective Document Drafting

In the previous sections, we let you in on the significance of common legal documents. Here, we give you the ins and outs of how to draft them.

When you prepare each of these documents, you should first consult your law firm's formbooks or document files for samples. After you input a document into your office's form file database, place a copy of that document into the document files for future reference.

This section shows you some techniques you can use to draft specific documents. The sample documents in this chapter follow Colorado rules, which, like those of most states, are similar to the federal rules.

WARNING

As a paralegal, you should consult your state's rules to find out the precise formats that your state requires.

Commanding attention: Format of a demand letter

You'll find a wealth of rules, and even whole books, that have been written about proper ways to format a letter. Some paralegals prefer to follow a strict structure to be satisfied that they're doing the work right, and plenty of material is available in bookstores and libraries to fill this need. For most paralegals, however, following some simple rules, using good judgment, and having pride in appearance will suffice. And spell-check isn't bad either!

TIP

A good demand letter should include the following factual information:

>> The **facts** surrounding the incident for which the plaintiff is demanding settlement

>> A **settlement proposal** of either a specific dollar amount or specific action

>> The **time period** in which the defendant must respond

TIP

Keep the following appearance guidelines in mind when you put together demand letters:

>> **Vary the letter's margin widths depending on its size.**

- Short letters: Give very short letters wide left and right margins (usually 1.75") with a few extra lines placed before and after the date line. Place the body of the letter (address through signature line) at the page's optical center, which is slightly above the exact center of the page.

- Medium-length letters: Give medium-length, one-page letters margins of 1.25" to 1.5" and a little less space before the date line.

- Long letters: Give longer one-page letters 1" margins left and right. Place the date line two lines below the letterhead, and begin the address line two lines below the date line.

>> **Avoid making an orphan of the signature block on the second page of a letter.** Often, you can fit the body of a letter nicely on one page, but the signature block sometimes spills over onto a second page. To avoid the orphan signature block, you can make the margins wider and force some of the text (preferably a full paragraph) to the second page.

>> **Always put a colon after the salutation line, even if you use only a first name, like this:**

- Dear Ms. Gogetter:

- Dear Ima:

>> **Don't number the first page but number the second and succeeding pages of any letter.** The style and placement of page numbers doesn't matter, but your office probably has its own procedure, so be sure to ask how they want it done.

>> **Begin the complimentary close with a capital letter and end with a comma, like this:**

- Very truly yours,

- Yours truly,

>> **Place about five lines between the complimentary close and the name of the attorney.** This gives plenty of room for the signature.

>> **Reveal the identity of the letter writer by presenting his initials in the block following the signature block.** Capitalize the writer's initials and leave the word processor's initials in lowercase. For example, if Pat Paralegal were creating a letter for Ima Gogetter, Pat would type "IG:pp" after the signature block.

Follow the initials with a statement of whether there are enclosures and whether copies have been sent to others. Place these revelations underneath the initials and flush with the left margin. Here's an example of the ending of a letter that contains enclosures with copy information (the *cc* used to stand for *carbon copies* back in the olden days before computers and copy machines; now it can stand for *courtesy copies*):

IGG:pp

Enclosure

cc: Rip U. Awff, Esquire

REMEMBER

Figure 10-1 shows you how all these features come together in a sample demand letter to Worst Deal's insurance company. (You can find a copy of the demand letter online.)

Ima Gogetter
Attorney at Law
511 Law Office Lane
Denver, CO 80203
(303) 555-5555 FAX (303) 522-2222
www.imagotetter.com
ima@gogetter.com

January ___, 20___

Agatha Agent
Lots of Bucks Insurance Company
444 North Agents Way
Denver, CO 80202

RE: DEMAND FOR SETTLEMENT
             Your insured: Worst Deal, Inc.

Dear Ms. Agent:

Wendell Worst, agent for Worst Deal, Inc., has informed our office that Lots of Bucks Insurance Company provides coverage for Worst Deal. This office has been retained by Kelley Klutz to pursue his remedies for negligence against Lots of Bucks Insurance Company in the Denver County District Court. On December ___, 20___, Mr. Klutz slipped and fell in the aisle of Worst Deal causing severe injuries to his legs and spine and resulting in a broken left hip. It is Mr. Klutz's contention that Worst Deal improperly and negligently maintained the floor at the time of Mr. Klutz's injury.

Mr. Klutz has had to undergo surgical operations and physical therapy and has lost the equivalent of two months of wages. His condition will require future physical therapy and time off from work.

This letter serves as a demand for settlement in the amount of Two Hundred and Fifty Thousand Dollars ($250,000.00) to be paid by certified funds, no later than February ___, 20___. This settlement amount and any future correspondence should be sent directly to the undersigned.

I trust that you will give this matter your most serious attention and will assist in avoiding additional attorney's fees and court costs by accepting this settlement proposal. Please have your attorneys contact my office if you should have any questions.

Very truly yours,

Ima Gogetter

Ima Gogetter
IGG:pp

FIGURE 10-1:
A sample
demand letter.

Making your case: The complaint

The format of a complaint (which, in some states and in certain types of lawsuits, is called a *petition*), varies from state to state, but all complaints should include a caption, text, and a *subscription* (the attorney's signature).

Because you personally serve a complaint on the defendant, it doesn't include a *certificate of mailing* (a statement certifying that you placed the document on a particular date to a specific address). You also file a certificate of personal service with the court.

We cover all of these items in the following sections.

Identifying the action: The caption

The caption states the court in which the action is filed, the case number, the name of the document, and the names of the parties to the action. A line on the document usually separates the caption from the text of the complaint. Each state has a specific format you should follow for the captions of legal documents.

REMEMBER

Most states provide Web sites where you can find the proper caption format. We include links to these sites online.

Telling the story: Text

The text of a complaint must include the following elements in the form of numbered paragraphs in the order that they're listed here:

1. An opening paragraph

2. A statement of jurisdiction and venue

3. A statement of the general allegations against the defendant, which include the specific elements of the offense and the resulting damages

4. A prayer for relief

IN THE BEGINNING: THE OPENING STATEMENT

The opening statement introduces the complaint and explains its purpose. The legal community is slowly changing its format to include clearer, more precise language that omits unnecessary legalese. Old expressions such as *whereas* and *wherefore* don't appear as often as they used to. Even the time honored introductory phrase, "Comes now the Plaintiff, by and through his attorney . . ." is giving way to more straightforward wording, "The Defendant, by his attorney. . . ."

A LITTLE CONFIRMATION: ESTABLISHING PARTIES AND JURISDICTION

The first numbered paragraph of the text usually identifies the parties with names and addresses and states facts to support the alleged jurisdiction of and venue for the action. For example if the plaintiff brings the lawsuit in a federal district court and relies on diversity of citizenship to give the court jurisdiction, the opening paragraph of the complaint will allege the plaintiff is a citizen of one state, that the defendant is a citizen of another state, and that the amount in controversy exceeds $75,000.

THE HEART OF THE MATTER: STATING THE CASE

The body of the complaint asserts in numbered paragraphs statements that present the case in a logical and sequential order. There's a difference of opinion on how much detail is needed in alleging the facts on which the plaintiff bases her recovery. The Federal Rules of Civil Procedure (FRCP) and most state rules have come a long way from the old days and require very little factual detail. The discovery process usually fleshes out many of the specific facts in the lawsuit. In a negligence action, alleging that on a certain date, at a described place, the plaintiff slipped and fell on the floor of the defendant's business, which resulted in crushing the plaintiff's hip, required him to seek medical help and miss work, and which also resulted in incurred expenses of a specified amount is usually sufficient.

TIP

Each paragraph in the complaint should state the allegations as succinctly as possible. A good guideline for you to follow is to include only one allegation per paragraph.

MONEY MATTERS: THE PRAYER FOR RELIEF

The complaint concludes with a *prayer for relief* or *ad damnum clause,* which is a short summary of the plaintiff's request. This statement may be as simple as, "Wherefore, the plaintiff demands judgment against the defendant in the sum of Two Hundred Fifty Thousand Dollars ($250,000.00) with interest, attorney's fees, and costs." Or it may consist of several pages of demands. The prayer for relief may also be more generally worded like this, "The plaintiff demands judgment against the defendant in an amount to be determined at the time of trial, including interest, attorney's fees, and costs."

The big finish: The subscription

The *subscription* is the attorney's signature block. It must contain the attorney's name, registration number, mailing address, and phone number. Many states also require that the plaintiff's name and address appear opposite the subscription.

REMEMBER

In Kelley Klutz's case, Worst Deal's insurance company has failed to respond to the demand letter by the designated date, so Ima Gogetter's paralegal, Pat, drafts a complaint like the one shown in Figure 10-2. (This sample complaint is also included online.)

DISTRICT COURT,
COUNTY of DENVER, COLORADO

Plaintiff: Kelly Klutz,

v.

Defendant: Worst Deal, Inc.

☐ **COURT USE ONLY** ☐

Ima Gogetter
511 Law Office Lane
Denver, CO 80203

303-555-5555
FAX: 303-522-2222
ima@imagogetter.com
Registration #: 1212

Case Number:

Div.:   Ctrm.:

COMPLAINT

The plaintiff, Kelley Klutz, by and through his attorney of record, Ima Gogetter, for his Complaint against Defendant alleges as follows:

1. Plaintiff is a citizen of Colorado, residing at 444 Clumsy Lane, Denver, Colorado, 80211. The action occurred in the state of Colorado, county of Denver.

2. Defendant is incorporated to do business in the state of Colorado, with the principal place of business located at 150 North Accident Way, Denver, Colorado, 80213, and the defendant's registered agent is Wendall Worst, who can be served at that address.

3. On December __, 20__, the plaintiff was shopping for electronics in the defendant's store when he lost his balance and slipped and fell in the aisle of the store, suffering the injuries and damages described below.

WHEREFORE, the plaintiff prays for judgment against defendant in an amount to be proven at the time of trial, including medical bills, lost wages, pain and suffering, costs expended in filing this suit, interest from the date of the commencement of this action, expert witness fees, attorney's fees, and for such other and further relief as to this Court may seem just and proper.

THE PLAINTIFF DEMANDS THAT THIS ACTION BE TRIED TO A JURY.

Plaintiff's Address:
444 Clumsy Lane
Denver, CO 80211

Respectfully submitted,

_____

Ima Gogetter, #1212
Attorney for Plaintiff

FIGURE 10-2:
A sample complaint with the Colorado caption format. Remember to check the correct caption format in your state.

Striking back: The answer

When Worst Deal receives service of Mr. Klutz's complaint, Worst Deal's attorneys respond with an answer. State law or court rules generally govern the time period a defendant has to respond, which is also spelled out in the summons. Within the specified time limit, as a paralegal for the defendant's attorney, you may draft the defendant's answer to the plaintiff's complaint. You then present it to your supervising attorney for approval and signature and file it with the court. The components of an answer pretty much mirror those of a complaint: The answer begins with the same caption as the complaint and ends with a subscription. The text of the answer usually begins with an introductory statement followed by the defendant's allegations.

Within the allegations, the defendant either admits or denies the allegations the complaint has raised. In forming responses for your attorney's client, make sure you provide a specific admission or denial for every allegation. To cover your bases, include an allegation such as the following: "All other allegations of the plaintiff's complaint that are not specifically admitted are denied."

WARNING

Be sure to address every allegation in the plaintiff's complaint. All allegations that are not specifically denied are deemed admitted.

REMEMBER

You should also include any affirmative defenses the defendant wishes to make under the specific heading of affirmative defenses. An example of an affirmative defense might be that the plaintiff caused or contributed to her own injuries. You end the text with a clause similar to the plaintiff's prayer for relief that requests that the case be dismissed, that the plaintiff recover nothing, and that the costs of defending the claim be awarded the defendant. Figure 10-3 shows a sample answer. (This sample answer is also included online, along with an example of an answer and a third-party complaint and an answer to a third-party complaint.)

After the subscription, include a certificate of mailing or certificate of service to be signed by whoever mails the answer to the other parties or to the attorneys representing the other parties. This certificate functions as a verification of service of the document by mail or hand delivery. Any document that isn't personally served on another party must contain a certificate of service.

DISTRICT COURT, COUNTY of DENVER, COLORADO	
Plaintiff: Kelly Klutz, v. **Defendant: Worst Deal, Inc.**	☐ **COURT USE ONLY** ☐
Rip U. Awff Attorney for Defendant 430 Herald Square, Suite 1022 Denver, CO 80203 303-555-3333 FAX: 303-522-3333 counsel@ripawff.com Registration #: 1444	Case Number: 00CV1002 Div.: 10　　　　　　　Ctrm.: 2

ANSWER

The defendant, Worst Deal Inc., by and through its counsel, Rip U. Awff, for its Answer states and alleges as follows:

1. Defendant is without knowledge or information sufficient to form a belief as to the truth of the allegation contained in paragraph 1 of the Complaint, and therefore, denies this allegation.

2. Defendant admits the allegation contained in paragraph 2 of the plaintiff's Complaint.

3. Defendant denies the allegations contained in paragraphs 3, 4, 5, 6, 7, 8, 9, 10, and 11 of the plaintiff's Complaint.

4. All other allegations of the plaintiff's Complaint that are not specifically admitted are denied.

AFFIRMATIVE DEFENSES

5. The Complaint fails to state a claim upon which relief can be granted.

6. The plaintiff's own negligence contributed or caused his injuries.

WHEREFORE, the third party plaintiff prays that the plaintiff recover nothing by reason of his Complaint and that the plaintiff's Complaint be dismissed.

Defendant's Address:
150 North Accident Way
Denver, Colorado 80213

Respectfully submitted,

_____
Rip U. Awff, #1444
Attorney for Defendant

FIGURE 10-3:
A sample answer with the Colorado caption format.

FIGURE 10-3:
(continued)

© John Wiley & Sons

The defendant may also include within the answer a third-party complaint. The allegations of this complaint come after the answer's affirmative defenses and bring another party into the action.

Presenting a formal analysis: The memorandum of law

The *legal memorandum* is among the most commonly used documents of the paralegal profession. Through legal memoranda, paralegals convey information to clients and witnesses, analyze complex legal problems, and present the client's case to others.

Legal memoranda may be internal or external. You send an *internal memo* to your supervising attorney or other member of the law office staff but send an *external memo* outside of the law office to the opposing counsel, the court, or both. The major difference between an internal memo and an external memo lies in how you present the case. Internal memos anticipate all legal issues by portraying both sides of a client's case, favorable and unfavorable. External memos, such as trial briefs or memoranda in support of motions, convey only the favorable points of a client's case.

WARNING

Even though the external memo conveys the favorable aspects of a client's case, it can't ignore dealing with on-point law that may contradict the client's case. The rules of professional conduct say that an attorney may not fail to mention any legal authority he knows about just because that information is bad for the client. (You can find more on the rules of ethics in Chapter 15.)

REMEMBER

The following sections walk you through the different parts. For a complete example of a memorandum of law, see the online content.

The components of a legal memorandum

The parts of a legal memorandum include a caption, a statement of the assignment, a statement of facts, a list of issues, an analysis of the issues, a conclusion, and, in many cases, recommendations.

THE CAPTION OR HEADING

The caption (like the one in Figure 10-4) includes information indicating who the memo is addressed to, the name of the writer, the date the memo was written, the case name and number if available, and a brief explanation of what the memo is about.

INTEROFFICE MEMORANDUM OF LAW

TO: Rip U. Awff, J.D.

FROM: Chris Cutter, Paralegal

DATE: January ___, 20___

RE: Motion for Summary Judgment, *Kelley Klutz v. Worst Deal, Inc.*

OFFICE CLIENT: Worst Deal, Inc.

OFFICE FILE NUMBER: CV 11196

DOCKET NUMBER: 07CV1002

STATEMENT OF ASSIGNMENT: Mr. Awff has asked me to research the primary authority supporting a motion for summary judgment in favor of Worst Deal, Inc., and to assist in deciding whether this motion should be filed against the plaintiff.

© John Wiley & Sons

FIGURE 10-4: The caption of a memo of law, including a statement of the assignment.

THE ASSIGNMENT

This one-sentence statement describes the purpose of the memo. It's sometimes included in the caption (refer to Figure 10-4).

THE FACTS

This section briefly outlines the facts of the case that you'll use in the legal analysis. For an example, see Figure 10-5.

FACTS: On December __, 20__, the plaintiff, Kelley Klutz, a married, thirty-year-old construction worker, was shopping at our client's electronics store. While in the aisle of the Karaoke machine section of the store, he allegedly slipped and fell on a portion of the floor that he states was wet.

Our client, Worst Deal, Inc., had purchased new tile from Slippery Tile Company, Inc., which was installed in the store on October __, 20__. This tile was represented to be slip-free even when wet. Our client has stated that the safety representations from Slippery Tile Company, Inc., constituted the primary reason for the purchase and installation of the tile. Based upon our investigation and research, we filed a third-party complaint against Slippery Tile Company, Inc.

In response to interrogatories and deposition questions, plaintiff admitted that for "just a few seconds" before his apparent slip and fall he had seen the sign that our client had placed in the aisle warning customers that the floor may be wet due to a recent washing. The sign, which read "Caution—Wet Floors" on each of its two sides, was freestanding on four metal tubular legs, and measured 14" by 14" square on each side. The background color of the sign was yellow, and the lettering was black. Each letter was 4" high and 1.5" wide. The sign is in our possession and will be introduced as an exhibit if this case goes to trial. Plaintiff also stated that he had been shopping at Worst Deal at least three times before the day of the accident and that he had seen this same sign in the store on one other occasion.

Within approximately two minutes of the plaintiff's fall, the department manager, Jeff Standing, aided Mr. Klutz. In his deposition, Mr. Standing stated that he did not witness the fall nor did he think that anyone else witnessed the plaintiff's fall. He asked Mr. Klutz to remain still because Mr. Klutz told him that his hip was painful and that he couldn't move his leg. Mr. Standing then went to the customer service counter and briefly informed the store owner, Wendell Worst, of the occurrence. Mr. Worst called for an ambulance, and Mr. Standing returned to attend to Mr. Klutz.

The ambulance arrived within ten minutes of the occurrence and transported Mr. Klutz to the nearest hospital. Mr. Klutz was treated for a broken left hip, had a pin placed in his hip, and was released with the aid of crutches five days after his admission. Copies of the complete ambulance and hospital records are in our client's file.

This interoffice memorandum will examine the propriety of a summary judgment motion and the possible defenses that the plaintiff may raise to the motion. The critical fact that is not disputed is that the plaintiff saw the warning sign prior to his alleged slip and fall.

FIGURE 10-5: A statement of facts.

THE ISSUES

The issues section lists the important questions of law and presents the issues as questions to be answered in the analysis. (See Figure 10-6 for an example.) The attorney often provides the issues, but as a paralegal, you may have to formulate issues on your own to submit to your supervising attorney for revision or approval.

FIGURE 10-6:
A statement of
the issues.

© John Wiley & Sons

THE ANALYSIS

Analysis is the process of answering each issue through a careful and thorough application of the law to the facts of the client's case. Figure 10-7 provides a portion of a sample analysis.

THE CONCLUSION

The conclusion summarizes the answers to the questions posed by the issues. The conclusion, like the one shown in Figure 10-8, should be based on the legal analysis and shouldn't contain any information that hasn't been discussed in the analysis section.

THE RECOMMENDATIONS

Based on the conclusion, this section proposes what steps should be taken on behalf of the client (see Figure 10-9). You generally only find this section in internal memoranda.

ANALYSIS:

1. Is our client's Motion for Summary Judgment likely to be granted?

Our client's Motion for Summary Judgment is likely to be granted since the plaintiff has admitted that he saw the warning sign prior to his alleged slip and fall. The relevant case law for the purposes of this motion is outlined in the case of *Drake v. Lerner's Shops of Colorado, Inc.*, 145 Colo. 1, 4, 357 P.2d 624, 626 (1960) where the Colorado Supreme Court stated:

> In order to establish a *prima facie* case of negligence, plaintiff's evidence must establish the existence on the premises of an unreasonable risk of harm to her as an invitee. The mere existence of risk is not sufficient. Some degree of risk is present in our every activity and if existence of hazard alone were the standard it would mean that the happening of an accident would be sufficient to raise the presumption of negligence and the landowner would be an insurer of the safety of his patrons. Such is not the law. The condition created by the conduct or activity of the landowner must pose an appreciable risk of harm. The defendant's conduct must threaten harm.

In *Drake*, the plaintiff testified that she walked out of a clothing store, failed to observe a warning sign, and failed to observe a five-inch drop-off to the sidewalk, which caused her fall and subsequent injuries. In upholding a directed verdict for the defendant, the court stated that "[c]onsidering the evidence in a light most favorable to the plaintiff, it cannot be said that the condition about which she complains was such to create an appreciable risk of harm. A step down five inches is not a hazard, which of itself suggests likelihood of harm. . .." *Id.* at 5, 357 P.2d at 626.

In our client's case, the plaintiff admitted that he had shopped at Worst Deal several times prior to the accident and had seen the "Caution—Wet Floors" sign in the aisles at least once prior to his alleged slip and fall. Furthermore, he admitted to having seen the sign immediately prior to his slip and fall and was thus aware of the potential harm. Under *Drake* alone, the court would be bound to grant our client's summary judgment motion.

FIGURE 10-7:
A portion of a legal analysis of an issue.

CONCLUSION:

Because there appear to be no material facts in dispute in this matter and the law appears to support a ruling in favor of our client, the granting of our Motion for Summary Judgment is likely. Although the plaintiff may request to amend his complaint to include new facts, there seems to be little doubt that the material facts of this case are agreed upon by both parties.

FIGURE 10-8:
A conclusion to a memo of law.

RECOMMENDATIONS:

Our client should be consulted and informed of our intent to file a Motion for Summary Judgment. Immediately prior to filing the motion, each of the authorities set forth in this memorandum should be shepardized and updated on Westlaw. Please inform me if there is any further research on this case that you would like me to do.

FIGURE 10-9:
A recommendations section of a memo of a law.

The process of legal analysis

The focal point of the memorandum of law is the analysis. Legal analysis is the means of providing an answer to an issue through careful application of the points of law of applicable statutes and previous cases to the specific facts surrounding the client's case. If you get good at analyzing the law, you'll be invaluable to your employer.

Through legal analysis, you apply a relatively unchanging body of law to the specific facts of your client's case (refer to Figure 10-7). You apply law to facts because law changes far less frequently than facts do.

REMEMBER

To conduct a thorough analysis of an issue, perform these four steps:

1. **Introduce the analysis by restating the issue to be analyzed and then listing the elements of the pertinent legal authority.**

    Analysis of a previous case requires a very brief, two- to three-sentence explanation of its relevant facts and issue. Analysis of a statute requires isolating its most important elements.

2. **Isolate the court's decision in the precedent case.**

3. **Carefully apply the precedent authority to the facts of the client's case.**

By comparing and contrasting the facts and issues of the precedent case with the facts and issues of the client's case, you determine whether the precedent case's decision applies to the client's case. By analyzing the important elements of a statute, you show how the client's case applies to the legislative intent of the statute.

4. **Based on the application of the legal authority to the facts and issues of the client's case, present a conclusion that answers the issue.**

You may derive the conclusion from an analysis of several different cases and statutes or from an analysis of just one case or statute.

TIP

In presenting support for an answer to an issue, concentrate on legal authority, such as cases and statutes, rather than on feelings or unfounded opinions. Base your conclusions on a thorough analysis of the law.

If the supervising attorney provides specific cases and statutes to analyze, discuss all the authority provided. Internal memos of law may include an analysis of legal authority that's detrimental to the client's case to help the attorney anticipate the opposing party's case.

Exerting your will: Motions

The format of a motion strongly resembles that of a pleading. Just like all other documents filed with the court, the motion begins with a caption. The text of the motion consists of an introductory statement, a list of reasons why the court should grant the motion, and a request that the court grant the motion. Like answers, motions must contain certificates of service. Figure 10-10 contains an example of a motion for summary judgment.

When you draft a motion, you also prepare a notice to set hearing on the motion, a memorandum of law or brief in support of the motion, and a proposed order to accompany the motion. All these documents are headed with the caption of the case, ended with a subscription, and completed with a certificate of service. Here's more about the purpose of these documents:

>> **Notice to set hearing:** You send the notice to set hearing to the opposing parties to notify them of the time and place for the setting of the hearing on a motion.

DISTRICT COURT, COUNTY of DENVER, COLORADO	
Plaintiff: Kelly Klutz, v. **Defendant: Worst Deal, Inc.**	□ **COURT USE ONLY** □
Rip U. Awff Attorney for Defendant 430 Herald Square, Suite 1022 Denver, CO 80203 303-555-3333 FAX: 303-522-3333 counsel@ripawff.com Registration #: 1444	Case Number: 00CV1002 Div.: 10　　　　　　　Ctrm.: 2

MOTION FOR SUMMARY JUDGMENT

The defendant, Worst Deal Inc., by its attorney, Rip U. Awff, moves for summary judgment against Plaintiff, pursuant to the Colorado Rules of Civil Procedure, Rule 56, and as grounds for this motion, states as follows:

1. The pleadings, exhibits and affidavits on file show that there is no genuine issue as to any material fact and the moving party is entitled to a judgment as a matter of law.

2. The plaintiff slipped and fell on recently cleaned tile in the defendant's store, and a conspicuous "Caution—Wet Floors" sign was positioned beside this tile.

3. Based upon defendant's answers to discovery, it is undisputed that the existence of the "Caution—Wet Floors" sign was known and apparent to the plaintiff prior to and at time of the incident.

4. As a matter of law there can be no liability by the owner/occupier of a premises for injuries to others from conditions that are obvious and known to the plaintiff. *Drake v. Lerner's Shops of Colorado Inc.*, 145 Colo. 1, 357 P.2d 624 (1960).

WHEREFORE, pursuant to Rule 56, the defendant requests that this court grant its Motion for Summary Judgment in this action.

Defendant's Address:
150 North Accident Way
Denver, Colorado 80213

Respectfully submitted,

_____

Rip U. Awff, #1444
Attorney for Defendant

FIGURE 10-10:
A sample motion for summary judgment.

FIGURE 10-10:
(continued)

© John Wiley & Sons

>> **Notice of hearing on motion:** When the hearing has been set and if your attorney's client is the *movant* (the moving party), you prepare a notice of hearing on motion, which has a similar format to the notice to set hearing on motion.

>> **Memorandum of law in support of the motion:** You draft a memorandum of law in support of the motion to present the points of law in support of the motion. In it, you state the purpose of the motion, the burden of proof, and the reasons that the movant is entitled to have the motion granted. You substantiate each of these points with an analysis of the applicable law as it relates to the facts of the case.

>> **Order:** For those courts that require an order, the movant submits a prepared order in hopes that the court will rule in favor of the movant's motion. The text of the order states that the motion has been granted and provides a signature line for the court.

REMEMBER

The sample motion for summary judgment in Figure 10-10 and a sample memorandum of law in support of the motion for summary judgment, notice to set hearing, and order are included online.

Playing detective: Disclosure and discovery

As a paralegal, you may get involved in the disclosure and discovery process by preparing proper disclosures in accordance with the rules of civil procedure. You may also be assigned to choose appropriate questions for interrogatories, coming up with admission statements for the request for admissions and making lists of necessary documents for the request for production of documents. You can also assist your supervising attorney in digesting the deposition document.

Preparing written discovery

Written discovery documents begin with the caption of the case. The text includes an introductory statement that provides the time limit that the other party has to respond to the discovery request. Depending on the type of discovery document, the text then continues with a list of interrogatories, statements to be admitted, or items to be produced that are relevant to the issues of the case. Usually, these lists are quite lengthy, requiring the other party to spend a great amount of time and effort to fulfill the conditions of the discovery. So, many state courts put limits on the number of interrogatories and sets of interrogatories a party can submit. These documents end with a *subscription* (the attorney's signature) and a certificate of service.

REMEMBER

You can get an idea of what an interrogatories document looks like in Figure 10-11. Examples of this and the other types of discovery documents are online.

TIP

Interrogatories, request for admissions, request for mental or physical examinations, and request for production of documents may be sent as separate documents or they may be combined in one series of documents. They seek to get as much information from the other side as possible prior to undertaking expensive discovery like depositions.

Digesting depositions

Depositions usually take place after the parties have responded to written discovery. The *deponent* (the person being deposed) may be a party or a witness to the action. As a paralegal, you may serve the deponent with a subpoena and a notice of deposition (similar in form to a notice to set) and send the notice of deposition to all the parties in the action. Through the use of a subpoena *duces tecum*, the deponent may be required to bring specific items (like company records, medical records, and so on) with him to the deposition. Depositions usually take place in the attorney's conference room where a certified or registered shorthand reporter swears in the deponent. Any objections to questions made by counsel during the deposition are preserved for a judge's review, and the oral testimony is transcribed for use in the court trial.

The attorney may ask you, as the paralegal, to *digest* the transcribed deposition. No, you don't eat the transcript! To digest a deposition, you use a memorandum of law to summarize the deposition for your supervising attorney. Your supervising attorney dictates the form of the digest. For instance, the attorney may want a 500-page deposition to be synthesized into a 5-page summary, or the attorney may want you to summarize only certain issues discussed in the deposition. If the deposition has been video recorded, you may assist in determining which portions would be best to show at trial.

DISTRICT COURT, COUNTY of DENVER, COLORADO	
Plaintiff: Kelly Klutz, v. **Defendant: Worst Deal, Inc.**	☐ **COURT USE ONLY** ☐
Rip U. Awff Attorney for Defendant 430 Herald Square, Suite 1022 Denver, CO 80203 303-555-3333 FAX: 303-522-3333 counsel@ripawff.com Registration #: 1444	Case Number: 07CV1002 Div.: 10 Ctrm.: 2

DEFENDANT'S FIRST SET OF INTERROGATORIES

The defendant, Worst Deal Inc., by and through its counsel, Rip U. Awff, and pursuant to CRCP Rule 33 requests Plaintiff, Kelley Klutz, to respond to the following interrogatories within thirty (30) days of service of these interrogatories.

1. State the name of the person answering these interrogatories.

2. How many times before the morning of December ___, 20___, had you entered the Worst Deal store at 150 North Accident Way in Denver, Colorado?

3. Approximately how long before your fall on December ___, 20___, did you see the bright yellow sign warning you of a possible wet floor in the Karaoke aisle of Worst Deal?

4. Etc.

DATED: _____ day of _____, 20___.

Defendant's Address:
150 North Accident Way
Denver, Colorado 80213

Respectfully submitted,

_____
Rip U. Awff, #1444
Attorney for Defendant

FIGURE 10-11:
Sample
interrogatories.

```
                    CERTIFICATE OF SERVICE

I certify that a true and correct copy of the foregoing Defendant's First Set of Interrogatories was served this ____
day of _____, 20__, by placing them in the United States mail, first class postage prepaid, addressed as
follows:

Ima Gogetter, J.D.
511 Law Office Lane
Denver, Colorado 80203


                                          _____
```

FIGURE 10-11:
(continued)

Handling trial documents

If a case goes to trial, you usually prepare a trial notebook for your supervising attorney. The trial notebook contains the information your attorney needs to successfully conduct the client's case during trial. The contents of the trial notebook vary but usually include copies of pleadings and motions, witness lists, deposition digests, a copy of the trial brief, which outlines the arguments of the client's case, and jury instructions. As a paralegal, you may be especially helpful in putting together the documents concerning the jury.

Jury instructions

When both parties have rested their cases, the judge gives the jury a series of instructions that explain the legal principles it should use when it deliberates. Often, attorneys make suggestions to the judge regarding what instructions they'd like the jury to hear. The paralegal often gets tagged with preparing the suggested jury instructions, and many law offices have sets of instructions for each type of case they try. So, from these sets you choose the instructions that apply to the case on trial and present them in written form, numbered and double-spaced.

REMEMBER

You can find sample jury instructions online.

Special verdict form

Sometimes, a jury will be asked to complete a *special verdict form*. This form contains questions that the jury must answer in rendering its verdict. The form begins with the case caption, presents several questions, and ends with the signatures of all the jury members or the *presiding juror* (the foreperson). Again, as the paralegal, you may have a hand in preparing this form for your supervising attorney.

Chapter **11**

Elementary My Dear Watson: Legal Investigation

C ases don't just show up on the law firm's doorstep served on a silver platter ready to take to court. Too often, the attorney and paralegal need to discover and develop the facts of the client's case in order to effectively prepare for settlement or trial. This means doing a little detective work. As a paralegal, you may find yourself playing Sherlock Holmes or Nancy Drew to find important evidence. Your supervising attorney may also call on you to mark and preserve case evidence and organize it for trial.

In this chapter, we show you how to conduct the informal discovery process (as opposed to the formal discovery process we discuss in Chapter 6, involving submitting to the other party written documents, like interrogatories and requests for production, and conduction depositions). We give you tips on how to find supporting evidence for civil cases, how to mark the evidence and keep it safe for trial, and how to organize it to present the client's case in the most convincing manner.

Searching for Clues: Gathering Evidence

Many large law firms have professional investigators on their staffs to help uncover relevant evidence for their cases. But in a small firm or for a less complex case, guess who often becomes the primary fact finder for the attorneys? That's right. When you work as a paralegal, you may be involved in a little investigation work.

Through legal investigation, you can find information that helps with many aspects of a case. Here are a few of the way you'll use investigation:

» To assist you and your supervising attorney with preparing pleadings

» To define the type of questions you and your attorney present in interrogatories and at depositions

» To uncover evidence that the law firm uses in settlement negotiations and in court to strengthen the client's case

Obtaining evidence is the first, and sometimes hardest, step of the legal investigative process. Every investigation has an objective, so make sure you clearly understand why your employer is asking you to gather certain facts.

TIP

Your time is extremely valuable to the law firm, so make sure you correctly understand the assignment from your supervising attorney. Listen closely and take notes while your supervisor assigns tasks. You can never get too *much* detail regarding assignments, so don't hesitate to ask questions during every stage of an investigation project. Time is too precious to waste it on a vague purpose.

Most likely, your supervisor will ask you to obtain papers and photographs because these are two of the most unimpeachable sources of information you can find. Papers include any documents that support the client's version of the facts and may include letters, contracts, and public records. Photographs may be pictures of the scene of the event in dispute, or they may be pictures of evidence that isn't easily presented in court, such as a damaged car or a depiction of a serious personal injury as it appeared on the date in question.

TIP

Because their contents are virtually indisputable, original documents and photographs are easily admissible in court, so whenever possible obtain originals.

After you've gained experience in fact gathering and investigation, you'll probably develop your own unique style of obtaining evidence. Trial and error helps you determine which methods work best in certain situations, so you have to be persistent. All methods, though, should include spotting issues, forming checklists, and pursuing all kinds of information sources, all of which we cover in the following sections.

What are you trying to prove?
Spotting issues

You can focus your investigation by spotting the relevant issues of law and fact in a particular case. An *issue* is the legal controversy that litigation attempts to resolve. When parties disagree about some fact or legal conclusion, you'd say that that fact or point of law is *at issue.* You attempt to resolve issues of law through legal research (see Chapter 13); you try to resolve issues of fact through legal investigation.

There may be more than one issue in a case; in fact, most cases involve several issues. You generally see issues presented as questions. The purpose of a thorough legal investigation is to find the information you need to answer these questions. Often, your supervising attorney formulates the issues for you. Sometimes you'll have to come up with them yourself, especially if your investigation uncovers information that leads to new issues.

For instance, in the slip-and-fall case of Kelley Klutz outlined in Chapter 10, the following relevant issues may come into play:

>> Is Worst Deal negligent in the maintenance of its floor?

>> If Worst Deal is negligent, was this negligence the proximate cause of Mr. Klutz's fall and subsequent injuries?

>> Is Mr. Klutz contributorily negligent?

>> Is the tile company strictly liable for manufacturing and installing defective floor tile?

The opposing parties would probably disagree on the correct answers to these four questions, but knowing their actual answers is vital to the case. Your job is to uncover and verify through investigation the facts necessary to provide answers for each of these questions or issue statements.

What order will you follow?
Creating checklists

Based on the relevant issues of a case, you create and rely on checklists to begin the fact gathering process. A checklist merely lists questions to answer and duties to accomplish in a sequential order. Your mission is to answer the questions and take on those duties in order to fully complete an investigative project.

You don't have to make up a checklist from scratch. Other paralegals and attorneys have thought of these situations in other lawsuits, so you likely won't need to reinvent the wheel. A great source for sample checklists is the *American Jurisprudence Proof of Facts* (POF) series, which details the necessary facts you need for virtually any investigative project. You can find this series of formbooks in law school libraries and most county courthouse law libraries. POF is also available through access to Westlaw online legal research service. You should begin your research in the topical index at the end of the POF series. When you refer to this series, you'll find out how to prepare checklists for just about any type of lawsuit imaginable.

Over time, law offices compile their own sets of checklists for investigating common issues. For instance, your investigative project may require you to determine whether process was properly served upon the party named in the summons and complaint. You could use a checklist from your office's information base to form the basis of your fact gathering process.

If you create checklists for new issues, you add them to the existing lists in your office's workbooks for future use. As you become a successful fact gatherer, you'll create new chapters of checklists that correspond to each area of inquiry.

Generally, investigation checklists should cover the following:

>> Known facts and whether they can be proved or supported

>> Facts that must be corroborated by supporting evidence

>> The kind of evidence that must be gathered

>> The way evidence should be gathered

>> Where you may find evidence (like agency documents, personal records, personnel files, business records, medical records, and so on)

>> The best method of inquiry (such as by telephone interview, letter, personal interview, formal discovery, and so on)

>> The appropriate timeframe required to complete the investigation

Then you create more specific checklists that apply to each of main categories listed here.

Here's an example of the kinds of questions a checklist to determine proper service of process might include:

>> Was the process sufficient on its face?

>> Was the proper defendant named in the process?

- ❯❯ Was the named defendant served with the process?

- ❯❯ Was the person who served the process over 18 years of age?

- ❯❯ Was the process server a party to the action?

- ❯❯ Were there any documents other than the complaint served with the summons? If so, what were these documents?

- ❯❯ Were there any witnesses to the service of process?

- ❯❯ Was the return of service properly executed.

- ❯❯ Was the properly executed return of service returned to the correct court?

REMEMBER

When you create checklists, keep in mind that fact gathering evolves through the investigation process. Even the most structured plans of attack may end up as only guidelines. The plan you implement with a checklist may uncover unanticipated facts. Don't get discouraged if you merely stumble upon pertinent information. You might find a gold mine of information in some of the least expected places. That's part of the give and take of investigation. Don't leave any stone uncovered just because it's not on your checklist!

Who are you going to call? Sources of information

Working from the checklist (see the preceding section), you then seek to obtain the information necessary to answer the questions. You don't need a special degree in the field of investigation to find out some of the juiciest bits of information about people and events. Many of your best tools come from public sources.

TIP

Some of the most helpful sources of information are the ones that are most easily accessible. You'll be amazed at how much you can find out from conducting Internet searches, analyzing court documents, exploring public and business records, interviewing experts, and using more creative alternatives.

Searching the web

You usually begin investigative fact gathering with a search of the Internet. Search engines and telephone calls may turn up addresses, land line phone numbers, and even ages of individuals, as well as phone numbers, addresses, and websites of businesses.

The easiest way to access published information is through the one of the numerous online directories, like www.whitepages.com, www.beenverified.com, www.anywho.com, www.ussearch.com, and www.superpages.com. If one of these websites doesn't produce the information you're looking for, you may find it in the crisscross directory provided by Cole: www.coledirectory.com. Criss-cross directories may list the owner of a telephone number even when the number is unlisted.

The online content at www.dummies.com/go/paralegalcareer2e provides links to several companies that will search national public records for you for a fee.

Another avenue for accessing personal and company information is social media. Conducting searches on Facebook and LinkedIn may reveal elusive cell phone numbers and information about an individual's work history or a company's employees. You may also obtain extensive information about a person's educational background and find helpful connections.

Analyzing the obvious: Court documents

Court documents filed in the case are excellent source information. You can start your search by consulting the case pleadings (such as the complaint, answer, reply, and any third-party complaints and answers). If you work for the defense attorney in a personal injury case, you can get all of this from the plaintiff's complaint: the location of the incident, who was involved in the incident, the damages claimed, and salient details about the plaintiff's lifestyle, family, and job. The attorney may then use this information to determine whether she should suggest an all-out fight against the claim in court or focus primarily on settlement. Similarly, a paralegal for the plaintiff's attorney may use information from the defendant's answer to delve more deeply into the investigation of the plaintiff's claim.

Of course, discovery documents — such as interrogatories, requests for admission, requests for production of documents, and deposition digests — provide excellent information about a case, and your job may be to sift through it all to find what's pertinent for your attorney.

You may find some precious gems of information in the court documents of other civil cases that the opposing party has been involved in. Usually pleadings, motions, and affidavits are part of the public record, but discovery documents don't often end up in the court files.

Delivering the data: Records

Hospital, school, court, motor vehicle, and military records contain information that is usually easily admitted as evidence in court and that even eyewitnesses have trouble refuting. You can find quite a bit of information just by accessing public records. For instance, if you work for the defendant's attorney in a personal injury case, you'll probably retrieve the records from the hospital where the plaintiff received treatment. Hospital records indicate the types of injuries the plaintiff suffered, the treatment the plaintiff received, and the cost of the treatment. This kind of information is good to know if the suit goes to trial, and it can also influence the defense if it decides to settle.

The key is knowing where to go, so become familiar with the kinds of records kept by the county clerks, local school districts, the tax assessor's office, and other offices and agencies. Table 11-1 summarizes some of the sources for records and the kinds of information the records contain. If you don't know where to find information, contact governmental agencies.

REMEMBER

The online content contains a list of state and federal agencies that may provide vital information for an investigation project.

TABLE 11-1   ## Sources of Information

Source	Type of Information
Police department incident or offense reports	Facts of an incident and the names, birth dates, addresses, and telephone numbers of the participants
Arrest records and warrants	Name, address, birth date, physical description, Social Security number, and fingerprints of the accused
Traffic accident reports	Location and time of the accident; names, addresses, and birth dates of the driver and passengers; driver's license numbers; and automobile registration numbers
Telephone and cell phone company records	An individual or business's full name, address, land line or cell phone number, length of phone service, record of calls and location, and number of extensions
Post office	An individual's full name, address, post office box number, and any forwarding addresses
Credit card companies	An individual's employment and credit references and information regarding the types of charges an individual makes
County assessor's office	Dimensions and taxable income on real property and information about property improvements
Health department records	Names and maiden names of a child's parents, their occupations and ages, and name of the child's physician
Public school records	Past and present records of students and possibly their photographs
Professional trade association and union records	List of members' names and their addresses and telephone numbers
Banks and other financial institutions	An individual's full name, address, occupation, sources of income, expenditures, personal and business references, net worth, and handwriting samples
Moving companies	An individual's forwarding address

(continued)

TABLE 11-1 *(continued)*

Source	Type of Information
Bureau of Vital Statistics	Birth certificates (which contain an individual's full name, birth date, place of birth, time of birth, and parents' names) and death certificates (for name, birth date, last known address, and cause of death of the deceased)
County clerk's office	Marriage license records (for an individual's marital information, birth date, signature, and last known address), divorce records (for an individual's marriage date and location, separation date and location, children's ages, community property, signature, and place of employment), civil files (for name changes, property liens and property descriptions, and the types of civil cases in which an individual is involved), criminal files (for transcripts of preliminary hearings, probation officer reports, subpoenas issued in a case, and names of attorneys who are involved in the case)
Election commission	A registered voter's full name, address, occupation, political affiliation, spouse's name, and most recent location of voter registration
Credit reporting agencies	An individual's full name, address, birth date, occupation, present and former addresses, credit rating, and marital status, as well as information regarding whether an individual owns or rents a home and documentation of personal and professional references, banks and financial institutions, and names of relatives
U.S. Citizenship and Immigration Services (www.uscis.gov)	Full name, address, occupation, age, physical description, marital status, signature, photograph, and date and manner of entry of an alien
Federal Aviation Administration (www.faa.gov)	Aircraft ownership information
Department of Motor Vehicles	An individual's full name, address, physical description, birth date, vehicle information, operator's license number, photograph, and signature
Utility companies	An individual's name, address, and prior addresses, as well as information regarding who's responsible for paying an individual's bill
Secretary of state	Information regarding corporations (registered agents, officers, and status), assumed names, and liens filed (Uniform Commercial Code, or UCC)

When you locate the appropriate records, be very polite to the office personnel you deal with. If you act impatiently or abruptly with the records staff, the person on the other end of the line will usually make it difficult for you to collect any information at all. If politeness doesn't work, then you may want to announce yourself as a paralegal and mention the attorney or law firm you represent. Most public employees are fairly willing to accommodate attorneys and law firms they're familiar with, so it doesn't hurt to name-drop.

But don't use an overly authoritative tone — it can often backfire. Although public employees are generally willing to help, they don't respond well to perceived threats. In fact, it may just result in some feet dragging.

TIP

Be specific when requesting records. That shows that you know what you're talking about and helps the person on the other end find the records you need. Instead of simply asking for Kelley Klutz's hospital records, ask for Mr. Klutz's hospital records from the admittance date of December 30, 2018, to a release date of January 8, 2019. Specific requests improve the chance that the clerk will pull the correct file. Imprecise requests waste everybody's time.

Chatting up: Conversations with people in the know

Every paralegal comes across a situation for which there's no available answer. If this happens to you, you may need to consult sources other than witnesses or parties to the action.

Community members like courthouse employees, city hall employees, reporters, experienced legal investigators, and even local gossips have a vast amount of knowledge and are usually willing to share the information with someone who appears interested in learning about it.

TIP

Obtaining information from disinterested sources may require more elaborate social skills. If somebody knows and trusts you, he'll usually open up to you. So, take time to establish professional relationships with people who are good sources of information and are familiar with the legal process. Sometimes, you can even get some helpful insight into the character of a judge from a person who makes a hobby of observing trials.

For more about how to conduct an interview, see Chapter 12.

REMEMBER

The online content at www.dummies.com/go/paralegalcareer2e provides links to several companies that will search national public records for you for a fee.

Keeping Track: Identifying and Protecting Evidence

Evidence comes in two basic forms: testimonial and tangible. Testimonial evidence is oral evidence, the kind presented by the spoken word of witnesses and experts. Tangible evidence consists of documents, photos, and other items you can hold or touch. (For more about evidence, consult Chapter 7.) One of your duties as a paralegal may be to mark and protect evidence so it's ready for trial.

Leaving your mark: Identifying evidence

After you obtain and verify tangible evidence, you need to carefully mark each item. Usually this means designating the evidence with your initials and recording the evidence in a journal or on a spreadsheet. You may have to assign each item its own unique number to assure that you can identify the evidence when you need it. When you follow a uniform procedure, you increase the chances that the court will rule to admit the evidence into court.

TIP

Although you can't really file and maintain testimonial evidence, you're still responsible for keeping track of testimony. Record names, addresses, and phone numbers of witnesses and experts in the evidence journals or spreadsheet. Maintaining good records results in more effective evidence.

On guard: Protecting evidence

After you mark tangible evidence, take measures to keep it safe. Wrap or bag it to keep the evidence from being destroyed, harmed, or altered in any manner. And keep a log that records everyone who takes a piece of evidence from safekeeping so that you know where evidence is if it's not in its protected location. To protect the client's chances for victory, you have to preserve evidence that may be easily altered (like original documents) from tampering and modification. Place this kind of evidence in a locked safe or safe-deposit box to guarantee its preservation.

WARNING

If a court isn't confident about the way evidence has been preserved, the court could easily throw it out, which means your attorney can't present it at trial. Not only does this adversely affect the client's case, but it could also ruin the reputation of the attorney and law firm. Careful identification and preservation of evidence is crucial.

Keeping Order: Organizing the Evidence

Your final step in working with evidence is to organize it so that the evidence establishes the chain of events of the client's case. Well-organized evidence tends to support a good story line and persuade listeners. Disorganized evidence detracts from the continuity of a story. If a piece of evidence doesn't directly support the client's story, you have to provide a logical explanation for the incongruity.

When you work as a paralegal, you'll probably organize evidence in three different ways to get the most impact from it: chronologically, by version, and by inconsistencies. We cover each of these in the following sections.

Setting a time frame: Chronological organization

Order the evidence chronologically by linking each piece of data to the rest in the order that the related action occurred. Chronological ordering of evidence helps promote the accuracy of the client's version of the story. It also makes the most sense to the fact finder (usually the jury) at trial.

Chronological ordering of evidence provides an important aid in the ultimate resolution of the case, and it assists in maintaining the consistency of the investigation process. When you chronologically order the information as you uncover it, you can more easily define the gaps of information that require you to conduct further research.

Getting the story straight: Organization by versions

Every story has more than one side. Organizing evidence as it relates to different versions of a story helps you keep track of which piece of information goes with which version of the case. So, you'll more likely be prepared to help your supervising attorney use the evidence to strengthen the client's case and also rebut the opposition.

Noting discrepancies: Organization by inconsistencies

After you've ordered the evidence chronologically and by version, you may find some inconsistencies in the information. You can organize these inconsistencies into checklists to prepare for further investigation. In this way, investigation continues throughout the litigation process. You prepare investigation checklists for one issue, diligently draw upon the sources of information to answer the questions on the checklist, and prepare the products of the investigation so that they'll be valuable to the client's case. Often, investigation of one issue uncovers new issues and new checklists. You may need to conduct further investigation in order to answer new questions as they come up. The investigation process usually doesn't end until the case is settled.

» **Interviewing witnesses**

» **Preparing clients and witnesses for giving testimony**

Chapter **12**

Chewing the Fat: Legal Interviewing

You'll find that you often get the most valuable information for a case when you interview clients and witnesses. Paralegals often have an advantage over their supervising attorneys when it comes to conducting interviews. Clients may be less intimidated by paralegals and find them to be more sensitive and more approachable than attorneys. So, you may be able to gain more information from a client or witness in an interview than an attorney can.

The majority of the interviews you hold serve one of two purposes: to gain information about a case from a client or witness or to prepare the client or witness to give testimony. This chapter shows you how to set up an interview with a client or witness, gives you ideas for the types of questions you ask, and provides tips on how to prepare clients and witnesses for testifying at trial.

Gauging Whether the Case Is Valid: Initial Client Interviews

The first and, perhaps, most important interview for any case is the initial client interview. The primary goal of the initial client interview is to gather enough information to determine whether the client has a valid case and to develop a proper investigation of the case if it turns out to be valid. Your supervising attorney may trust you to perform this important task. At the very least, you may be present during the interview to take notes and provide support to the client and your supervising attorney.

Successful client interviews require proper preparation. The initial interview provides the client with the first, and probably most lasting, impression of the law firm, so you must present yourself as a competent and caring professional. To make for a comfortable client and an enlightening interview, you, as the interview director, set the stage, control the discussion, and provide a natural ending point.

Setting the mood

You need to keep a couple things in mind when you set the stage for a client interview. The room you choose and the way you position those involved in the interview within that room can affect the success of the interview.

The room where you hold the interview should be comfortable and free of clutter with a room décor that doesn't detract from the matter at hand. A good choice would be a conference room, a general meeting room, or the office of an attorney or paralegal.

WARNING

Law libraries and reception areas make bad choices for an interview. You don't want the client's interview interrupted by an attorney or paralegal wandering into the law library trying to do some legal research. Even worse, you definitely don't want to hold a client interview in a public area where other clients, messengers, and delivery people could happen by. Your client needs to trust the law firm's ability to keep her affairs confidential.

After you settle on a location for the interview, you need to consider the arrangement of the people in the room. Usually, interviews are set up in one of three basic seating arrangements:

>> **The interviewer and interviewee face to face across a desk (see Figure 12-1A):** This arrangement is the most formal of the three. Corporate clients may prefer this type of meeting with attorneys in their law firm to discuss company litigation, but other clients may find this situation too intimidating and formal.

>> **The interviewer and interviewee face to face at an angle on a corner of a desk (see Figure 12-1B):** This arrangement is more personable than the preceding one but still maintains a professional atmosphere. This position allows you to share documents very easily with the client, and it allows you to lend support during emotional or traumatic episodes.

» **The interviewer and interviewee side by side (see Figure 12-1C):** This arrangement offers the most personable, unimposing atmosphere. You can either eliminate the desk and table completely and converse from the comfort of two cozy chairs, or you can sit side by side at a table. Sitting at a table gives you space to work with when you have documents to discuss. This arrangement may limit your eye contact with the client, but because the client may feel less intimidated with this arrangement, he may feel more comfortable giving out information.

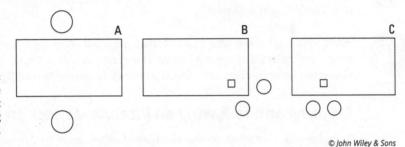

FIGURE 12-1:
You have options when it comes to seating arrangements.

© John Wiley & Sons

After a while, you'll instinctively know the best location and seating arrangement for interviewing clients. Then, you'll be able to focus on preparing for the content of the interview rather than its setting.

REMEMBER

If you adopt a more casual interview style, don't get too complacent about how you conduct yourself. Although the content of the interview is important, first impressions are lasting. How your client perceives the law firm in the initial interview setting will make a huge difference in building and maintaining credibility with the client. The relationship you develop with the client in the initial interview sets the tone for rest of the litigation process.

Directing the content

Before you interview anyone, you need to have a plan. Know what you want to accomplish from the meeting and put it in writing so you have something to refer to as you move through the interview.

Relying on a checklist

TIP

Before you meet with clients or talk to them on the phone, create a checklist of items you need from the clients as well as a list of questions they have to answer. You can mark items off the list as you receive the information. With a checklist, you can be certain you've covered all the important topics. It also gives you a subtle tool for containing an interview if the client starts to veer from the topic.

Many clients love to tell you their life stories, but time is a valuable resource in a law office. You'll be pressed for time just like everyone else on staff, so you'll generally have a specific amount of time allotted for a client interview. Not only does the checklist help you to keep the client focused on the task at hand, but it also gives you a polite way to bring an interview to a close. Review your checklist with the client at the onset of the interview so she knows what you plan to cover during the interview. The client knows the interview is over when you've worked through all the questions.

REMEMBER

The client is often just as concerned about time as you are. In cases where an attorney charges clients by the hour, clients usually don't want to spend too much time discussing trivialities!

WARNING

Don't be so rigid about your checklist that you don't allow the client to stray a little. When you let the interviewee go off on a tangent, you may get some information that you would never have uncovered had you stuck to the checklist religiously.

Creating and following an interview checklist

Organize your checklists so that the flow of information has some continuity. Use any information you may have about the case before you see the client to formulate your questions and organize the interview. Ask background questions first to establish a foundation. Then use the logical sequence of events as a guide for ordering the questions you ask about the event or incident in question. For example, in divorce, estate, and other legal matters that concern finances, you gather information on a client's assets and debts. It's customary to ask about assets first and then use the asset information as a guide for gathering the information on debts.

TIP

Successful client interviews use a combination of *open-ended questions* (ones that can't be answered with a simple fact or "yes" or "no," like "What did the accident scene look like?") and *closed questions* (ones that ask for simple answers, like "Was the car damaged in the front?"). The open questions allow the client to tell the story, while the closed questions help bring focus and additional detail to the interview.

REMEMBER

Online at www.dummies.com/go/paralegalcareer2e we've provided you with an extensive sample checklist that you could use for the initial client interview in a divorce matter. You can customize this list for other situations.

TIP

You can break the content of the interview into four stages:

1. **Secure background information.**

   Ask questions about the client's biographical data and other information about the client that's pertinent to the case. You can find checklists of background questions for all kinds of cases in the *American Jurisprudence Proof of Facts*

(POF). (You can find out more about this helpful resource in Chapter 11.) For example, if a client is seeking assistance with a drunk driving charge, you'd ask about the client's driving record to get insight into his driving background.

2. **Find out what happened immediately before the event.**

   In the pre-event stage of questioning, ask the client to thoroughly explain the circumstances leading up to the incident in question.

3. **Find out what happened during the actual incident.**

   The initial interview focuses on the event stage, which may be the most emotional part of the interview for the client. Be prepared to handle the client's anger, sadness, or fear as he recalls the details of the event. Pay close attention; sometimes seemingly insignificant details can have a crucial bearing on the success of a case.

4. **Discovering what occurred after the event.**

   Have the client finish the accounting with information about what happened immediately after the event and what relevant matters have occurred up to the time of the interview. This information helps you determine the client's damages and the extent of his pain and suffering.

Here's a sample scenario to help you work through the initial client interview process. Suppose your supervising attorney asks you to interview a prospective client by handing you a memo like the one in Figure 12-2.

MEMO

TO: Pat Paralegal
FROM: Ima Gogetter, Esq.
DATE: January __, 20____
RE: Initial Client Interview of Cary Careless

Cary Careless has contacted our firm. He is in need of legal representation because of an auto accident in which he was involved. You are to meet with Cary to gather information about the accident as well as general client information.

All we have been told so far is that Cary hit another car. He has been cited for reckless driving and manslaughter charges and a civil action may be pending.

Attached is a copy of the police report of the accident. Please study this summary before the interview to assist you in your information gathering.

FIGURE 12-2: An attorney's memo requesting an initial client interview.

The memo includes a police report. Sometimes the law office will have preliminary information you can ponder before you meet the client. Figure 12-3 shows you the narrative report referred to in the memo.

Based on the information provided to you and using the four stages of an event as a guideline, you may come up with a checklist of questions like the following to ask Mr. Careless in the initial interview. *Note:* You ask follow-up questions based on the answers you get for the original questions.

>> **Background questions**

1. Full Name

2. Contact information: address, phone number, Social Security number, date of birth (Client is only 18. Does he live with his parents? If not, what are his living arrangements?)

3. Attend school?

4. Employed? If so, where? How long?

5. When did he receive his driver's license?

6. Any citations on record?

7. Does he own the car? If not, whose car was he driving?

8. Who carries insurance? What type and amount of coverage?

>> **Pre-event questions**

1. Why were you driving on that road? Where were you going?

2. What was your physical condition? Were you tired? Taking any medications with or without prescription? Consumed any alcohol? Any illegal or nonprescription drugs?

3. Any physical limitations? Eyeglasses? Hearing aids?

4. Were you in a hurry for any reason?

5. Did you know the speed limit?

6. What were the road conditions?

7. What was the weather like that day?

8. What was the general condition of the car you were driving? Had it been serviced recently?

9. What are the names and ages of the two passengers in your car?

10. What is your relationship to the two passengers in the car?

11. Why were they traveling with you?

≫ Event questions

1. What time of day did the accident occur? What was the weather like at the time?

2. Explain your version of the accident. Take this one step at a time: Speed? Position of passengers? Radio or other music playing? What were the other passengers doing? Anyone on a cell phone? Anyone eating?

3. Was the road familiar or was it one you hadn't driven on before?

4. When did you see the other car?

5. Was there a stoplight or stop sign? A yield sign? Do you know who had the right of way?

6. When did you realize how serious the accident was? How did your passengers react?

7. When did the police arrive? How were they summoned?

8. Relate your conversation with the officer at the scene.

9. Anyone go to the hospital? How were they transported?

10. Did you contact your family? The family of other passengers in the car?

11. Did you take photos of the scene?

≫ Post-event questions

1. Describe your injuries.

2. Have you received any medications? Any ongoing care? What is your prognosis?

3. When did you learn of Ms. Fortunate's hospitalization? Have you received grief counseling or other ongoing psychological support?

4. Do you understand your responsibilities and/or the choices you will have to make?

5. Has your insurance agent contacted you?

6. Has Ms. Fortunate's family or attorney attempted to contact you?

The success of any interview depends upon the client's ability to provide the necessary information. One means of persuading the client to talk is to have him explain the stages in story fashion. If possible, encourage the client to recount the events in chronological order and avoid interrupting the client during the account. At the end of the client's story, summarize the chain of events and repeat it to the client. This gives the client the chance to correct any of your misperceptions and allows the client to recall additional details to fill in the original account.

FIGURE 12-3:
A narrative police report in the Cary Careless case.

© John Wiley & Sons

Ending the initial interview

Before you end the initial interview, ask whether the client has any additional questions about the case. The odds are pretty good that the client won't remember every single detail about the incident or her actions during the first interview, so encourage her to contact you or your supervising attorney if she remembers something else or has additional questions. Before the client leaves the initial interview, be sure to tell her to refrain from discussing the case with anyone other than members of the law firm.

TIP

Right after the client leaves your office, take a few moments to summarize the interview. While your memory is fresh, record the date and time of the interview and jot down a statement of the pertinent facts of the case, your evaluation of the client, a list of documents and other evidence that may help the case, a list of potential witnesses, and other pertinent information.

Completing the Story: Witness Interviews

You conduct witness interviews in much the same way you do client interviews. The major difference between the two is that you go into the witness interview with a more definite goal for the interview.

WARNING

Before you interview any witness, you must first determine whether that witness is represented by an attorney in the case. If so, get the attorney's consent *in writing* before interviewing the witness.

As in the initial client interview (see the previous sections), you'll have a checklist of questions prepared in advance. To give you an idea of the kinds of questions you may ask a witness to an accident, we return to the Cary Careless incident (see "Creating and following an interview checklist," earlier in this chapter). Imagine your supervising attorney hands you the memo in Figure 12-4.

MEMO

TO: Pat Paralegal
FROM: Ima Gogetter, Esq.
DATE: January __, 20__
RE: Cary Careless Matter: Witness Nathan Nosy

We received a call today from Nathan Nosy alleging that he witnessed Cary's auto accident. Mr. Nosy claims that Cary was consuming what appeared to be alcohol in his car before the accident. We need to uncover as much information about Mr. Nosy's allegation as possible. You can contact him at the Cozy Creek Retirement Center, which is located on the same block as the accident site. He is elderly, so you can schedule an appointment during the middle of the morning.

It is within your discretion to select the meeting site for this interview. Remember to ascertain all the facts about the allegation. And determine as much as possible about the credibility of Mr. Nosy.

FIGURE 12-4: Attorney's memo requesting a prospective witness interview.

© John Wiley & Sons

To complete the assignment, you first find out whether Mr. Nosy has an attorney to represent him in the Careless matter. Then you choose a location for the interview. You may call the retirement center where he lives to find out if they have a quiet, comfortable room where you could talk to Mr. Nosy, especially if he doesn't live alone. After you've established the site and scheduled an interview with the witness, you prepare a set of questions like the ones in Figure 12-5.

WITNESS INTERVIEW CHECKLIST

Name: Nathan Nosy
Date: February ___, 20__
Location: Cozy Creek Retirement Center
Time of interview: 10:30 a.m.

[Make sure the room is comfortable for the witness. Make sure he is seated comfortably and has water and other creature comforts. Perhaps start the interview with small talk, like questions about how long Mr. Nosy has been at Cozy Creek, about his family, past history, and so on. During the interview note his attention level and demeanor, and check for any problems he may have remembering dates or names.]

What is your full name? Date of birth?

What is your address? Phone number? The address/phone number of your nearest relative?

Where did you work before your retirement? What was your occupation?

Are you on any type of medication? What types? For how long?

Do you have any difficulties seeing or hearing? Have you undergone any recent testing for vision or hearing? What is your vision? (Does he wear glasses or a hearing aid?)

Do you recall the date of the incident?

What was your location at the time of accident? In your room? At your window?

What was the weather condition at the time? Could you see clearly? What was the lighting like?

What made you first notice Mr. Careless? What drew your attention to him?

Do you remember the color of the car? The color of Mr. Careless's clothing at the time? How tall would you say Mr. Careless is? Do you recall the color of his hair?

Was there anybody with you when you observed Mr. Careless? Were you engaged in conversation with anyone at the time? Was your television on? What shows do you like to watch or what were you watching that day?

Did you notice anybody else on the street at the time of the accident?

Please describe for me Mr. Careless's behavior before he drove the car. What was he doing? Was he holding anything?

What did you see that made you think he was drinking alcohol? Can or bottle? Brown bag? Color or design of container?

Can you give me your impression of Mr. Careless during the time you observed him? How long did you observe Mr. Careless?

Did you see the accident? If so, describe what you saw happen.

What is your opinion of young people? Do you have grandchildren? How old are they? Do you know anyone of a similar age as Mr. Careless?

Did you tell anybody else about your observations at the time? Please give me their names, addresses.

[Thank the witness for his help and express appreciation for his time and efforts. Also give him my business card in case he thinks of anything else that might be helpful to either side.]

FIGURE 12-5:
Checklist for a
witness interview.

TIP

As you conduct the witness interview, note whether you think the witness would provide effective testimony in the event of a trial.

Preparing Clients and Witnesses for Testimony

Now that you've interviewed your office's client and the prospective witnesses, you know exactly what they're going to say during questioning if they're deposed or in court if the case goes to trial, right? Wrong! One of the best ways to sink your client's case is to let your client or any of your witnesses get on the stand without training them for questioning.

WARNING

Never assume that people you've interviewed will say the same things under questioning that they've told you in an interview. Witnesses can freeze up and get flustered when they're under oath and facing questions from attorneys.

To prepare clients and witnesses for testimony during a deposition or trial, let them know the purpose of the questioning. Give them a thorough description of the questioning process and provide them with insight into the opposition's perspective and how the opposition may use the answers they give to make its case. Here are several time-tested pointers to give to a client or witness, especially if she's giving testimony to a jury:

>> **Tell the truth.** Telling a lie may lose the case. In a lawsuit, as in all other matters, honesty is the best policy. If you tell the truth, nobody can cross you up. And you could face criminal perjury charges for intentionally lying under oath.

WARNING

Never tell a client or prospective witness to say anything under oath that's untrue. Not only is it against professional ethics to encourage a witness to lie, but you could also be prosecuted for perjury or witness tampering.

>> **Don't guess.** If you don't know the answer to a question, don't speculate. Simply state that you don't know the answer.

>> **Understand the question before you give an answer.** You can't possibly give a truthful and accurate answer unless you understand the question. If you don't understand the attorney's question, ask him to repeat it.

>> **Take your time.** Think about a question before you provide an answer. Take as much time as you need to formulate your answer, but keep in mind that if you take too long to answer a question, the jury may think you're making up an answer.

>> **Answer only the question that's asked.** Don't volunteer any information that isn't required by the question.

>> **Make yourself heard.** Don't chew gum, and keep your hands away from your mouth.

>> **Answer audibly rather than with gestures.** It's easier for the court reporter to record a "yes" than a head nod.

>> **Don't look to the lawyer for help when you are on the stand.** If you look at your lawyer during questioning from the opposition, the jury may interpret this as a sign you're being untruthful.

>> **Beware of questions involving distances and time.** If you provide an estimate, make sure you clarify that you're estimating. Think clearly about speeds, distances, and intervals of time, and make reasonable estimates.

>> **Know your vital statistics.** Your truthfulness may be suspect if you can't recall basic information about yourself, like your address, how old you are, and when you were married.

>> **Don't argue with any lawyer who questions you.** Maintain as much composure throughout the process as you can.

>> **Don't lose your temper no matter how hard you're pressed.**

>> **Be courteous.** Showing good manners is one of the best ways to make a good impression on the judge and jury.

>> **Avoid making jokes and wisecracks.** A lawsuit is a serious matter.

>> **Address the jury during questioning.**

>> **Dress conservatively so as not to distract a jury.** Nose rings and tank tops may send the wrong message to the jury. Dress for trial as though you're attending a job interview. Suits, dresses, and sport coats and slacks in dark blue, brown, or black are good options.

In addition to going through this list with clients and witnesses, you'll probably prepare them for specific questions they can expect to answer.

TIP

To avoid unpleasant surprises, you should try to anticipate the questions the opposition will ask of your clients and witnesses and give them a mock questioning to help them form their answers before the trial or deposition.

REMEMBER

One of the most important factors in the success of your client's case is the quality of the evidence that your office's legal team presents to the jury. A big part of that evidence consists of witness testimony. The more credible your client and witnesses appear to the jury, the better your office's chances for a successful outcome in the litigation.

Chapter **13**

Burning the Midnight Oil: Legal Research

You may find your most challenging yet rewarding responsibility as a paralegal is the hours you spend conducting legal research, whether in a law library or online. Legal research is a critical component in the success of civil and criminal law suits. Understanding legal research provides you with a passkey that opens doors to virtually every legal issue that might arise in the typical law office or freelance paralegal practice.

But by the same token, legal research has been known to result in endless hours of frustration, especially if you're new at it. You must access an extensive amount of material that grows larger by the day. And because the law invariably changes, the legal material you find today may not appear in the same form tomorrow. It's subject to continuous revision and updating. You may get so inundated with legal material that you reach the point of sensory overload!

TIP

Approach legal research with a certain amount of open-mindedness and flexibility. You'll rarely encounter a single-issue research problem. Even though you may think that you have only one topic to research, the specific issue could quickly multiply into numerous related questions as the research project progresses.

WARNING

Legal research can be addictive. When your supervising attorney assigns you to research a given issue, you need to focus your allotted time on the precise question, or you may find yourself returning to legal resources more often than is efficient or practical for your firm.

Conducting Legal Research

When you tackle research for the first time, you may find that simply beginning the process can be the major obstacle to thorough and efficient legal research. You can usually spot neophyte paralegals in the law library quite easily. They're the ones listlessly roaming the stacks like zombies. This may seem like a natural state for you at first. However, as you become accustomed to the inner sanctum of the law library or online legal research, you'll rapidly develop a routine. With time, this routine becomes so ingrained in your research style that the question of *where* to begin researching becomes academic. Before long, you'll join the ranks of seasoned legal research veterans who find it to be immensely enjoyable and challenging. Many paralegals find themselves thriving on the rigors presented by complex legal research problems.

This section focuses on conducting traditional research. Even if your law firm primarily uses online research tools, make sure you're familiar with the steps involved in finding law in traditional law books to have a better understanding of the process.

TIP

Chapter 8 provides more detail on the major sources of primary and secondary authority you seek for through legal research. Pay particular attention to those authorities listed in Table 8-1 for an overview or review of these sources. Familiarize yourself with as many of them as possible to increase your effectiveness in performing legal research.

Searching for applicable law in four easy steps

The odds are you won't find a magical, universally accepted approach to complete and thorough legal research. But many paralegals, law students, and attorneys use a simple approach that involves the following four steps:

1. **Begin the research process by consulting legal dictionaries.**

   Ballentine's Legal Dictionary and Thesaurus, Black's Law Dictionary, Words and Phrases, and William Statsky's *Legal Thesaurus/Dictionary* are examples of some of the most popular tools you'll use to come up with as many terms pertaining to the legal research problem as possible. Compile a comprehensive list of terms that appear to relate to the issues of the case. Include synonyms, antonyms, and other relevant expressions. This process is known as *cartwheeling*.

2. **Determine which court jurisdiction the research problem involves.**

   You need to figure out whether the research problem involves the federal or state court system. From there, you establish the specific level of court you're dealing with in either system.

3. **Discover the applicable law.**

   The kinds of law resources you consult depend on whether you're researching on the state or federal level. We give you more information about the specific resources listed here later in this chapter in "Tools of the Trade."

   If the problem is a state court matter, research these resources:

   - Consult major legal encyclopedias. Obtain a better understanding of the nature of the case and obtain primary case and statutory leads through *Corpus Juris Secundum* and *American Jurisprudence, 2d.*

   - Obtain more leads in *American Law Reports* (ALR). You can supplement the material from the legal encyclopedias by checking this other secondary legal resource.

   - Find a digest topic, or topics, from West's "Outline of the Law," which is located at the beginning of each of West's digests. The topics will lead to applicable state, regional, and federal digests, which in turn direct the researcher to primary authority.

   - Locate as many on-point court decisions from the state supreme court, appellate court, and federal court cases as possible and read the complete decision in the appropriate reporter. Remember that you might have a hard time finding on-point federal court cases when researching a state court matter because federal court jurisdiction differs from state court jurisdiction.

   - Apply any pertinent provisions of the state constitution and statutes as well as the U.S. Constitution and U.S. Code to the facts.

   If the problem is a federal court matter, expand your research:

   - Consult encyclopedias, ALR, and digests as you would for a state case.

   - Find and apply as many on-point federal court cases as possible. You can find the relevant federal court decisions handed down by the U.S. District Courts in the *Federal Supplement.* You can find cases coming from the U.S. Court of Appeals in the *Federal Reporter.* Locate any cases from the U.S. Supreme Court in the *United States Reports* (the official reporter of U.S. Supreme Court decisions), the *Supreme Court Reporter*, and the *United States Supreme Court Reports, Lawyers' Edition.*

- Apply any pertinent provisions of the U.S. Constitution, U.S. Code, and applicable state constitution and statutes to the facts of the problem.

4. **Shepardize or otherwise validate each of the primary authorities you've found.**

To make certain that what you've found is still *good law* (that is, that subsequent court decisions haven't overruled, modified, or reversed any of your authorities), use Shepard's citations. Sheparizing may also point you toward additional on-point statutes or cases. ***Note:*** If you have access to Westlaw or Lexis Advance, you should consult these online update services because they're usually more current than the Shepard's volumes you find in the law library.

When you look up cases in Shepard's to determine if they're still valid or to find other cases that may have followed or otherwise approved of the decisions, you're doing what's called *Shepardizing,* or checking the current status of a case.

Reining in the research process

Following an approach that includes the steps outlined in the preceding section allows you to successfully meet the challenges of legal research without resorting to too many aspirin tablets. Your main concern with legal research will soon become not where to *begin* a project, but when to *end* it. After you're in a law library or logged in to an online legal research database, you may discover that you're so inundated with information and so intellectually stimulated by tracking down the answers to the research problem that you lose track of time. Don't get locked inside the library!

Answer these four guiding questions regarding how much time you spend on a research project:

» **Have you found authority on-point?** Like finding a needle in a haystack, the object of any legal research problem is to narrow in on mandatory primary authority that relates to your research problem. It may take 2 hours to find applicable law or it may take 20. But after you locate mandatory primary authority and properly validate it, you just need to integrate that authority into the research memo and present it to your supervising attorney.

» **What is your legal research deadline?** When you're working under the gun to find the right case, the time constraint itself becomes a much more common determinant for ending a research project than finding the most applicable mandatory authority. Many law offices function in crisis mode, and the pressure of the deadline may preclude complete legal research.

WARNING

Unfortunately, because most law offices have a heavy workload, many attorneys are famous for waiting until the last minute to give research projects to their paralegals. So, much of the time, you'll need to hustle to get in the most research in a limited amount of time. Very simply, your research task ends when your time runs out.

» **Have you exhausted all available research sources?** Paralegals and attorneys have ethical and financial incentives to perform the most thorough research possible in the quest for the answers to research problems. If the resources you find in the law library or with Westlaw and Lexis Advance consistently point you to the same cases or statutes, you can be pretty sure you've found the most pertinent law for your case.

» **Can the client afford to pay for more of your time?** One final factor governs your decision on how far to research an issue, and that's the amount of retainer the client has provided or is willing to provide to the firm. When you're assigned a research project, immediately check to see if your supervising attorney has suggested a time limit and report the status of your research to the attorney. Sometimes an attorney wants you to continue your research and won't bill the client for the hours you go over.

Relying On Tools of the Trade

In addition to knowing where to begin and how to end legal research, you need to get to know the five main tools of legal research:

» Legal encyclopedias

» *American Law Reports* (ALR)

» Digests

» Reporters

» Shepard's citations or KeyCite

» Westlaw or Lexis Advance online legal research

TIP

With the increasing popularity of online legal research, some paralegals have never opened up a law book, but we strongly suggest that you learn how to perform legal research in a law library before you rely on online legal research. Westlaw and Lexis Advance may be too expensive for some smaller law firms, sole practitioners, or law students to use continually, and you never know when you'll be in a situation that requires you to access the law through traditional means. So, do yourself and your supervising attorney a favor and learn how to research from the texts before you go online.

The five main research tools comprise the heart of many law libraries and are exceptionally useful for performing background research on a topic, understanding a research topic, finding leads to primary authority, and validating the primary authority after you've located it.

Establishing a foundation with legal encyclopedias

Legal encyclopedias, like *Corpus Juris Secundum* and *American Jurisprudence, 2d*, help you get a broad understanding of the legal issue you're researching and the relevant facts surrounding that issue.

First you find the general topic in the encyclopedia and scan through the text until you uncover a specific topic that matches your research problem. Then you consult the footnotes to find applicable cases as well as the current updated authorities in the pocket part, which literally appears in a pocket at the end of the book.

WARNING

Don't neglect to look in the pocket part of any legal research text. That little supplemental booklet in the back of the main volume contains any updates and new cases that have come out since the time the main volume was published.

Corpus Juris Secundum

Corpus Juris Secundum (CJS) lists very broad categories by titles and subsequently narrows them into more specific subdivisions. Within each title, the subdivisions are numbered by section. CJS organizes the sections within each title like this:

>> Definitions and general topic information

>> Individual elements and requirements

>> Procedural and evidentiary subtopics

You can find topics in CJS either through the title outline or the index. Near the front of each CJS volume is a topic outline that includes all the titles in the CJS series. After you find a relevant topic in the outline, you access the particular volume that includes that title. From there, you narrow the general title to a subtitle that's relevant to your research problem. At the beginning of each title, you find an even more detailed outline that contains more specific information about the issue you're researching.

You can use the index to research CJS. The index alphabetically lists titles, subtitles, and cross-references. The index approach helps if you already know the vocabulary related to the legal topic you're researching.

American Jurisprudence 2d

American Jurisprudence 2d (Am. Jur. 2d) contains organization strikingly similar to CJS, but because it's a relatively newer publication it has more stuff. Am. Jur. 2d provides two items that CJS doesn't have:

>> **New Topic Service,** which contains topics that have been added after publication of the topic volumes

>> **Table of Statutes, Rules, and Regulations Cited,** which enables the researcher to do further research on the topic if the researcher already knows the federal statute, regulation, or court rule that governs a particular situation

TIP

Legal encyclopedias provide excellent secondary sources for you to begin your legal research with. But you have to research beyond the information discovered in legal encyclopedias to finish your research projects.

Analyzing topics with American Law Reports

Each volume of *American Law Reports* (ALR), except for the index volumes, contains case opinions and articles entitled *annotations*.

TECHNICAL
STUFF

In general, an *annotation* is a collection of explanatory notes and commentary on a topic of law.

The ALR annotation technique has evolved from the selective case system of legal reporting in which only cases of general legal significance are reported. The editors of ALR analyze and interpret these cases and place them into a current legal context. Today, each ALR annotation begins with the complete text of a recent appellate case that illustrates the annotated point of law. The annotations have become so informative and comprehensive that they have far eclipsed the importance of the illustrative cases in the reports.

The ALR staff writes or edits information in the ALR entries. This information includes a summary of the decision, headnotes, a listing of the appearances of counsel, several sample briefs of counsel, and the case opinion. Following the case opinion, you find the annotation, which collects and analyzes the law pertaining to the legal issue that relates to the annotated article.

Most ALR annotations include the following information:

>> Total Client Service Library (TCSL) or West Key Number System references

>> A table of contents for the annotation

>> An index to the annotation

>> A table of jurisdictions represented in the annotation

>> The text of the annotation

TIP

When Thomson Reuters took over publishing ALR, it added the West Key Number System to the annotations. Prior publications use a similar system called the TCSL. We talk more about the West Key Number System in "Digging through digests," later in this chapter.

You can use three main research approaches to find specific topics in the ALR volumes:

>> **Search by index.** The Index to Annotations and the pocket parts lead to the specific legal category that relates to the issue you're researching.

>> **Search by digest.** The digests lead to synopses of the cases included in ALR by topic. The first and second series have their own digest, and the third, fourth, fifth, sixth, seventh, and federal ALR have a unified digest.

>> **Search by computer.** Computer databases like Westlaw and Lexis Advance lead to ALR annotations.

After you find references, you can use the Annotation History Table to see if the annotations have been overruled or supplemented since the annotation was published.

REMEMBER

Overall, ALR is an excellent source for beginning virtually any legal research problem. One major limitation is that it lacks comprehensiveness. Unlike encyclopedias and digests, ALR doesn't discuss every area of law. However, ALR *does* annotate topics of law that are contemporarily significant. Also, ALR discusses them in a very thorough manner with references to cases from every jurisdiction that's taken a position on the cited topic. The series is an indispensable research tool!

Digging through digests

You use digests to find relevant cases by topic. Thomson West is the primary publisher of digests, and its key-number digests are fundamental to the legal profession. Digests contain small summaries (much like the headnotes in reporters) of the points of law (arranged by topic and assigned a key number), but don't contain the actual text of the law.

West's digest system assigns a permanent key number to a specific point of case law, and every point of case law has its respective key number. The organization of the West Key Number System generally follows West's *Outline of the Law*, which includes seven main divisions of the law and 414 subdivisions. You can answer most research questions by finding references to the pertinent case law in the key number digests and then examining the resulting primary authority in the appropriate reporter. Key Number Digests are among the most significant creations for accessing case law.

To use West's digests, access the topic names and key numbers through one or more of the following means:

>> **The Descriptive Word Index:** This index is usually located in the first volume of the set and refers to a topic name and a key number.

>> **The Topic Outline:** If you're already familiar with the topic being researched, use the outline because it further breaks down the listed topics to help you more precisely define your research.

>> **The West Key Number System:** You can use this system to access a topic anywhere within the digest system, because after you find a key number that fits the topic, you can use it to transfer from one reporter to another, or from one digest to another.

>> **The Table of Cases:** This table is usually located in the last volume of the set and is helpful if you know the name of an on-point case but don't know the case citation.

In most cases, the West Key Number System is the fastest, most universally accessible approach to researching any digest or reporter. You can use the West Key Number System to find cases on a specific topic in any other jurisdiction included in West's digest system. All you need to remember is the topic and key number for reference when you move back and forth between jurisdictions.

West's digest system contains a number of different volumes available for research purposes. The West system digests federal court decisions, federal issues (in different specialized reporters), and regional decisions. The Key Number Digests also include state digests that cover all states except Utah, Nevada, and Delaware.

TIP

Although digests cover courts all across the country, use the most specific digest for your research problem. In other words, if you want to find case law that applies in an individual state, focus on that particular state's digest before turning to the regional digests.

Rummaging through reporters

Digests point you to relevant cases and summarize their decisions, but you find the actual case decisions in a reporter. There are federal, regional, state, and topical reporters. In most reporters, the case begins with *headnotes*, which are short summaries of important legal issues within the opinion. You can use the headnotes to identify the issues of a case and maybe locate additional relevant authority by using the key numbers associated with the headnotes to refer back to the digest.

WARNING

Headnotes aren't part of the official opinion, so don't quote them as authority in your memos.

Following the headnotes is a case synopsis, which summarizes the entire case opinion. After the synopsis comes the entire official case opinion. When you include case references in your memos, quote from the official opinion you find in the reporter.

TIP

Some reporters (like U.S. Reports) don't contain headnotes and case synopses.

Keeping current with case citators

After you've found on-point primary authority, you have to validate that authority. *Shepard's Citations*, along with similar validation services such as West's KeyCite, provides a method of checking the status of a case in light of more recent legal developments. A citator provides a list of references to sources that have cited the cases you find. For instance, if your research exposes on point case, like *Land v. Hill*, 70 Wash.2d 80, 644 P.2d 43 (1961), you need to find out whether the case is still good law (that is, whether any subsequent cases have overruled or reversed the original case). To accomplish this important task, you look up *Land v. Hill* in a Shepard's citator to find all the cases that have cited *Land v. Hill*, how those cases have treated it, and any history relationship between the cited case and the citing cases.

REMEMBER

Validating is checking the current status of a case. You validate cases by looking them up in Shepard's or using Westlaw's KeyCite to determine if they're still valid or to find other cases that may have followed or otherwise approved of the decisions.

Shepard's Citations

To use Shepard's, first locate the appropriate citator. Because a Washington state court decided *Land v. Hill*, look in either the set of Shepard's that covers the *Pacific Reporter*, which is *Shepard's Pacific Reporter Citations*, or the set covering

Washington cases, *Shepard's Washington Citations,* to find the appropriate volume of Shepard's. There is a set of *Shepard's Citations* for nearly every existing reporter.

After you've found the correct set of *Shepard's Citations,* consult the page that lists the volume and page number of the case you're Shepardizing. In the appropriate volume on the specified page, you'll find the list of cases that cite the Shepardized case. The first of the listed cases is the *parallel citation,* which is a cross-reference to another publication that sets forth the Shepardized case and is shown in parentheses.

After parallel citations, the column lists cases that have a history relationship to the Shepardized case. These cases generally involve the same parties, the same facts, or the same litigation as the cited case. The history relationship is shown by history letters, which are abbreviations indicating what happened to the case on further appeal. For instance, if the citing case set aside *Land v. Hill,* the Shepard's notation indicates *Land* was vacated on appeal. History letters may also indicate other locations where the same case or a connected case has been reported.

Next, Shepard's lists cases that don't involve the same parties, facts, or litigation but have made reference to the cited case. The citator arranges these cases chronologically by jurisdiction from least current to most current. The citator may list many jurisdictions, and it arranges cases within each jurisdiction chronologically.

TIP

Here are several of the key abbreviations indicating history and treatment analyses:

>> **r = reversed.** The case has been reversed on appeal.

>> **a = affirmed.** The case has been affirmed on appeal.

>> **o = overruled.** The case is no longer valid authority as it has been overruled by a subsequent court decision.

>> **q = questioned.** The continuing validity of the case is questionable.

>> **c = criticized.** Another court disagrees with the case.

>> **l = limited.** The case has been limited to its facts and will not be extended to other facts.

Shepard's shows many other abbreviations. You can find a complete listing in the front of each volume of *Shepard's Citations.*

TIP

Shepard's also enables you to narrow Shepardizing to those points of law that are most relevant to the research. You can save a lot of time by Shepardizing a particular headnote number. If you see a small raised or superior number before the page number of the citing case, that's the *headnote number* that the citing case discusses. If you're interested in just one particular headnote from the case you're Shepardizing, you can check out those cases that reference your headnote and ignore the others!

After you examine the case listings in the main volumes of Shepard's, check for additional citing references in any of the supplements to the particular citator you're using. You can find supplements in the gold or red pamphlet volumes or in white advance sheets. If you're Shepardizing a case that was decided in a state for which Shepard's publishes *Shepard's EXPRESS Citations*, you'll need to check for citing references in that publication as well. *Shepard's EXPRESS Citations* provides the most current citing references to a case and summaries of many of the treatment and history analyses that discuss the nature and impact of the citing judge's comments.

WARNING

As with any other type of reporter, digest, or citator, you must check the most current publications to verify that your research is accurate and your legal authority is still valid. Including in a brief a case decision that a later court has overruled, reversed, or otherwise called into question is a nightmare. At best, your opponent will draw the court's attention to this shortcoming, thus applying a liberal dose of egg on your supervising attorney's face. At worst, this practice could bring the attorney ethical condemnation from the court or bar association!

No Shepardizing job is complete until you check all relevant and the most up-to-date volumes of Shepard's. The best way to determine whether you've accessed all the necessary volumes, supplements, and advance sheets is to read the front cover of the most current publication, where it says "What Your Library Should Contain." This legend lists every publication you should consult to thoroughly Shepardize authority, including *Shepard's EXPRESS Citations* in states that it's published for. Studying "What Your Library Should Contain" is sometimes referred to as *reading the box.*

As you use Shepard's citators more frequently, you become familiar with the format of the books and the table of abbreviations in the front of each volume and supplement. Shepard's also has an online service available on Lexis Advance.. When you use Shepard's correctly, you know you've consulted all relevant authorities and your research is current and thorough.

Westlaw's KeyCite

Westlaw offers KeyCite, an online validating tool that integrates with the West Key Number System to provide current history for state and federal cases in the national reporters and many unpublished decisions, state and federal statutes and regulations, and administrative and IRS decisions. When you find a case using Westlaw, you can immediately see its current history and complete headnotes so you don't waste a bunch of time reading a case that no longer provides valid legal precedent. (For more information about using Westlaw online research, see the "Westlaw" section later in this chapter.)

Through KeyCite tabs, you can discover the following:

>> **Negative Treatment:** This tab displays a list of all event that could negatively impact a piece of law you've discovered, such as whether a case or law has been reversed or overruled on appeal.

>> **Citing References:** You can access a list of all cases that refer to the case you've found by selecting this tab.

>> **History:** This tab clearly outlines a case's history

>> **Graphical KeyCite and Graphical Statutes:** These tabs clearly display the evolution of a case or statute.

KeyCite uses flags to clearly warn you about negative history. A red flag at the top of the case means the case is no longer good law for at least one of its points of law. A yellow flag tells you that the case has some negative history but hasn't been completely reversed. You can also set up KeyCite Alert to receive updates on a case you've found and warn you of any current negative treatment.

Opting for other resources

Legal research doesn't have many shortcuts. However, prior to accessing the five legal research tools, you should examine all available office form files and copies of previously prepared briefs on the same topic as you currently research a project to obtain leads to primary authority. You can also consult experts on the topic or other attorneys who've successfully litigated similar cases for leads to the proper primary authority. Other attorneys often accommodate a paralegal's request for copies of briefs and other documents. This invaluable resource can jumpstart your often-overwhelming research project.

TIP

Your supervising attorney should reimburse experts for copy charges and other reasonable expenses incident to providing helpful information. And, to promote good will, you should offer to send a copy of the resulting briefs to the attorney who has contributed his expertise. Receiving leads and sample briefs from others who have been successful in similar litigation saves a firm and its client a considerable amount of time and money. Rarely do attorneys refuse to provide information to other attorneys. However, if the attorneys get overly protective of their work, you can always contact the clerk of the court where the previous action was filed and request copies of the pertinent documents from the court. Of course, be prepared to pay premium copying costs to the clerk!

Getting Technological: Computerized Legal Research

In the last quarter-century, the art and science of legal research has undergone changes of revolutionary proportions. In that time frame, attorneys and paralegals have transformed their research practice from one of primary, or sole, reliance on books toward a blend of text and computer legal research. Many law firms now rely exclusively on computer resources for all their research needs. Computers and the practice of law are becoming increasingly interdependent. Today, computerized legal research in the form of paid online research services, such as Westlaw, Lexis Advance, and Bloomberg Law, have made legal research almost easy.

Westlaw

Virtually any research you can do manually in a law library you can also perform on Westlaw, which makes any manual task much less time-consuming through the speed of computers and the convenience of having all research sources in one location: the computer terminal.

Although computerized legal research is expensive to access, it offers great flexibility and convenience for paralegals who lack adequate law libraries. Research databases allow paralegals to access a law library through their computers. And Westlaw, with its unique access to the West Key Number System, is one of the most effective research databases on the market.

Westlaw makes learning how to perform conduct online legal research pretty pain-free with its free trial access and training sessions. You can sign up for access with a paid subscription plan tailored to your specific needs. New databases and features appear on Westlaw regularly and products such as Westlaw Next use common language searches to streamline your research tasks.

TIP

To get answers to questions and keep pace with the new additions to Westlaw, you can contact West reference attorneys toll-free at 800-733-2889, seven days a week. Refer to the earlier section on Westlaw's KeyCite if you want more information.

Lexis Advance

The databases under the Lexis Advance umbrella provide attorneys and paralegals with just as much power to conduct legal research as Westlaw. Lexis Advance allows the user to find case law, statutes, administrative rules, court rules, and a plethora of other legal resources. In addition, the Lexis Advance web-based service also provides access to news and business sources.

You access Lexis Advance pretty much the same way you do Westlaw. You first formulate your search query before signing on to Lexis Advance. Database services often charge the law firm by the minute, so make sure you know what you're looking for prior to logging on!

After you've signed on, select a source of material where you want to conduct your search. You can search in certain areas of law, such as administrative law, constitutional law, or criminal law. You may limit your search to a particular jurisdiction, such as federal bankruptcy court decisions or only those court cases from a particular state or region. Or you can search the entire U.S. legal system.

Finally, Lexis Advance allows you to Shepardize your case to validate your results. Shepardizing your case ensures that you've found the latest cases and that subsequent court decisions have not overruled or reversed the authority you've found. It also helps you to find additional on-point authority.

And just as Westlaw has telephone support, Lexis Advance also has trained attorneys to assist you 24/7.

Bloomberg Law

Relatively new to the online research field is Bloomberg Law. This comprehensive subscription-based option is a viable alternative to the more expensive Westlaw and Lexis Advance products online legal research site that facilitates access to primary and secondary source material, time-saving practice tools and analytics, and more with an emphasis on law in a business context.

The online content contains links to Westlaw, Lexis Advance, Bloomberg Law, and other companies that offer online legal research subscription services.

The Internet

Many law school law libraries are available online, and social media, newsgroups, and email provide access to global communication. New information becomes available on a daily, and even hourly, basis. Attorneys and paralegals are finding that they can do a tremendous amount of legal research on the Internet.

You might want to simply experiment with some of the sites on the World Wide Web. One example is the Internet Legal Research Group (www.ilrg.com). This site organizes, categorizes, and indexes helpful legal websites and provides access to more than 2,000 downloadable legal forms and documents. Other sites such as Law Guru (www.lawguru.com) provide the user with a database of answers to commonly asked legal questions. Still other sites such as Findlaw (https://lp.findlaw.com) provide the user with court rules, statutes, court cases, and forms.

One word of caution — many of the sites on the Internet charge user fees to access the information that you find most useful for legal research, and the free information may be outdated. Plus, addresses for websites can change with little or no advance notice.

Although many privately run websites charge a fee to users of their material, a fair number of sites provide their information free of charge. Generally, government and educational sites provide access to state and federal statutes, cases, court rules, and more commonly used legal forms.

The online content contains a list of websites you can access on the Internet for legal research and other law-related information.

Citing Cases Properly: Citation Format

When your research reveals on-point authority for a case, you'll need to tell your supervising attorney and others about it, usually in a written memo. So, you need to know how to cite authority properly in memoranda, briefs, and any document the law firm files with the court or submits to opposing parties. Proper citation format follows a uniform system throughout the legal world. It conveys the minimum information readers need to quickly find a cited case in the law library.

Proper citation format is especially critical in briefs submitted to the court, because judges readily equate improper citation format with laziness, sloppiness, or both!

A Uniform System of Citation (also known as *The Bluebook*) has long been viewed as the official guide to proper citation format. *The Bluebook* traditionally has been a soft-cover, spiral-bound book that's literally blue in color. *The Bluebook* contains citation formats for hundreds of different kinds of materials and abbreviations for hundreds of sources of information. It includes two citation systems, one for official documents and another for informal documents. You should be primarily concerned with learning the format for official documents, so be careful to access the correct quick reference table in *The Bluebook*.

You can find out more about *The Bluebook* and see excerpts from its pages at www.legalbluebook.com.

You may find a more user-friendly citation manual to be the *ALWD Citation Manual*, published by the Association of Legal Writing Directors. You can find out more about this manual at www.alwd.org/. Also, make sure to ask your supervising attorney or the person who assigned you the research project which citation format that she would like you to use in your memos.

Citing statutes

The Bluebook gives a simple format for citing statutes. Keep the following rules in mind for federal statutes. In the official publication *U.S. Code,* write the volume number first, then write U.S.C., then the section number, and finally end with the supplement information in parentheses, like this: 42 U.S.C. § 1983 (Supp.III 1979). Avoid citation to the unofficial publication, although *A Uniform System of Citation* does recognize these styles: 12 U.S.C.A. § 635F (West Supp. 1981) and 8 U.S.C.S. § 43 (Law. Co-op. 1980).

A separate section of *A Uniform System of Citation* contains the format for citing each state's statutes. You can easily find the citation format for a specific state by locating the state name in the table of contents and going to the proper page number.

Citing cases

A properly cited case is a joy to behold! It allows the supervising attorney, opposing counsel, or judge reading your memo to quickly access the cited material in the law library. When you cite a case correctly, you provide your reader with the following information:

>> The parties to the litigation

>> The court that decided the case

>> The year the case was decided

>> The publications where the case can be found and the volume number and page number of the publication where the case can be found

TIP

The following case citation is complete:

> *Konas v. Red Owl*, 158 Colo. 29, 404 P.2d 546 (1965)

It states the parties involved in the action (*Konas v. Red Owl*). It states which court decided the case (the Supreme Court of Colorado). It provides the year the case was decided in (1965). It shows the publications where the case can be found (158 Colo. 29, 404 P.2d 546). Note that the first citation (158 Colo. 29) to the official Colorado Supreme Court reporter (*Colorado Reporter*) comes first. The first number (158) is the volume number, the next entry (Colo.) is the abbreviated publication name, and the second number (29) is the page number. The citation to the West regional reporters (in this case, Pacific Reporter, 2d, volume 404, page 546, as indicated by 404 P.2d 546) follows, even though most readers might be more likely to access the regional reporter to retrieve the case.

You need to <u>underline</u> or *italicize* the case name and separate it from the publication information by a comma. Also separate different publications by commas. Finally, put the date of the case in parentheses.

REMEMBER

Nobody memorizes *The Bluebook*. It is, after all, a book! And much of it addresses citation format for international and foreign materials that you'll probably never need to know. Judges and even your supervising attorney may have a citation style that slightly differs from *The Bluebook*. So, if you use a citation format that differs slightly from *The Bluebook*, just make sure it's consistent and informative.

» Selecting the jury

» Presenting the case

» Collecting on judgments

Chapter **14**

Where the Rubber Hits the Road: Trial Performance

P roperly preparing for and carrying out the various tasks involved in trial practice require enormous amounts of the paralegal's time and energy. When your employer specializes in litigation, you'll concentrate on making sure your supervising attorney is ready for trial, and you'll be on hand to assist both during and after trial. In this chapter, we describe the trial process from developing a trial notebook and selecting a jury to presenting a case to a court and collecting a judgment.

Creating the Ultimate Source of Information: The Trial Notebook

Even before you know whether the client's case is going to trial, your office should begin to develop a *trial notebook* (which contains all the information and documents pertinent to a client's case). Make no mistake about it: The best law firms get the jump on early trial preparation, and the paralegal plays a fundamental role in that process. It's all about preparation and organization. A good trial notebook provides the tool any attorney needs to be a winning professional.

The first thing you do when getting ready to put together a trial notebook is read the client's file from cover to cover to get a firm grasp on all the facts of the client's case. As you go through the file, record notes about anything that doesn't make sense or requires future follow-up. Pay attention to what isn't in the file, such as medical or other expert witness reports, lab reports, and so on. Keep a sharp eye out for anything that will help you locate witnesses, and make notes of their names, addresses, and other identifying information.

When you have a handle on the facts of your client's case, you organize the information in a logical fashion so your supervising attorney isn't fumbling through a mass of information to find case details while working on the case in the office or the courtroom.

TIP

Trial notebooks may be paper based, electronic, or a combination of both. We outline the process for compiling a paper notebook here, but many law offices use trial notebook software programs and apps so that they can access information on a laptop or tablet. Electronic notebooks may integrate online legal research programs and may allow for evidence to appear on courtroom monitors. Even if you rely entirely on electronic data organization, print out a copy of the notebook for trial or mediation just in case you encounter Wi-Fi or Internet connection issues.

Arranging the trial notebook is sort of like putting together a binder for the first day of high school when you had to make divisions for all your classes. Here's how you build it:

1. **Get a three-ring binder wide enough to hold the amount of documents you expect to accumulate and organize over the life of the case.**

   Usually, the bigger the case, the bigger the binder.

2. **Get dividers with large tabs and label them for the various sections of the trial notebook.**

   These sections roughly follow the order of events in the case as it plays out in court and usually include the following:

   - Civil Pleadings/Criminal Charging Documents
   - Pre-Trial Motions

- Jury Selection/*Voir dire* Examination (see "Selecting the Jury: The Paralegal and *Voir dire*," later in this chapter)

- Opening Statement

- Witnesses (Direct Examination, Cross Examination, Rebuttal)

- List of Exhibits

- Jury Instructions

- Closing Argument

- Evidence

- Legal Authority

- Trial Notes

- Post-Trial Motions

- Miscellaneous

3. **Include a trial preparation checklist in the front of the notebook.**

   Figure 14-1 shows a sample trial preparation checklist for a criminal case that you can use to guide the way that you gather evidence and store it in your files. The person responsible for collecting each document initials the sheet when it makes its way into the trial notebook.

4. **Insert case documents into the appropriate sections of the notebook.**

TIP

As reports, witness statements, and the like filter into the office, use a highlighter or marker to note the following information for each document:

>> **Who:** Names, addresses, and phone numbers

>> **When:** Dates and times

>> **What:** Discoverable material and physical evidence

>> **Where:** Locations (for maps, photos, and the like)

In anticipation of trial motions and other court procedures, prepare blank documents before the trial starts. If the attorney needs to make a motion or suggest jury instructions in court, the attorney can do so very quickly both verbally and in written form. Having these documents ready at the attorney's beck and call makes you appear very professional.

TRIAL NOTEBOOK CHECKLIST: CRIMINAL	
Task	**Responsible Person's Initials**
All police reports (initial and additional reports)	
Property reports	
Photo log	
Photos and/or videotapes	
Crime lab reports	
Search warrant and return	
Vehicle identification sheet/vehicle invoice sheet	
911 tape	
CAD report	
Medical reports (victim and/or defendant)	
Autopsy report	
Defendant's criminal history	
Victim/witness criminal history	
Restitution information from victim or crime victim fund or Department of Social Services	
Polygraph results	
Identification—latent prints reports	
Witness list/order	
Discovery response	
Photo montage	
Exhibit log	
Constitutional rights card	
Search consent card	
Other: _____	

© John Wiley & Sons

FIGURE 14-1:
A trial preparation checklist, like this one for a criminal trial, should go in the front of your trial notebook.

TECHNICAL STUFF

Trial notebook preparation also includes organizing evidence. As a paralegal, you need to make sure that each and every item is ready for production at trial, accompanied with the necessary supporting documentation. Usually, you complete the evidence organization along with the trial notebook. You can store your side's evidence electronically or in folders and boxes and gather it in one place for safe-keeping. Each item of evidence consists of the original, any necessary copies, and notes on its history, including how and when it was found, how it was handled from its finding to the day of trial, and the names of the individuals involved in each step. You should then index the evidence collection so that at trial the attorney can instantly access any required piece of evidence. (For more about collecting and organizing evidence, see Chapter 11.)

Selecting the Jury: The Paralegal and Voir Dire

The first step of the actual trial process for a jury trial is jury selection. *Jury selection* whittles down a large pool of potential jurors to 6 or 12 final jurors and alternates through a question-and-answer process called *voir dire*. Jury selection plays a crucial role in getting a fair and impartial jury for the trial. Attorneys question members of the jury pool to eliminate individuals who may be prejudiced in deciding the case. These questions also serve a second purpose: They're the attorney's first chance, even before opening arguments, to display the central themes of the case to prospective jurors. As a paralegal, you should assist your supervising attorney in preparing *voir dire* questions in advance to use with the jury pool, questions that may very well be key to the outcome of the case.

REMEMBER

Three primary goals of *voir dire* include the following:

>> Eliciting information about the biases of potential jurors

>> Educating the jury about factual and legal concepts of the case

>> Establishing a rapport with the jury

In important cases, your firm may call in a jury selection specialist to investigate the entire pool of potential jurors, which could consist of hundreds of people. The jury consultant advises attorneys on which jurors are likely to be sympathetic to one party or the other.

TIP

Paralegals with psychology or communication backgrounds often operate freelance businesses that specialize in jury selection consultation.

During *voir dire*, attorneys ask the members of the jury pool questions that address their qualifications to sit as jurors. Given a large jury pool, attorneys usually direct questions to the whole group. Based on the responses they get, the attorneys may then question individuals. Although lawyers never want to intentionally embarrass a potential juror, sometimes they have to delve into someone's personal life. Personal inquiries help your firm weed out those jurors who might view your client's case unfavorably.

Following is a sample list of *voir dire* questions directed to the group of potential jurors that you can adapt to fit many criminal or civil cases. Naturally, you alter the questions depending on the subject matter of any particular case.

>> Is there anyone here who hasn't read the juror's handbook?

>> Has anyone sat on a jury before?

>> Has anyone heard anything about this case?

>> *<Names of individuals>* may be called as witnesses in this case. Does anyone know any of these potential witnesses? Does anyone know the plaintiff, the defendant, the attorneys, or the judge in this case?

>> This event allegedly occurred in *<name of area>*. Does anyone live near or is anyone familiar with this area?

>> Has anyone ever been involved in or witness to the types of events surrounding this case? Does anyone have relatives or close friends who have been involved in or witnesses to the types of events surrounding this case?

>> Does anyone have a personal interest in the outcome of a case of this nature?

>> *For criminal trials:* Is anyone employed in law enforcement or in the justice system?

>> *For criminal trials:* Has anyone ever had a bad or unpleasant experience with a police officer?

>> Does anyone have religious, personal, or philosophical views that would interfere with sitting as a juror in this particular case?

>> Does anyone have strongly held opinions about the nature of this case that would prevent you from following the law in this case?

>> Is there anyone who cannot agree to follow the law and instructions as given to you by the court, whether you personally agree with them or not?

>> Is there anyone who doesn't understand that a juror's job is to weigh the testimony of each witness, which means determining truth in the event that the parties disagree on an account of the facts?

>> This case may involve some complicated facts. Is there anyone who has a problem with the time it may take to sift through testimony and evidence to attempt to sort fact from fiction?

>> Would you refrain from voicing your opinion if it were unpopular with other jurors?

>> Would you listen fairly to the viewpoints of other jurors and give them a chance to persuade you?

>> Is there anything about this trial, as it has been described to you, that makes anyone uncomfortable about sitting as a juror?

>> Can anyone think of any reason why you could not be a fair and impartial juror?

After attorneys have questioned prospective jurors about the case, they may exercise *challenges* to excuse those jurors whose biases would make them least favorable to the client's position. You can assist the attorney so that she can intelligently challenge jurors for bias or otherwise. State law governs how attorneys may challenge prospective jurors.

TIP

Challenges to prospective jurors fall into one of three categories:

>> **Peremptory challenges** require no reason to excuse jurors.

>> **Challenges for cause** must be made for a specific reason.

>> **Challenges to the array** involve the removal of the entire panel of jurors.

Rebelling without a cause: Peremptory challenges

Peremptory challenges, as the name implies, are those that don't require the lawyer to give a reason for excusing a prospective juror. The juror could be giving the lawyer funny looks or could be overly friendly with the opposing lawyer. Your supervising attorney may exercise the peremptory strike because he has a gut feeling that a juror would be bad news for the client.

TECHNICAL STUFF

There are lots of reasons why attorneys may not want a particular juror sitting in judgment of their clients. A lawyer can challenge a juror for reasons ranging from the juror's wearing too much makeup to the juror's not being able to converse in complete sentences. However, the U.S. Supreme Court has held in the case of *Batson v. Kentucky* (1986), that a lawyer can't exercise a peremptory challenge to a prospective juror based on race, unless there is some other race-neutral reason for excusing that juror. The courts have extended *Batson* to also apply to challenges based on gender and ethnic background.

You don't get to have as many peremptory challenges as you want — otherwise, there would probably never be enough jurors in the pool to satisfy each side in a lawsuit. Depending on whether you're involved in a civil or criminal case, each side to the lawsuit gets a certain number of peremptory challenges. For example, some states allow the parties to exercise three peremptory strikes in a civil case, and attorneys in a criminal case may have as many as six or more peremptory challenges. If the case is heard in a court of limited jurisdiction, or if the final jury panel consists of 6 instead of 12 jurors (for a criminal misdemeanor case), the parties may be limited to only three strikes. If there are two or more defendants, each defendant may get an additional challenge, and the prosecution might get an extra one as well.

Making a good excuse: Challenges for cause

Each side to a lawsuit is entitled to an unlimited number of challenges for cause. A *challenge for cause* is one that lawyers use to kick off a prospective juror for bias, whether implied or actual. Implied bias shows up when, for example, a potential juror is a family member or close friend of one of the parties. Actual bias occurs when a potential juror states that she can't be fair to one or both of the parties. One classic example might be a rape victim who is called to sit as a juror in a criminal rape case. Although the juror could conceivably be fair, it's far more likely that she would have an extremely difficult time hearing the facts of the case and keeping them separate from her own experience.

Each party has an unlimited number of challenges for cause. As long as the attorney can articulate a clear reason why a particular juror can't be fair, the court will excuse that juror for cause.

WARNING

Jurors who hold preconceived ideas about the nature of a case may not necessarily be disqualified for bias. If they demonstrate that they can set aside their prejudices to render a fair verdict, the court may not see cause to excuse these jurors.

Dismissing the kit and caboodle: Challenges to the array

A *challenge to the array* occurs when one of the parties requests the court to disqualify the entire pool of prospective jurors. A challenge to the array is also known as a *challenge to the venire*. A party may exercise a challenge to the array only in highly unusual circumstances. You might see this type of challenge at play when irregularities or illegalities occur — for example, if the clerk or jury administrator uses some means other than random selection or if he purposely calls in a panel of completely biased prospective jurors. Challenges to the array don't happen very often; if you ever see this occur in one of your attorney's cases, consider buying a lottery ticket!

Monitoring the pool

As the lawyers exercise their challenges with jurors and particular jurors are stricken from the panel, new jurors from the pool, or *venire*, may be brought forward to take their place and the makeup of the jury box changes. You can help your supervising attorney during this process by noting potential jurors' reactions to questions and observing how they relate to attorneys for both parties. And, while the attorney focuses her attention on questioning one prospective juror, you can watch the reactions of the others.

You may keep track of the panel for the lawyer by drawing a schematic juror seating chart. When a successful challenge has removed a particular juror from the box, you write the name of the next juror in that same location in the box. This allows your supervising attorney to always know which jurors are sitting on the panel at any one time.

REMEMBER

Figure 14-2 is one example of a schematic diagram you could use to assist the lawyer in the jury selection process. The jury panel seating chart is also available online at www.dummies.com/go/paralegalcareer2e.

Case Name:	_Plaintiff v. Defendant_	Trial Date:	_____
Cause No.:	_____	Trial Judge:	_____
Cause of Action:	_____	Plaintiff's Attorney:	_____
Verdict:	_____	Defense Attorney:	_____

Juror No. 6	Juror No. 5	Juror No. 4	Juror No. 3	Juror No. 2	Juror No. 1
Juror No. 7	Juror No. 8	Juror No. 9	Juror No. 10	Juror No. 11	Juror No. 12

Alternate No. 1	Alternate No. 2

FIGURE 14-2: A jury panel seating chart can help your supervising attorney keep track of the jurors.

© John Wiley & Sons

Your supervising attorney may also rely on software to assist with _voir dire_. Existing programs help attorneys keep track of juror and offer predictions regarding a prospective juror's potential biases.

Keeping Track of Witnesses

Often, the paralegal is responsible for ensuring that the party and witnesses are ready for trial and that they get to the proper courtroom on time. You should let witnesses know the time and place of the trial, any traffic conditions they might expect, and parking areas and fees if they drive. The party calling the witness needs to make sure that the witnesses are paid for their time as well as mileage.

You should provide your office's client with the same information you provide the witnesses, and review with the client the plan for his activities during the trial. Usually, your supervising attorney handling the litigation will want the client to be beside the attorney in court for the entire trial. You should also discuss with the clients proper dress, demeanor, and nonverbal communication required to make the right impression on the judge and jury.

The supervising attorney will probably want to meet with as many of the witnesses as possible and, without actually coaching them, practice with them the line of questioning. Paralegals frequently participate in the witness preparation process; Chapter 12 has some helpful hints you can use in preparing the client and any witnesses for what they might expect in court.

You should help your supervising attorney determine the order that she'll call the witnesses in to testify. She may choose an order that helps tell the story chronologically, or, to make sure she starts and ends her case on a positive note, she may slip the testimonies of weaker witnesses in between the testimonies of stronger witnesses. You can help determine which witnesses are more persuasive than others.

You may want to prepare a master witness list for use in trial preparation, but the master witness list comes in especially handy during the heat of the trial battle. Having witness contact information at your fingertips is critical, because your attorney may have to call a witness unexpectedly. Updating witness information is easy when you can rely on electronic trial notebook software applications.

REMEMBER

Figure 14-3 is one example of the type of master witness list you may use to assist your supervising attorney at trial. The master witness list is also available online.

LIST OF WITNESSES

Witness Name	Witness Address	Home Phone (or cell phone)	Work Phone	Summary of Testimony:	Associated Exhibits
Joe Blow	123 South Elm Street Anytown, New York	555-5555	555-5555	Describes Injuries; Identifies Defendant	Ex. Nos. 1-5

FIGURE 14-3: A master witness list can come in handy. You never know when you'll need a witness's contact info.

© John Wiley & Sons

Weighing Testimony: The Paralegal's Take on the Jury's Reaction

Because the attorney focuses on the witness during examination, he cannot effectively evaluate the jury's reaction to the witness's testimony. This places you, as the paralegal, in a unique situation. Although your supervising attorney questions witnesses, you provide vital assistance by simply paying attention to what's going on with the jury.

During trial, you take notes on witness testimony and evaluate the jury's reaction. Most courtrooms don't have the capability to instantaneously produce transcripts of the trial testimony, so your notes are invaluable to the attorney. They give him a check on what was actually said in the trial. Your notes of the proceedings remind the attorney of what areas need to be covered or followed up through the remaining witnesses. You further demonstrate your true value to the attorney by providing him with helpful hints on what points the jury felt particularly positive or negative toward. Your suggestions to the attorney often show him where he may have missed something important. You contribute a second set of eyes, a second set of ears, and even more brainpower to evaluate the proceedings.

Preparing Questions for the Attorney

Immediately before trial, the legal team begins writing speeches. The attorney prepares opening and closing arguments to emphasize to the judge and jury the overall point of the case. These oral arguments should be emotional and persuasive, and the attorney is likely to recruit you for practice and suggestions. He may also request your help in formulating questions for direct-examining witnesses.

TIP

Use these four steps to prepare questions for direct examination:

1. **Review the trial notebook for all documents related to a particular witness.**

   These documents include, but aren't limited to, witness statements, notes from witness interviews, and deposition transcripts.

2. **Summarize all knowledge of the witness in an outline.**

3. **Keep track of the witness's testimony in rough chronological order.**

4. **Formulate a question that will elicit each important element of the witness's story for the court.**

In addition to developing questions for the attorney to ask witnesses, you should also anticipate the other side's testimony long before they testify to it at trial. This preparation allows you to help your attorney develop a line of cross-examination questions. Anticipating the opposition's testimony is somewhat akin to playing chess. You need to figure out your moves ahead of time. If the other party says x, your attorney needs to be able to ask follow-up questions a, b, and c. If the other party answers with y, you need to come back with questions d, e, and f. This demonstrates to your attorney, and especially to the other party, that your trial team is thoroughly in control of the proceedings. Likewise, every time the opposing counsel examines a witness, you should take notes to prepare questions on the spot for your attorney to use in cross-examination and redirect.

Settling Up: Preparing the Cost Bill

You're still not done when your client wins a judgment against the other party. A judgment is the final determination of the rights and obligations of the parties toward each other. If neither party appeals the judgment within a certain period of time, generally 30 days, the judgment becomes final. After the final judgment comes back in your favor, you need to notify the other side regarding its legal obligation to cough up and pay the piper. They usually don't take it upon themselves to pay up, and they have no incentive to perform unless you tell them in the legal format of a cost bill. The cost bill is a summary of all the items the other side owes you now that the lawsuit is terminated.

TIP

The cost bill generally includes the following items:

>> **Special damages** (medical bills, auto repair bills, and so on)

>> **General damages** (like pain and suffering or embarrassment)

>> **Punitive damages** (if allowed and ordered)

>> **Attorney and paralegal fees** (if allowed by law)

>> **Filing fees** (paid to the court)

>> **Court costs** (set by statute or court rule)

>> **Process server fees** (for service of summons and complaint)

>> **Expert witness fees** (big bucks!)

>> **Court reporter fees** (for depositions and so on)

>> **Jury demand fee** (set by statute or court rule)

In some cases, it's not entirely uncommon for the costs and fees associated with the litigation to far exceed the amount of damages recoverable.

Blood from a Turnip: Collecting a Difficult Judgment

Winning a judgment from another party in court and collecting on that judgment are entirely separate tasks. Unless the losing party is an insurance company or other large entity, your attorney probably won't receive an immediate payment for a client's judgment, which means you have to do some collection work.

For nearly every case, you have to find and quantify the assets of the losing party. To promote this process, you may draft *interrogatories in aid of judgment* (which are questions directed to the judgment debtor about her assets). In fact, the process of quantifying the opponent's assets is so important that you may complete that task before the client files the suit rather than after. There's no point in winning a judgment that you can't collect.

Assets exist in many forms. All the following assets might be useful sources of revenue for a party collecting a judgment:

>> Bank accounts

>> Real estate

>> Business and personal property

>> Debts owed to the debtor by a third party

>> Business ownership

>> Financial instrument ownership, like stocks and bonds futures

>> Good-will ownership in a business and its trademarks

>> Intellectual property rights ownership, like copyrights, patents, and trade secrets

>> Future income

>> Cash holdings (Dishonest people have escaped from paying debts by eliminating their assets, hoping that those investigating them would forget to inquire about the retained cash.)

REMEMBER

This list is only a partial one, and each item on it is very broad. Thus, you should feel quite challenged when investigating for collections. You can find websites that offer to provide asset searches for a fee. Some of these sites are listed online at www.dummies.com/go/paralegalcareer2e.

WARNING

Internet asset search services largely assume the relative transparency of the target of the investigation. If a person tries to beat the system by putting bank accounts in false names, transferring assets to relatives, or moving assets off shore to nations that don't financially cooperate with the United States, the resulting asset search can be very time consuming and difficult.

The point: If your legal team has gone so far as to prevail over the other side in court, you've demonstrated your tenacity and should be able to find creative ways to beat them in the asset recovery game. As a paralegal, you may be instrumental in the recovery efforts.

Chapter **15**

The Official Word: Ethical Codes for Legal Professionals

Attorneys and paralegals are considered legal professionals. Paralegals perform many of the same tasks as attorneys and have similar responsibilities to the attorney's clients. For this reason, as a paralegal, you'll be expected to know and abide by the rules of professional conduct in your jurisdiction. In most states, these rules are very similar to the American Bar Association (ABA) Model Rules of Professional Conduct. Most of these rules apply to both lawyers and paralegals.

Additionally, paralegals must follow other special rules that define the types of duties they may perform. Essentially, paralegals may do anything an attorney does except give legal advice, set fees, and try cases in a court of law. Some states allow laypersons (people who aren't attorneys) to fill out forms for clients for certain types of legal matters, like bankruptcy, as long as they don't give legal advice about the form and don't suggest to clients what type of forms they need. And, as we discuss in Chapter 5, some administrative courts allow paralegals to represent clients. But, for the most part, all the work you do as a paralegal must be supervised by a practicing attorney, so you have to abide by the ethical codes and considerations that apply to members of the bar.

To help you adhere to the ethical requirements of the paralegal profession, this chapter explains the most pertinent ethical rules provided by the ABA and national paralegal associations.

Doing What's Right: The Importance of Ethics

It's no secret that many people have doubts about the ethics of legal professionals. Dozens of books, Web sites, and even daily calendars are based entirely on lawyer jokes. These jokes rarely question the intellect of lawyers but focus almost exclusively on ethical considerations. A common line of jokes compares lawyers and sharks; invariably the shark gets the better treatment in the comparison!

The reality, of course, is that lawyers and paralegals are representative of the culture at large and, therefore, reflect the ethics of the culture. You can find legal professionals who are ethical and those who are unethical. And sometime the line that separates them can be fuzzy.

TECHNICAL STUFF

The reason that the legal profession is singled out for criticism may be that legal professionals represent clients in an adversarial system. If you're involved in a legal battle, your perception is that the legal team that's working hard for your side is honest and the tough tactics they use are necessary. The lawyers and paralegals working for the other guy must certainly be corrupt and dishonest and the tactics they use unethical. If they were honest, they would simply admit that your position should prevail and give you the settlement you deserve, right?

REMEMBER

As a paralegal, your primary professional responsibility is to your supervising attorney. But the attorney is first and foremost responsible to the client, so as a representative of your supervising attorney, you're responsible to the client as well.

Defining ethics in the field of law

Ethics in law is different from the ethics you may have discussed in a philosophy class. Legal ethics aren't the ethics of Plato, Kant, and Rousseau. When lawyers are brought before state bar ethics boards, they aren't asked to defend their views of right and wrong. Instead, it's their behavior, especially in relation to their clients, that needs explaining. So, state bars and other related associations refer to the ethical standards for the legal field as "rules of professional conduct" or "codes or professional responsibility." You should think of them in this way, too — as codes for how to behave properly.

The philosophical sort of ethics isn't usually applied to attorneys and paralegals because the practice of law is particularly concerned with determining right and wrong. Legal professionals serve as tools their clients use to prevail in the legal system. The primary concern of you and the attorneys you work for is putting on the best case for the client, and that case may not necessarily be one that promotes a general good. You may even find that you sympathize with, and would rather be associated with, the other side.

Personal ethics might tell you not to argue for the client if you don't believe in his case. For example, you and your attorney may think that a client your attorney has agreed to represent in a personal injury suit is a real jerk. But if the client has a legitimate case, the rules of professional conduct that govern the legal profession obligate you to provide that client with the best legal services possible, despite your personal feelings. Likewise, in criminal law, even though your attorney may think the client is guilty of the crime charged, the attorney must work to provide the best defense for the client. This issue is one you have to get used to when you work as paralegal.

TIP

If you want to be a philosopher, you should choose another profession. Very few paralegals get to pick and choose the cases they work on. You can choose your specialty and the attorneys with whom you work, but you'll probably have to work on the cases you're assigned. If you find the client to be morally offensive, some of the rules of professional conduct prohibit you from revealing any damaging personal information you may know about the client to anyone other than your supervising attorney (whom you're required to tell everything about a client to). So when we talk about ethics in law, we're really talking about professional responsibility to clients, the court, and the public, and *not* necessarily judgments of right and wrong or justice and injustice.

REMEMBER

Legal professionals work for clients, which is the heart of what it means to be a lawyer or a paralegal. This is true whether you work for the district attorney's office or for a private practice on behalf of individual clients. In all areas, at all levels, attorneys and paralegals first and foremost work for their clients. This concept unites everyone in the legal profession. The essence of ethics is fair treatment of the client, and most ethical problems arise when a legal professional fails to uphold a duty to the client.

Going too far: The unauthorized practice of law

As a paralegal, you perform many of the same tasks that attorneys do, but you're not an attorney. You probably haven't graduated from law school or passed the bar exam, so you're not licensed to practice law. Although foregoing law school means you don't have to live with a huge student loan debt (or the knowledge that you've just spent three years of your life performing uncompensated legal research assignments in the law library!), it also means that you can't actually represent clients or be responsible for cases.

A paralegal must always work under the supervision of an attorney who's a licensed member of the bar. That attorney is ultimately responsible to all clients and for all cases. Even though, in recent decades, a few states have expanded the types of duties paralegals can perform, licensed attorneys are still the only legal professionals who can give legal advice, set fees, and represent clients in most courts.

WARNING

Anyone, including an experienced paralegal, who takes on clients without a law license may be found guilty of the unauthorized practice of law, which is a very serious offense. The penalties vary from state to state and may include jail terms of one year or longer and fines of $5,000 or more, in addition to repayment of all monies taken from unsuspecting clients. Those who experience the harshest penalties for unauthorized law practices are those individuals who pretend to be attorneys or who admit they aren't attorneys but still offer legal services. As a paralegal, if you unknowingly overstep your authority, you probably won't face the full extent of penalties, but sanctions are possible so all paralegals should know and follow the laws of their jurisdictions regarding who's authorized to practice law.

TIP

The most important thing for you to remember as a paralegal is that you must work with an attorney on behalf of that attorney's clients. You should think of the clients as "your clients" because you owe them the same duties and consideration that you would as an attorney. But you must remember that you aren't allowed to advise and represent clients of your own; you must work under the supervision of a licensed attorney.

Following the chain of responsibility

In general terms, if an action is unethical for an attorney, it's unethical for a paralegal. Duty to the client, the court, and the public applies to both types of legal professionals. There are, however, some differences in the level of responsibility. Chief among them is that, ultimately, the attorney is responsible to the client and is responsible for the paralegal's behavior.

Paralegals can perform such tasks as interviewing clients and witnesses, preparing documents, and drafting documents without being guilty of the unauthorized practice of law because they're working under the supervision of a licensed attorney who's answerable for their actions. So, your supervising attorney is ethically bound to make sure you act ethically and professionally and to refrain from asking you to perform any task that isn't within your scope of duty. Ultimately, the attorney determines what is and isn't ethical based on her knowledge of the rules of professional conduct.

Even though your attorney supervises your work and has the ultimate responsibility to the client, you must be very aware of your role in maintaining an ethical standard in the law office. Your responsibilities are to refrain from the unauthorized practice of law, to perform the duties assigned to you by the attorneys you work for, and to uphold the ethical requirements of attorneys in your jurisdiction.

So, although you won't be required to take the same ethics examination lawyers take, ethics plays an important part in your paralegal training. Ethics is the cornerstone of legal practice and without high ethical standards the system breaks down. Clients must be able to trust the lawyers that represent them, and also trust their lawyers' staffs.

REMEMBER

Your supervising attorney is responsible for your actions, so be very careful about the way you handle yourself. Your actions affect you, the reputation of your supervising attorney, and the reputation of the firm you work for.

Abiding by the Rules of Professional Conduct

In most states, the ethical rules that apply to legal professionals are called the *Rules of Professional Conduct.* These ethical codes comprise the central source of rules governing the behavior of legal professionals. Each state's supreme court has the authority to admit attorneys to practice law and to regulate those attorneys after they're admitted. Increasingly, state supreme courts have also claimed authority over regulating and disciplining (if not yet licensing) paralegals.

Attorneys are *self-regulating,* which means that they're bound by rules of conduct that have been written by lawyers and judges. And disciplinary panels composed of lawyers regulate them.

The largest organization of lawyers in the country has had the biggest impact on the standards of professional conduct. The American Bar Association (ABA) is probably the most powerful force in the legal profession. The ABA's Model Rules of Professional Conduct serves as the basis for codes of conduct in most states. The Model Rules and the state codes based on those rules define the appropriate conduct of a legal professional. The rules don't discuss how a lawyer, and therefore the paralegal, should *feel* about a given situation; they describe how they should *act* in dealing with clients and legal staff to maintain the integrity of the legal profession.

REMEMBER

You can access the complete and most current version of the ABA Model Rules of Professional Conduct at `www.americanbar.org/groups/professional_responsibility/publications/model_rules_of_professional_conduct/model_rules_of_professional_conduct_table_of_contents/`. The link to this site is also available online at `www.dummies.com/go/paralegalcareer2e`.

Preserving the client-lawyer relationship

The first topic covered in the ABA Model Rules of Professional Conduct concerns the client-lawyer relationship. Because the representation of clients constitutes the heart of the legal profession, it's no surprise this topic would come first. And because most ethical problems emanate from this relationship, it's fitting that this topic has two times more rules devoted to it than any other topic in the rules.

Rules in this first topic (Rules 1.1–1.16) provide guidance to legal professionals in the areas of:

>> Confidential communications

>> Fees

>> Conflict of interest

>> Duties to former clients

>> Duties to clients with diminished capacity

>> Safekeeping property

>> Declining or terminating representation

>> Duties to prospective clients

TIP

Here is a summary of the model rules that are most important to you as a paralegal:

>> **Rule 1.1 states that an attorney has to provide competent representation to a client.** Attorneys and their staffs must perform adequate research for, and give proper attention to, each client's case.

>> **Rule 1.2(d) says that an attorney can't advise a client to do things that the attorney knows are criminal or fraudulent, even if these activities would help the client's case.**

>> **Rule 1.3 maintains that an attorney has to represent a client with reasonable diligence and promptness.** Undo feet dragging in carrying out the activities related to a client's case is unethical.

>> **Rule 1.5(a) claims that the fees an attorney charges must be reasonable.** Determining what's reasonable depends on the amount of experience the attorney has, the complexity of the case, the location of the law practice, the potential costs incident to the case, and other considerations.

>> **Rule 1.6 prevents an attorney and any member of the legal staff from revealing information relating to a client's case.** The only exceptions to this rule are if the client agrees to the disclosure or if the attorney has reason to believe that the disclosure would prevent a client from committing a criminal act that would likely result in someone's death or substantial bodily harm.

WARNING

When you work as a paralegal, you must not give out any information about a client's case (including mentioning that a specific person is a client) to anyone, even family members. You're also obligated to make every effort to insure that a client's confidential information is safe from public view, so all case documents need to be locked up at the end of the day, away from the eyes of janitorial staff or any other individuals who may be in the office during or after hours.

>> **Rule 1.7 states that an attorney can't represent a client if there's a conflict of interest.** In other words, an attorney can't get involved in a case that would adversely affect another client. The two exceptions are if the attorney reasonably believes that his involvement in another case wouldn't harm a relationship with another client or if the attorney tells both of the clients affected about the risks of multiple representation and both clients agree to go ahead with having the same attorney.

This issue comes up in divorce cases when an attorney who has represented both spouses on matters while they're married is asked by one spouse to represent him or her in the divorce.

>> **Rule 1.8(a) prevents an attorney (and, therefore, a legal staff member) from entering into other business deals with clients.** Exceptions may occur in these circumstances:

- When the client understands the written terms of the transaction and agrees that they're fair and reasonable

- When the client has the opportunity to get advice about the business deal from another attorney who isn't involved in the transaction

- When the client agrees to the terms of the business deal in writing

>> **Rule 1.15 requires that an attorney hold clients' property in separate accounts from the attorney's own property.** This rule regards any money an attorney collects from outside entities on behalf of a client, like debt payments designated for a client, any refundable legal fees, or any monies a court awards to a client. For instance, if an attorney performs collection work for a client, any payments the client's debtors make to the attorney's office have to be deposited in an account that's separate from the law office's general account.

>> **Rule 1.16(a) states that an attorney has to withdraw from a case in the following circumstances:**

- When continuing the case would violate any of the ethical rules or other laws

- When the client dismisses the attorney

- When something about the attorney's physical or mental condition significantly weakens his ability to provide competent representation for the client

Other areas of the model rules concern clients or potential clients. You should be aware of these rules, too, most specifically Rule 7.3, which prohibits an attorney from soliciting business from a prospective client who hasn't approached the attorney on her own. This rule can get pretty complex in its application. There's a fine line between advertising one's services and soliciting business, and the rules allow attorneys to advertise. The distinction is that advertising is directed to a general audience who may seek legal counsel in the future. Improper solicitation usually occurs when an attorney personally offers services to an individual who is in obvious immediate need of legal services — the clichéd notion of "ambulance chasing."

Dealing with others in and out of the law office

Rules regarding law firms and contacts made with people outside the law office include several topics of great importance to paralegals. Rule 5.3 says that an attorney may not help a nonattorney engage in the unauthorized practice of law. A paralegal is a nonattorney, so this disciplinary rule directly relates to the use of paralegals in the law office. What the rule means is that attorneys may *not* ask or allow paralegals to do the following:

>> Represent themselves as attorneys.

>> Perform tasks that only attorneys may do, like give legal advice, argue cases in court, or establish legal fees.

>> Perform legal work without attorney supervision.

If an attorney asks you to take on a duty that may be considered the unauthorized practice of law (such as draft a pleading without her supervision), you should politely remind her that you aren't allow to perform that task without attorney supervision.

You should be aware of some other model rules that relate directly to law-office activity. Rule 3.1 prevents an attorney from bringing a frivolous claim or asserting a frivolous defense. It's unethical for an attorney to file a case that she doesn't think has a valid cause of action or to put forth a defense that isn't justified. It's especially unethical for an attorney to file a case for the sole purpose of maliciously injuring another party.

REMEMBER

As a paralegal, your duty is to your supervising attorney, and it's his job to uphold the ABA model rules. If a client asks you to violate an ethical rule or you're aware of violations committed by another person in your office, report the incident to your supervising attorney. He's responsible for handling the situation. If your supervising attorney violates the rules of ethics, you may report the violation to another attorney in the firm and let her handle it. You are under no obligation to report the actions of your supervising attorney to anyone outside the firm.

Regarding communications with other parties, Rule 4.2 prohibits an attorney (and the legal staff) from communicating with the opposing party about the subject matter of the case if the attorney knows the party has attorney representation. Attorneys and their staffs may only contact the attorney for the opposing party when the other attorney consents to direct client communication. So, don't make contact with opposing parties if they have their own attorneys.

The model rules also regulate attorney communications with the court. Rule 3.3(a) states that an attorney may not knowingly

>> Make false statements to the court about the facts or law related to a case.

>> Neglect to tell a court about laws or other authority that opposes a client's position if the other side doesn't bring up the law or authority. (If an attorney knows about a law that is unfavorable to his client's case, he may present the adverse authority and then show how it's substantially different from his client's. This rule isn't intended to prevent an attorney from representing the client's best interests.)

>> Offer false evidence.

REMEMBER

As a paralegal, you need to make sure that your efforts in the law office don't break any of the tenets of Rule 3.3(a). So, for example, if your legal research discovers legal authority that adversely affects the client's case, you must bring that authority to your supervising attorney's attention.

Maintaining the integrity of the profession

As a paralegal, you're responsible for helping to maintain the integrity of the legal profession. Rules regarding honesty and decency require you to refrain from engaging in dishonest, criminal, or unprofessional behavior, *and* to report the unethical behavior of other legal professionals. For instance, Rule 8.3 requires that attorneys who know that another attorney has seriously violated one or more of the ethical rules must report the attorney's conduct to the appropriate disciplinary body.

TIP

Your primary duty is to report unethical behavior to your supervising attorney so that she can inform the appropriate authority.

Other topics of the model rules apply mainly to practicing attorneys. For example, rules governing the way in which an attorney provides legal advice or serves as an arbitrator don't apply to you because, as a paralegal, you usually won't be engaged in these practices. However, on the whole, the ABA Model Rules of Professional Conduct of each state apply to paralegals as well as practicing attorneys. The good news is that, although you should be familiar with the rules governing attorneys, most of the important ethical considerations that apply to paralegals are also covered in rules specific to paralegals that we discuss in the following section.

REMEMBER

As a paralegal, you're required to follow the same code of conduct that attorneys do. Your violations of this ethical code may result in disciplinary action against the attorneys you work for. Such discipline would likely make other attorneys unwilling to hire you as a paralegal!

Sorting through the Codes of Paralegal Associations

Although paralegals must adhere to the ethical codes designated by the ABA, perhaps the best sources of ethics information for paralegals are paralegal organizations. Chapter 2 provides lots of information about organizations like the National Association of Legal Assistants (NALA), the National Federation of Paralegal Associations (NFPA), and other associations that are composed of and created for paralegals. Many of these associations have created ethical guidelines specific to paralegals. These codes closely mirror the ABA Model Rules of Professional Conduct but focus on areas that are most relevant to paralegals.

Applying the standards of the National Association of Legal Assistants

The National Association of Legal Assistants (NALA) is one of the largest national associations of paralegals. NALA works to maintain the integrity of the paralegal profession. One of its functions is to outline ethical standards to maintain the reputation of the paralegal profession through the Model Standards and Guidelines for the Utilization of Legal Assistants – Paralegals.

REMEMBER

The important standards set forth by NALA are *not* laws; they are merely guidelines as set forth by a large organization. So, for instance, NALA's statement that a paralegal should have a certain number of hours of paralegal education or work experience is merely its interpretation of an ideal standard — it's *not* a legal requirement. Currently, only one state, California, mandates any sort of education or work experience requirement for paralegals.

REMEMBER

You can access the full version of NALA's Model Standards and Guidelines for Utilization of Legal Assistants – Paralegals at `www.nala.org/sites/default/files/modelstandards.pdf`. This link is also available online at `www.dummies.com/go/paralegalcareer2e`.

Defining the qualifications of a paralegal

The first section of the NALA code deals with its definition of a legal assistant or paralegal. NALA defines paralegals as individuals with the training and expertise to work in substantive and procedural areas of the law on tasks that would otherwise be completed by a licensed attorney.

The next section of the code defines NALA's qualifications of a paralegal. As we mention in Chapter 1, there are two ways to train to be a paralegal: education and on-the-job experience. The NALA code defines the standards of training that the organization feels should be required of all paralegals.

REMEMBER

NALA has come up with its own definition of a paralegal. It doesn't set laws for regulating paralegals on either the state or federal level. So, don't think you can't be hired if your particular qualifications don't exactly match NALA's standards.

Designating the duties a paralegal can perform

The NALA code says that, in general, a paralegal can perform any task that is properly delegated and assigned by an attorney. The attorney must remain ultimately responsible both for the task and for supervising the paralegal. Paralegals interview clients, maintain records, perform investigations, draft documents, conduct legal research, write legal memos, assist attorneys in settlement conferences and at trial, and much more.

Relating to the client

Several of the NALA guidelines deal with the appropriate relationship between paralegals and clients. Many of these guidelines mirror those of the ABA's Model Rules of Professional Conduct. You must maintain confidentiality, avoid conflicts of interest, and act in a professional manner to forward the interests of the client.

Paralegals must also follow some guidelines specific to paralegals. For example, at the outset of any communication with clients, paralegals are required to disclose the fact that they are legal assistants and not attorneys. Paralegals are not allowed to establish attorney/client relationships, set legal fees, give legal advice, or represent a client before a court (except under special circumstances).

REMEMBER

These guidelines were developed by the NALA based on the accepted practice in many jurisdictions. The attorney and the paralegal are required to know specific state laws regarding the use of paralegals.

Knowing the National Federation of Paralegal Associations code

If you join a local or state paralegal association, you'll probably become affiliated with the National Federation of Paralegal Associations (NFPA). As we discuss in Chapter 2, NFPA is a federation comprised of individual members and paralegal associations from throughout the United States and Canada.

Like NALA (see the earlier section), NFPA is also committed to upholding the integrity of the paralegal profession. In fact, NFPA's Model Code of Ethics and Professional Responsibility is very similar to NALA's Model Standards. That makes things easier for you and other paralegals!

The difference between the codes is really one of emphasis. NALA calls its standards "guidelines," while NFPA refers to them as "rules." NFPA seems to be less interested in answering common ethical questions and more focused on describing proper professional conduct. The first three sections of the NFPA code calls on paralegals to maintain a "high level of competence," a "high level of personal and professional integrity," and a "high standard of professional conduct." Although these sections contain much the same information as the NALA guidelines, they're more detailed as to the kinds of behaviors a good paralegal should avoid.

The online content also contains this link to the entire contents of NFPA's Model Code of Ethics and Professional Responsibility: `www.paralegals.org/files/ Model_Code_of_Ethics_09_06.pdf`.

The NFPA code includes a *rule* (which, in this case, means a suggestion, not a legal mandate) that each paralegal aspire to contribute a certain number of hours per year of pro bono work. Your contribution should be directed toward helping persons of limited means or the organizations that help such persons. The code also directs you to support efforts to improve the legal system.

The NFPA code also includes model guidelines for enforcing its code. The guidelines include recommendations for associations to structure a "disciplinary committee." This committee would be called to hear allegations of misconduct by a paralegal and would be composed mainly of other, experienced paralegals.

Cracking the codes of other organizations

Other paralegal organizations and associations have their own codes of ethics. These codes are usually similar to the ones NALA and NFPA have written (see the earlier sections). NALS (see Chapter 2) has a code of ethics called the NALS Code of Ethics and Professional Responsibility ; the code is similar to NALA's and NFPA's, but it's shorter and less specific. The AAPI code contains just ten canons that, like the other codes, hold paralegals to the highest level of professional behavior.

You can read the NALS code at `www.nals.org/page/history`. A link to the code is also included online. Some state paralegal associations tie their ethical codes to specific state laws and are, therefore, more pertinent than the codes of national organizations. The online content provides a list of many of these local associations.

Maintaining ethical standards is crucial when you work as a paralegal. By adhering to rigorous ethical codes throughout your career as a paralegal, you'll stay out of legal and professional trouble and uphold the reputation of the paralegal profession. Most importantly, you'll provide your office's clients with the professional legal service that they deserve.

BEYOND THEORY: REAL-WORLD ETHICS

Codes of ethical standards present important guidelines, but their application can be difficult in the real world. In your paralegal career, you may face situations where your personal ethics conflict with your professional ethics, or where you inadvertently do something unethical.

The requirement to keep information confidential can result in conflicts between personal and professional ethics. For example, you may work for an estate planning firm where a client informs you that he plans to kill himself as soon as his will is completed. You have a professional duty to keep a client's information confidential, but you probably feel an obligation to tell someone that your client is suicidal.

The person you turn to is the lawyer who's working with the client. Because the attorney is responsible for the client, you must tell the attorney what you know about the client and leave it up to the attorney to inform the appropriate authorities (under the exception that revealing the client's confidence will prevent serious and imminent bodily harm).

You may find yourself in the position of one of the authors, who, while he was working as a paralegal, learned from a client that the client had lied under oath at trial. The paralegal's duty was to report this information to the supervising attorney, who then reported the issue to the judge.

4

Identifying the Skills Paralegals Need to Soar

Ensure that your written communication in emails, letters, and legal documents expresses a clear and grammatically proper writing style.

Keep up with the ways that technology has advanced legal practice.

Maintain the proper running of a legal practice with clear systems for time management, efficient accounting, and client file organization.

Chapter **16**

Presenting a Clear, Concise Legal Writing Style

Writing legal documents is one of the most important things you do as a paralegal. Whether you're composing a letter, drafting a document, or writing a memo, you need to use a writing style that's grammatically correct and easily understood. Developing a good writing style requires practice, study, and hard work. However, if you get a handle on some basic rules, you'll be well on the way to great legal writing!

Legal writing may use more technical terms and Latin phrases than other types of writing, but legal writing shouldn't be confusing and long-winded. Somewhere legal writers have gotten the impression that big words and long sentences communicate importance and authority. In reality, big words and complicated sentences obscure your message and confuse your readers. Good legal writing is like good writing in general: clean, concise, and easily understood.

If your memos contain problems with grammar, punctuation, mechanics, or organization, you won't communicate effectively and your research will go to waste. This chapter focuses on showing you how to avoid the errors we've seen paralegal students make most when they draft documents and prepare legal memos.

Corresponding Carefully

Everyone who works in the legal field should understand the importance of communication. Communication can establish and preserve rights, it can be used to win an argument or reach an agreement, and it could even be used against your client as evidence in court. These are ample reasons for you to focus on careful correspondence.

As a paralegal you're working with a legal team on behalf of a client. As part of the legal team, you have to communicate in a way that effectively advocates the rights of your client. You must make sure that your communications never harm your client or your employer. Much of your communication will be written: documents, pleadings, letters, email, and, in some cases, text.

Written communication has permanence that verbal communication lacks. Any grammar mistakes that Shakespeare made in his plays and poems written 400 years ago are preserved today! Don't let that scare you too much — your letters and emails are unlikely to be read by students in the 25th century. However, the things you write and the way that you write them will be preserved.

Now that you understand the importance of written communication to your paralegal career, we want to focus on two forms of written communication that are often overlooked: letters and email.

Letters that impact

Great legal letters are written with a purpose in mind. Ask yourself, "What is the objective of this letter?" Letters should begin with an outline and end with proofreading.

But having a purpose in mind doesn't mean that you can't be cordial. Even a sentence or two of "small talk" can show your audience that your firm is concerned about more than just bringing in business. This is especially true in communicating with long-standing clients or business associates. Be sure to remain professional in all your communications, even with colleagues that you consider friends. You never know who may eventually read your letters.

TIP

Anything that you send on your employer's letterhead represents your employer and your clients. Be professional in your letters and never emotional. Even if you're replying to a letter that is angry or rude, you still must be professional in your reply. You should also never write anything in a letter that compromises the position of your client or can be used against your client or firm in court. The rule is: When in doubt have your supervisor or a trusted colleague review the letter before you mail it. A minute of review can spare you a lot of regret!

Effortless emails

Emails and texts have an ambiguous role in the modern workplace. They have taken the place of both phone calls and letters, and sometimes they move so quickly that they almost take on the form of a conversation. In these cases, you may not even think of them as a form of written communication. Make no mistake, emails and texts are written communication, and as high-profile cases involving corporations and government agencies demonstrate, careless emails and texts can come back to haunt the writer.

WARNING

Don't send lazy texts and emails! Treat any correspondence written on the job as letters. Use proper grammar, punctuation, and capitalization. Don't use the abbreviations you may use in your personal texts or emails. Spell-check your emails and proofread them. Have important emails proofread by the same people who look at your letters before you mail them. And save important emails as drafts before you send them. That way you can look them over once more before you click Send. *Remember:* Just like letters, texts and emails can't be "unsent."

Grammar: Grasping the Foundation of an Effective Writing Style

Like most people, you probably cringe at the prospect of studying grammar. The mere mention of the word often produces bad memories of diagramming sentences and memorizing complex rules. This section isn't a grammar lesson — don't worry! Although you may have hoped to leave the subject in the classroom, a precise understanding of grammar is fundamental for anyone who wants to write well. Fortunately, the essential rules of grammar are really quite logical, so bear with us as we tackle this unpopular subject — and return to this section whenever you're writing a letter or legal document and you're not quite sure which way to go.

Identifying the eight parts of speech

Your road to effective communication begins with constructing effective sentences. Sentences are made from words, and each word in a sentence has a function. In the English language, there are eight parts of speech: verbs, nouns, pronouns, adjectives, adverbs, conjunctions, prepositions, and interjections. We cover them all in more detail in the following sections.

Verbs

You can't have a sentence without a verb. The only part of speech that is capable of being a one-word sentence is a verb. The verb expresses the action of the sentence — a lot of work for a single word!

REMEMBER

There are essentially three categories of verbs. A verb can either be an action verb, a "to be" verb, or a linking verb.

ACTION VERBS

In your legal writing, you should use mostly action verbs. These verbs describe what the subject is doing. Use action verbs to form the most powerful and direct sentences.

TIP

You should use mostly action verbs in your legal writing. Passive verbs convey the state or condition of something and are essential when used sparingly, but action verbs form the most compact, direct, and understandable sentences. We discuss active and passive verbs in more detail in "Using active voice," later in this chapter.

THE "TO BE" VERB

The verb "to be" *(am, is, are, were, been,* and *being)* is like an equal sign. It equates the subject with a noun or adjective. For example: *Katy is a paralegal* means *Katy = a paralegal,* and *You are efficient* means *You = efficient.*

LINKING VERBS

You use linking verbs in the same way as the "to be" verb. Linking verbs join (or link) the sentence's subject to an adjective that describes the condition of the subject. Linking verbs are never followed by adverbs. Whereas the "to be" verb is merely an equal sign, linking verbs carry additional information or meaning. Common linking verbs are *feel, seem, appear, look, taste,* and *smell.*

Nouns

You're undoubtedly familiar with the common characterization of a noun as a "person, place, thing, or idea." And you probably know that a noun functions in a sentence in different ways. In the following sentences, the *subject* (Johnson) plays the principal role in the sentence; the *direct object* (opportunity) receives the action of the verb; the *indirect object* (reporter) receives the direct object; the *object of a preposition* (interview) and the *object in a verbal phrase* (candidate) serve as the receivers of the preposition or verbal; *appositives* (independent) clarify other nouns; and *predicate nouns* (woman) follow the verb "to be" and describe the subject.

> Being a candidate with few secrets, Johnson, an independent, provided every reporter the opportunity for an interview. She was an honest woman.

Pronouns

We now turn to a special type of noun, the pronoun. Pronouns rename nouns and provide a means for avoiding the needless repetition of names and other nouns in a sentence or paragraph. You need to know the three types of pronouns: personal, indefinite, and relative.

PERSONAL PRONOUNS

You're probably already familiar with the personal pronouns. They're used to rename specific nouns, and they take two forms.

>> **Subjective personal pronouns:** *I, he, she, it, we,* and *they*

>> **Objective personal pronouns:** *me, him, her, it, us,* and *them.*

As their names imply, you use subjective forms when the pronouns function as subjects or predicate nouns and objective forms when the pronouns function as an object.

TIP

Collective nouns, such as *group* and *jury*, are common in legal writing. In most cases, these nouns are singular; therefore, you use the pronoun *it* to refer to them. You also use *it* when referring to company names — for example, "The jury has not reached *its* decision regarding the trucking company and *its* negligence."

INDEFINITE PRONOUNS

Indefinite pronouns refer to generalities rather than specifics. Some common examples are *everyone, somebody, anything, each, one, none,* and *no one.*

REMEMBER

All indefinite pronouns are singular, which means that they require singular verbs — for example, "None of the cases *is* settled."

RELATIVE PRONOUNS

The third type of pronoun you need to know is the relative pronoun. Relative pronouns like *that, which,* and *who* link adjective clauses to the nouns they describe. *Who* refers to persons, *which* refers to animals and things, and *that* may refer to both persons and things.

Here's an example:

> She is a lawyer *who* is accustomed to winning. The cases *that* she handles are usually settled for large sums of money, *which* makes her a very rich attorney.

TIP

Note that the pronoun *that* introduces a restrictive clause, and *which* introduces a nonrestrictive clause. We discuss both types of clauses later in this chapter.

Adjectives

You could write without adjectives, but it would be boring! Adjectives describe and clarify nouns and other adjectives. Adjectives provide additional information and clearer descriptions of the words they modify. Choose them carefully because one precisely chosen adjective is more powerful than several vague ones.

Here's an example sentence:

> The demeanor of the *stern* judge cast a *somber* mood on the courtroom.

Stern describes the kind of judge, and *somber* describes the kind of mood. Without the adjectives, the sentence would be unclear:

> The demeanor of the judge cast a mood on the courtroom.

Adverbs

Like adjectives, adverbs also clarify, but whereas adjectives usually modify nouns, adverbs primarily modify verbs. You can form many adverbs by adding *−ly* to adjectives. However, adverbs include all words and groups of words that answer the questions "Where?", "When?", "How?", and "Why?"; adverbs can modify adjectives and other adverbs as well as verbs.

Here are some examples of adverbs:

> The jury *quickly* discussed the case.

In the preceding sentence, the adverb *quickly* modifies the verb *discussed.*

> The paralegal took lunch *outside.*

Here, the adverb *outside* modifies the verb *took.*

> The legal team researched the issue *yesterday.*

In this example, the adverb *yesterday* modifies the verb *researched.*

Conjunctions and prepositions

The previous sections cover the main elements of the sentence. But you need to link these elements together — and that's the job of the conjunctions and prepositions.

CONJUNCTIONS

You use conjunctions to join together words, phrases, and clauses. The three types of conjunctions are

» **Coordinating:** You're probably familiar with the seven coordinating conjunctions: *and, but, for, nor, or, so,* and *yet.* These are the words most people think of as "conjunctions." Example: The defendant neglected to file an answer *and* third-party complaint within the deadline, *so* the plaintiff prevailed.

» **Correlative:** This type of conjunction always appear in pairs: *either/or, neither/nor, not only/but also.* These conjunctions "correlate" two similar clauses in one sentence. When using the first two types of clauses, you must employ parallel structure. This means that the parts of the sentence joined by the conjunction must be grammatically equal. If you're not clear on parallel structure, turn to "Employing parallel structure," later in this chapter. Example: The trial court erred *not only* in allowing the defendant's testimony into evidence *but also* by failing to grant the defendant's motion to recuse.

» **Subordinating:** The third type of conjunction introduces dependent clauses and connects them to independent clauses. *Although, because, if, when,* and *while* are common examples of subordinating conjunctions. Example: *Although* the process server failed to serve process properly the first time, she successful served the defendant with the second attempt. As the name suggests, the dependent clause is made subordinate to the independent clause by the conjunction. Without the subordinating conjunction, the relationship between the clauses would be unclear and the sentence would be incorrect.

PREPOSITIONS

Whereas a conjunction links clauses *within* a sentence, a preposition joins a noun *to* a sentence. A preposition cannot function within a sentence without a noun, so you must always use a preposition in a prepositional phrase.

We would need several pages to list all prepositions, but common examples are *about, above, for, over,* and *with.* (You can think of a preposition as anywhere a little mouse can go: A little mouse can go over, through, under, around, and so on.)

WARNING

Bad legal writing glorifies *compound prepositions,* which are several prepositional phrases that work as one preposition. Compound prepositions, such as *at this point in time, with regard to,* and *by virtue of,* are weak and imprecise — if you find yourself reaching for a compound preposition, try to state your point in simpler, more definite terms. For instance, you can shorten *at this point in time* to *now,* you can shorten *with regard to* to *regarding,* and you can shorten *by virtue of* to *by.* Remember: Good legal writing emphasizes precision and clarity.

TIP

The proper use of conjunctions and prepositions can add style and a sense of flow to your writing. The improper use of these elements is jarring to your reader. Take the time to figure out when and how to use conjunctions and prepositions, and you'll be on your way to becoming a superior legal writer!

Interjections

Interjections are words that express emotion in the sentence. Rarely do legal documents or memos contain words like *wow, darn,* or *shucks* unless they're included in direct quotations.

TIP

However, some four-letter interjections do make their way into settlement negotiations. If you have to quote four-letter interjections in a document, quote them accurately. If the exact wording of the statement is unnecessary, paraphrasing may be more polite.

Recognizing the elements of a sentence

The eight parts of speech work together to form sentences, but the thrust of your sentences' information is conveyed by three main elements: the subject, the verb, and the element that the verb links the subject to. To locate the main idea of a sentence, you should focus on these three elements. Other information in the sentence may be important, but it isn't the main idea.

Subject, verb, and the third element

The *subject* is the main character of the sentence, the noun that carries out the action of the sentence or whose condition the sentence describes. The *verb* describes the action or links the subject and the rest of the predicate (which is the verb and all that comes after it).

Forceful writing includes an abundance of carefully chosen action verbs. Depending on the verb you use, the third important part of the sentence could be either a direct object, an adverb, an adjective, or a predicate noun. Placing the bulk of the sentence's message within the three main elements will improve the clarity and impact of your written work.

Your subject will always be a noun (person, place, or thing), so the number of possible sentence structures hangs on your sentence's main verb. Because there are four types of verbs (two kinds of action verbs, "to be" verbs, and linking verbs), there are four essential sentence structures:

» Subject + Transitive Verb + Direct Object: "The attorney argues the case."

» Subject + Intransitive Verb + Adverb: "The paralegal responds quickly."

» Subject + "To Be" Verb + Adjective or Predicate Noun: "The client is nervous."

» Subject + Linking Verb + Adjective: "The jury feels tired."

**TECHNICAL
STUFF**

Action verbs can be either *transitive* or *intransitive*. Don't let these names worry you! The distinction is simple: Transitive verbs can immediately be followed by a noun, and intransitive verbs can't. This is because a transitive verb requires that its action be received. Here's an example: *The court supported the motion.* On the other hand, a noun can't receive the action of intransitive verbs: *The appellate court agreed with the plaintiff's argument.*

Phrases and clauses

After you have your three main elements, the only possible additions to the sentence are more nouns, adverbs, and adjectives. These additions provide more information about the sentence's main message and appear as single words, phrases, or clauses.

Phrases and clauses are groups of words that work together to form a single part of speech, such as an adverb or adjective. Clauses contain their own subjects and verbs; phrases do not. A good understanding of clauses is essential to a good understanding of sentence structure and proper punctuation.

INDEPENDENT AND DEPENDENT CLAUSES

Clauses are either independent or dependent:

» **Independent clauses** are complete by themselves; no additional information is required.

» **Dependent clauses** express incomplete thoughts. Even though they contain subjects and verbs, they cannot stand alone as sentences without other information; they are sentence fragments.

Here's an example of a sentence with both an independent clause and a dependent clause:

When the jury reaches a decision, it will return to the courtroom.

The independent clause in the sample sentence is *it will return to the courtroom.* No other information is required to complete this thought. *When the jury reaches a decision* leaves the reader wondering. The information is incomplete, so it's a dependent clause.

TIP

To form a complete sentence, a dependent clause must be attached to an independent clause. The way you join the clauses depends on how the dependent clause functions within the sentence. The dependent clause that functions as an adverb begins with a subordinating conjunction and answers the questions *how, when, where,* or *why:*

> The client shot the man because he was attacking her.

On the other hand, an adjective clause usually begins with a relative pronoun to provide more information about the noun it modifies:

> Frederick is an employer *who insists on perfection.*

Dependent clauses may also function as nouns:

> The client was oblivious to how much time had passed since the accident.

RESTRICTIVE AND NONRESTRICTIVE CLAUSES

Dependent clauses can be classified as either restrictive or nonrestrictive, and distinguishing between the two can sometimes be tricky. But knowing the difference helps you with punctuation.

>> **Restrictive:** A restrictive clause is one whose presence is vital to the meaning of the sentence: "Steve never loses his cases *that involve dog-bite victims.*" The restrictive clause in this sentence provides essential information that pinpoints the particular type of cases Steve never loses. Without that clause, it would appear that the attorney never loses *any* cases!

>> **Nonrestrictive:** A nonrestrictive clause provides clarifying information, but its presence isn't necessary for the sentence to make sense: "Grace never loses her cases, *which involve dog-bite victims.*" The nonrestrictive clause makes a "by the way" statement; it provides additional information about what type of cases Grace handles. Her practice is limited to dog-bite victims, and she never loses a case.

TIP

Note that in the examples the restrictive clause begins with *that* and the nonrestrictive clause begins with *which.* Use commas to set the nonrestrictive clause apart from rest of the sentence. The restrictive clause is an integral part of the sentence and isn't set apart by commas.

WARNING

Bad legal writing often relies too heavily on the use of clauses. Clarify and simplify your sentences by replacing them with appropriate single words and phrases. You must also properly locate phrases and clauses within your sentence to emphasize the main elements of the sentence. Locating elements within the sentence is called *structuring the sentence.*

Sentence Structure: Positioning the Sentence's Elements

You form sentences from a subject, verb, and third element, using the four structures mentioned in the "Subject, verb, and the third element" section, earlier in this chapter. Varying your style is a good idea, but essentially all sentences appear as one of the four structures. You can then add descriptive elements to these basic structures.

The key is to construct your sentence so it conveys its message clearly and precisely. Ambiguity occurs when the sentence's descriptive elements cloud the main message either because they're too numerous or because they're improperly positioned. Generally, a clear, concise sentence contains *one* main message and an average of 25 words. Obviously, some sentences will be longer than 25 words and some will be shorter, but as a legal writer you should strive to convey a single message within 25 words.

TIP

If your sentence can logically be made into two complete sentences, consider breaking it up. Independent clauses can certainly be combined to form a sentence, but often two short sentences are clearer than one long one!

If you pay careful attention to the way your sentences are structured, you'll greatly improve the way people receive your messages. If you use the sentence construction techniques mentioned in this section, you'll produce more powerful writing.

Eliminating wordiness

Legal writing is plagued by wordiness. Historically, the writers of statutes and many case opinions held to the philosophy of "The longer the sentence, the better." Anyone who has tried to decipher the points of long-winded statutes and case summaries will attest that this just isn't so! As soon as a sentence has conveyed its point, your best bet is to end it and begin a new sentence.

The good news is that nearly all ABA-accredited law schools now contain a practical course on legal writing. In such courses, law students learn to write clearly and accurately using active sentences. Some of this training may filter into statutes, opinions, and legal briefs — and into the writing of the attorneys you work with!

TIP

Don't try to impress your supervisor, client, or judge by using long phrases that sound impressive. It is not the length of your phrases, but the strength of your arguments that impress.

WARNING

Be careful when you first try to simplify your writing. Sometimes efforts to shorten sentence length result in a series of choppy, disjointed sentences that read more like a reading primer for the first grade than a legal document! A treatment for this broken style is to discover the common element of the shorter sentences and create a slightly longer sentence that incorporates the other elements.

In the following sentences, the common element is *the client:*

> The client had been injured in a car accident.
>
> The client was distraught.
>
> The attorney decided to talk to the client.

The main idea of each sentence is very clear, but when you read the sentences together as part of a paragraph, the sentences read as if the author has the hiccups:

> The client had been injured in a car accident. The client was distraught. The attorney decided to talk to the client.

You can combine these sentences into one graceful sentence:

> The attorney decided to talk to the distraught client who had been injured in a car accident.

Another method you can use to smooth out choppy writing is to use the less important of two sentences as an introduction for the more important sentence:

> The jury awarded the plaintiff damages of $100,000. It based its decision on the testimony of the expert witness.

Which sentence do you think is more important to the client? You can restructure the sentence as follows:

> Basing its decision on the testimony of the expert witness, the jury awarded the plaintiff damages of $100,000.

The jury award forms the main clause and the incidental information of why they acted is the dependent clause.

TIP

You must work hard to avoid making your sentences too short and choppy *or too long and complex. Remember:* There is really only one way to improve your writing style: practice.

Positioning modifiers

Modifiers make up an important part of your writing, but you need to place them properly. Adjectives, adverbs, and other modifiers should be placed as closely as possible to the words they modify. This helps you avoid the problem of *misplaced modifiers,* which occurs when your modifier applies to the wrong word. When a modifier is misplaced, the results can be ludicrous:

> The paralegal placed the schedule of depositions to be held in October on the top of the desk.

The sentence conjures up a picture of attorneys and their clients conducting October depositions while sitting on a desk. Positioning the adverbial phrase *on the top of the desk* adjacent to the verb *placed* clarifies the meaning of the sentence:

> The paralegal placed on the top of the desk the schedule of depositions to be held in October.

Using active voice

The legal profession has begun to embrace using active voice. Legal writing texts include chapters emphasizing the importance of active voice in constructing clear arguments. Passive voice obscures the main idea of a sentence because it hides the subject. "Charles committed the crime" is more direct than "The crime was committed by Charles." In the first sentence, written in active voice, the subject is the doer of the action; the message is clear. In the second sentence, written in passive voice, the doer of the action is obscured and the message is weak.

Passive voice does have a role in writing. There are some occasions when the doer of the action is unclear or unimportant. For instance, you may use passive voice when you're not sure who committed an action, like when you're describing damages in a car accident case where the perpetrator of the accident has yet to be determined:

> The car was hit and dented on the left-front bumper.

Employing parallel structure

To improve your writing, you need to maintain *parallel construction*. This means that elements joined by a conjunction must be grammatically alike. Compare the following sentences:

> The students study to maintain good grade point averages, for increased knowledge, and because they enjoy the admiration of their peers.

Although this sentence is not awful, it could be improved by using similar grammatical forms for the elements that are linked by the conjunction *and*:

> The students study to maintain good grade point averages, to increase their knowledge, and to inspire the admiration of their peers.

The sentence is better balanced because all the elements joined by the conjunction are phrased as infinitives.

Punctuation and Mechanics: Mastering the Rules

Punctuation can be scary. Commas, semicolons, parentheses, and dashes. Where do they all go? Capitalization and quotation can be tricky, too. Actually, you can understand the rules of punctuation and mechanics with a little time and commitment. *Remember:* The proper use of punctuation and mechanics is essential to guide a reader through a sentence.

Rules for proper punctuation

The rules of proper punctuation may seem confusing, but when you have a working knowledge of some basic grammatical concepts, you'll find them easier to follow. Unlike some aspects of the English language, particularly spelling, the rules of punctuation are pretty logical.

Periods and question marks

The two simplest types of punctuation to use properly are periods and question marks. Periods end declarative sentences (like this one). Periods also follow initials, as in *Ph.D.* and *D. H. Lawrence,* and abbreviations, like *etc.* But you don't use periods for initials used in agency names, such as *ACLU* and *YMCA,* or for commonly used shortened forms, like *ad* (short for *advertisement*) or *memo* (short for *memorandum*).

Use question marks to end direct questions, such as, "Which document should I file first?" Don't use a question mark with indirect questions, such as, "He asked me which document had to be filed first." With indirect sentences, you're not *asking* questions, you're *reporting* questions that someone else asked. The only time you use a question mark to report someone else's questions is when the question is a direct quote:

> He asked me, "Which document has to be filed first?"

Commas

Although the period is the most often used mark of punctuation, the comma is the mark most often *misused*. You can't write properly without the comma. But you shouldn't simply add commas where you pause in a sentence. You add them in specific places for specific reasons.

SERIES

In a series of three or more expressions joined by one conjunction, put a comma after each expression except the last:

> Mary, Bill, and Joan prepared the petitions, filed them in court, and placed copies in the office files.

When stating firm names, omit the last comma:

> The firm of Goodwin, Spencer, Kolb and Weise represents the defendant.

TIP

Some employers prefer that the last comma be omitted in *every* series (not just in law firm names); be sure to follow the preferences of your supervisor.

OMITTED WORDS

Use a comma to replace words omitted from a sentence:

> The *Cupp* document was filed yesterday; the *Burton* document, today.

In the second clause, the comma replaces the words *was filed.*

SEPARATION OF CLAUSES

When you join two independent clauses with a conjunction (such as *and, but,* or *so*), place a comma before the conjunction:

> The bankruptcy suit was very complex, but the attorney had a skilled paralegal to help prepare the case for trial.

Also use a comma to set apart a beginning dependent clause:

> Because you've worked hard, you'll present a good case.

Do not use a comma when the dependent clause comes *after* the independent clause:

> You'll present a good case because you've worked hard.

PARENTHETIC EXPRESSIONS

When you include information that's important but not essential to the meaning of the sentence, set that information off with commas. Sometimes it's difficult to determine whether an expression is parenthetic or not, but the following classifications should help:

>> **Asides** consist of words like *however, in my opinion,* and *for example* and are set apart from the rest of the sentence: "For example, the trial court in the *Reschly* case, in my opinion, was biased toward the defendant."

>> **Appositives** provide additional information about a noun that is important, but not essential to the central idea of the sentence: "The attorney for the opposition, Mr. Gall, has a scheduled court date." *Mr. Gall* provides the reader with the attorney's specific name, without that information, the sentence is still true. If you use the name as part of a title, do not use commas: "Attorney Gall requested a court date."

>> **Titles and distinctions** that follow a name should be set off with commas: "Jason Venner, J.D., is the attorney for Pottila Trucking Company, Inc."

>> **Abbreviations** such as *etc., e.g.,* and *i.e.,* should be set off by commas: "Enclosed are the copies letters, emails, etc., mentioned in the warrant."

>> **Dates and place names** actually contain parenthetic information and should be punctuated accordingly: "Boulder, Colorado, is the venue for the trials, which are set to take place on May 25, 2006, and July 19, 2006." If the date is written 25 May 2006, commas are not necessary.

>> **Nonrestrictive clauses** are, by definition, parenthetic. A nonrestrictive clause always provides information that is not essential to the meaning of the sentence, so you should always use commas to set it apart: "The accident occurred in Missouri, where both the plaintiff and defendant reside." The second clause provides important information but is not essential to the sentence.

REMEMBER

Only important information that isn't essential to the sentence is included in a parenthetical phrase. Information that is interesting, but not important to the argument, shouldn't be included in the sentence at all.

Semicolons

A *semicolon* looks like a period placed over a comma (;). This definition is supposed to remind you that the break formed by a semicolon is more definite than a comma but less final than a period. Here are some instances for semicolons:

>> **Joining two independent clauses:** Because the semicolon forms a more definite break, you don't need a conjunction: "It is almost midnight; I cannot finish this brief before tomorrow morning." You use the semicolon instead of a period, because the sentences are related in thought — the reason you can't finish the brief is probably because it's almost midnight and you're out of time.

>> **Beginning a second clause with a conjunctive adverb:** Clauses that begin with conjunctive adverbs (such as *accordingly, also, besides, consequently, furthermore, hence, however, indeed, likewise, moreover, nevertheless, otherwise, similarly, so, still, therefore,* and *thus*) require a semicolon to separate them from another clause: "I should finish this brief tonight; otherwise, I will have to work on it during lunch tomorrow." Note that a comma comes after the conjunctive adverb.

>> **Separating an enumerated series or a series of expressions punctuated by commas:** Use semicolons when commas would be confusing: "The legal secretary's duties include (1) drafting and filing legal documents; (2) corresponding with clients and opposing counsel; and (3) organizing information within the office." Here's another example, "Valencia, Mayo & Braun; Walton & Walton, P.C.; and Fielding, Burgess and Lloyd are just three of the firms with which we regularly correspond."

Colons

Colons are unusual punctuation marks that can be used in unique ways. You can use colons in place of periods to separate two clauses, each of which could be a sentence. You can also use a colon to introduce a list of specifics, long appositives and explanations, or quotations that provide for the preceding clause.

A colon creates a more powerful impression than a comma and is more formal than a dash. But be careful to never use a colon to separate a verb from the third element or a preposition from its object:

She will be finished when she completes three projects: the deposition digest, the letter to Johnson & Brown, and the memo to her immediate supervisor.

Note that the following is *incorrect*:

She will be finished when she completes: the deposition digest, the letter to Johnson & Brown, and the memo to her immediate supervisor.

There are some special uses of colons that you should know for legal writing. Use colons in the salutation of a business letter, like this:

> Dear Ms. Thompson:

Also use a colon between the hour and minutes when indicating clock time (for example, "4:30 p.m.") and between a main title and its subtitle, as in "The book entitled *Legal Research: A Guide to the Law Library* will be available today after 4:30 p.m."

Dashes

Like colons, dashes introduce long appositives, but they're less formal and don't often appear in legal writing. More commonly they separate a beginning series from the corresponding clause. You also use them to indicate abrupt breaks in the continuity of the sentence, but only when other marks of punctuation are inadequate:

> Breakfast in bed, lunch by the pool, dinner by candlelight — such were the dreams of the overworked paralegal.

TIP

To create a dash on your computer, you can either type two hyphens (--), or you can actually enter a dash using your word processing program. If you use Microsoft Word 2003, you can go to Insert ⇨ Symbol, select the Special Characters tab, highlight Em Dash, and click the Insert button. (If you use dashes frequently, you can use the shortcut key shown in the Special Characters tab of the Symbol dialog box.)

WARNING

You should probably save the dashes for the fictional book you will write featuring an overworked paralegal who happens to be a superhero. Use more formal punctuation in your legal writing.

TECHNICAL STUFF

Another kind of dash, the en dash, is shorter than the em dash and longer than the hyphen. You can find more information on the difference between em dashes and en dashes in a style guide such as *The Chicago Manual of Style*, 15th Edition.

Parentheses

Use parentheses sparingly. They create a stronger separation than commas or dashes. You can use them to distinguish parenthetical information:

> The format of the caption on the complaint (called a petition in some states) varies from state to state.

You use them to distinguish the numbers in an enumerated series. In legal documents, they designate a numerical figure when it follows an amount that has been expressed in words:

The plaintiff requests damages in the amount of One Hundred Thousand Dollars ($100,000.00).

Parentheses are also used when transcribing legal testimony to designate the actions of the speakers:

MR. STEWART: Is this the document you signed? (hands Ms. Avery the contract)

The only punctuation marks that appear within parentheses are those that are essential to the parenthetical material. The rest of the sentence should be punctuated as it would be if the parenthetical information weren't there.

Mastering mechanics

Rules that govern the mechanics of writing include: how to form possessives, when to capitalize, when to italicize and underline, and how to quote others' material.

Forming possessives

Even if you're an experienced writer, you may still have difficulty with possessives. You should use the possessive form of a noun when the noun is immediately followed by another noun that it possesses. Here are the five rules for forming possessives:

» **Most possessives are formed by adding *'s* to the end of a singular noun.** This is true even if the noun ends in *s*. *Examples:* "Mrs. Ruddy's case"; "the jury's decision"; "Charles's opinion"; "Jack Johnson's letter."

» **If the possessive noun is plural and ends in *s*, only an apostrophe is added.** *Examples:* "The four boys' bikes"; "the three clients' wishes"; "the Joneses' front porch."

» **If you must use an appositive with a possessive case, apply the possessive form to the noun closest to the thing possessed, usually the appositive.** *Example:* "The patient, Mr. Jones's, surgery lasted several hours."

» **Memorize the possessive forms of proper pronouns (*my, his, her, your, its, our,* and *their* for pronouns preceding the noun; *mine, his, hers, yours, its, ours,* and *theirs* for possessive pronouns that occur at the end of a clause or that are used as a subject).** *Example:* "Yours is a very strong case; it is much stronger than mine." Note that none of the possessive pronouns contains an apostrophe. *It's* is a contraction of *it is,* and therefore rarely appears in legal writing. As opposed to proper pronouns, possessive indefinite pronouns do contain apostrophes: "Somebody's dog has chewed my carpet."

> **»** **The possessive form of a noun should almost always be used before a** **_gerund,_** **a noun formed by a verb + _–ing_.** *Example:* "I am concerned about our client's presenting himself well at trial." The phrase *our client presenting himself* may sound accurate, but it is not.

Capitalizing properly

Proper capitalization is like the law; the rules are there, but the interpretation and application of those rules is the subject of debate. The best advice is to capitalize words consistently and follow the preferences of your employer.

TIP

Within a sentence, capitalization is essentially based on one guideline: If a noun is the proper name of an individual entity, it should be capitalized; if it names a generality, it should be lowercase.

PROPER NAMES

Capitalize the name of a particular person, place, event, or thing and the degrees and titles that accompany a person's name:

> Professor Juan Ramirez
>
> Senator Sarah Grey
>
> President Hammond

But, professional titles that follow a name or stand alone should be lowercase:

> Juan Ramirez, a professor of geology, will speak tonight.
>
> The senator and the president will attend.

In one case, the title is designating a certain professor, Juan Ramirez. In the other case, the appositive provides information that Juan Ramirez is a professor.

LEGAL DOCUMENTS

Capitalize the official titles of specific acts, bills, codes, and laws:

> First Amendment
>
> Code of Civil Procedure
>
> Securities Exchange Act

General terms for legal documents are lowercase:

> The prohibition amendment was repealed, but many codes and laws that are equally useless are still in effect.

NUMBERS

In a legal document, a dollar amount should be written out and each word capitalized:

> The accidents resulted in damages totaling Eight Thousand Nine Hundred Forty-Two Dollars ($8,942).

In all other cases, the second number in a compound numeral should be lowercase:

> He moved to 432 East Fifty-second Street.

COURTS AND JUDGES

Probably the most confusing capitalization rule for legal writers involves references to courts and judges. Generally, you should capitalize the name of a court or judge if it's included in the full title of a specific entity; if it's a general term or stands alone, it's lowercase. Here are some examples:

> The most commonly recognized court of appeals is the U.S. Supreme Court.
>
> The case was heard by Judge Fairway's court.
>
> The judge will make her decision by the end of the week.

An exception to this rule occurs when the word *court*, standing alone, refers specifically to the presiding judge or officer:

> The Court's decision was to sentence the defendant to three (3) years probation.

The word *Court* in this sentence refers specifically to the judge.

TERMS OF GOVERNMENT

The words *government*, *administration*, *federal*, and *national* are capitalized only when they are included in titles:

> the National Socialist party
>
> *The Federalist Papers*
>
> the Veterans Administration

the federal government

a national pastime

City, state, county, and *district* are capitalized when they are part of proper names:

Oregon State

Jersey City

Denver District Court

Bowie County

They are lowercase when they stand alone

the state of Georgia

the city of Detroit

the entire district

the largest county

Full titles of boards, committees, departments, bureaus, and legislative bodies are capitalized, but general or incomplete designations are not:

The U.S. Senate approved a bill to provide more power to state senates.

ENUMERATIONS

Capitalize the first word of enumerations that are introduced by a colon and include full sentences:

There are three reasons for the decision: (1) The new proposal is more cost-efficient. (2) It provides for an increase in production. (3) It allows us to use existing facilities.

DIRECTIONS

Capitalize *east, west, north,* and *south* only when they name a section of the United States:

People who live in the Midwest tend to travel west for their vacations; people who live in the West tend to travel east.

Underlining and italicizing

As a paralegal, you'll need to know the rules regarding underlining and italicizing. Underline or italicize case names, book titles, and Latin terms, such as *quid pro quo, respondeat superior,* and so on. Here's an example:

A case that involved the concept of *respondeat superior, Dach v. General Casualty Co.,* is located on page 170 of the *North Western Reporter.*

TIP

Underlining and italicizing are interchangeable; however, italicizing is the preferred method.

Quoting

You can find the rules regarding the mechanics of quoted material in legal writing in *A Uniform System of Citation.* When quoting information from case precedents, paraphrase lengthy statutes and points of law and *never* quote case headnotes, prefatory statements, or an entire presentation of facts. (Of course, you must cite paraphrased material correctly, as you would direct quotes.)

Quoted material should be limited to especially important comments made by a key witness to an incident or a legal authority. However, any copied material that is set forth exactly as it's presented in the original *must* be designated by quotation marks or indentation.

SHORT QUOTATIONS

Generally, exact quotations that are shorter than 50 words are designated by quotation marks and included within the same paragraph as the introductory comments. Separate a full-sentence quotation from its introduction by a comma unless the introduction is an independent clause; in that case, you could use a colon. Look at these examples:

> The Court sentenced the defendant to life imprisonment stating, "All evidence reveals that the defendant is a habitual criminal incapable of being reformed."

> The following testimony of the defendant's sister best supports the judge's statement: "Lynn actually seemed proud of committing each crime."

LONG QUOTATIONS

Quotations over 50 words are usually separated from the introductory comments, indented on both sides, and single-spaced. Quotation marks are eliminated as shown in the following example.

> In reaching its decision, the Court stated the following:

> > The defendant did not permit the taxes to become delinquent. He was under no duty or obligation to pay the taxes. The default in payment of taxes was with the mortgagor, the predecessor in title of the plaintiff. . . .

ALTERED QUOTATIONS

Designate anything added to or deleted from an exact quotation. Words or letters added to a quotation for clarification are enclosed in brackets:

> We feel that it [the trial court's decision] should be upheld.

> The jury said, "[T]he defendant is guilty."

In the second example the *T* is added in brackets to show that is was actually lowercase in the original.

Indicate eliminated words with ellipses. For example, four dots end each quotation that eliminates the end of the quoted material but ends the sentence. (The first dot is the ending period of the sentence, following by the three dots of the ellipses.) Words eliminated from the middle of a quotation are designated by three dots.

Here's an example showing both an ellipses in the middle of a sentence and one at the end of a sentence:

> In reaching a decision, the jury considered "the defendant's clear assumption of risk . . . and his obvious negligence. . . ."

Always include a space between each dot and between the ellipses and the words after them. *Note:* When you're ending a sentence with an ellipses, you put the period up against the last word, and then you add the three dots of the ellipses.

If you add emphasis to any portion of a quotation, the words *emphasis added*, contained in parentheses, must follow the quoted material. The designation is placed after the ending quotation marks in a short quotation or after the period in a long one:

> The witness claimed in his letter, "There is *no way in hell* the defendant was innocent" (emphasis added).

> As stated in *Drake v. Lerner Shops of Colorado, Inc.*, 145 Colo. 1, 4, 357 P.2d 624, 626 (1960), to establish a prime facie case of negligence, the plaintiff must show that the defendant's actions caused the harm:

Some degree of risk is present in our every activity and if existence of hazard alone were the standard it would mean that the happening of an incident would be sufficient to raise the presumption of negligence and the landowner would be an insurer of the safety of his patrons. Such is not the law. The condition created by *the conduct or activity of the landowner must pose an appreciable risk of harm.* (emphasis added).

The preceding quote is also a great example of how long-winded legal writing can get!

PUNCTUATION WITH QUOTATIONS

Place common marks of punctuation, such as periods and commas, before an ending quotation mark:

> When she described the accused as a "lazy bum," she was not referring to his ability to hold a job.

Semicolons and colons go outside the quotation marks:

> The defendant said, "That jury had it in for me from the beginning"; he plans to appeal.

Organization: Structuring the Finished Product

Before you begin writing, you need to organize your thoughts. Longer documents require more planning, but even letters, emails, and short memos should begin with a plan.

The outline

Organization begins with brainstorming. Jot down ideas that seem to be important, compile them into major categories, and then provide more specific information about each category. You don't have to follow perfect outline form, especially if you're working under a tight deadline, but you must identify the major categories of information, the logical order of those categories, and the specific information that supports each category.

Different documents require different types of organization. Depending on the document, the information may be ordered chronologically, from general topics to specific, or from least important to most important. All documents must have an underlying purpose, a main point, substantiating information, and a conclusion. Each bit of information must be essential to the purpose of the written work. Writing is an ongoing process, so as you write you may reorder existing topics, add new ones, or delete unimportant ones as needed to advance your position. The outline is a tool, not a restriction.

TIP

As you being your paralegal career, you should make a point of showing your outline to your supervisor before you begin the actual writing. Your supervisor may not always have the time to review your outline, but a quick review can reveal any weaknesses and keep you from wasting your great writing skills on unnecessary points. As you become more experienced, you can probably do your own review of your outline.

The paragraph

When your outline is complete, you'll use it to construct paragraphs. Some elements of your outline may be discussed in a single paragraph, while others may require several paragraphs. Include an introduction, a body, and a conclusion in each paragraph you write. As with sentences, only include essential information.

TIP

Pay careful attention to sentence structure. Readers are more willing to read paragraphs containing clear, well constructed sentences, and they're more likely to continue reading paragraphs that contain a variety of sentence structures. Readers are also more willing to read paragraphs that flow easily from one to another. Lead the reader from one idea to the next by implementing careful transitions.

You can use any of a variety of transition techniques:

>> **Words like *furthermore, also, for example, first, next, finally, however,* and *therefore* show the relationship that paragraphs have to one another.**

>> **Referring to previous paragraphs by repeating key words and ideas or using words like *this, these, those,* and *that* ties together the thoughts of several paragraphs.** Don't use *this, these, those,* and *that* alone, however. "This has been very confusing for all of us" is ambiguous. The following is better: "This breakdown in communication has been very confusing for all of us."

>> **You can also provide transition by foretelling future topics by ending paragraphs with sentences that foreshadow what's coming next.** For example, you might end a paragraph by saying, "Another feature of our office management system is automated billing." The next paragraphs would then discuss automated billing.

Specific documents

Every written work has a purpose and every work has a reader. Focusing on who will read a document — and why — will make writing that document much easier. Letters should contain introductions, bodies, and conclusions. Begin each letter or memo by stating its purpose and noting any enclosures. Provide specific information, and close with a short summary and a recap of any action that is required by the receiver of the communication.

Briefs and legal memos are much easier to write if you organize the information into three parts: (1) The **introduction** includes the purpose of the document, a statement of the case, and a list of the relevant issues. (2) The discussion of each of the issues by careful application of law to fact makes up the **body** of the argument. (3) The **conclusion** summarizes the answer to each issue. All three elements are essential for a complete organization and a persuasive presentation of the argument.

REMEMBER

We include examples of legal memos in the online content at www.dummies.com/go/paralegalcareer2e.

The structure of court documents, like pleadings and motions, follows specific rules. Their introduction consists of the caption and the statement of purpose. The purpose is then more specifically outlined in the document's text, which explains the elements of the case or the kind of information requested, depending on the type of document. Finally, the purpose is summarized in the *ad damnum* clause. The text of a court document should contain all the elements necessary to achieve the desired result and nothing more. Its information should be clear and precise. (For more about drafting legal documents, see Chapter 10.)

Proofreading: Polishing the Finished Product

Your knowledge of grammar and sentence structure paired with proper punctuation and careful planning will result in powerful writing! Great writers utilize one other important tool: proofreading. Don't neglect proofreading because of time constraints or laziness. The process of proofreading can make a fair document good and a good document great. With a little practice and the use of available technology, proofreading can become a nearly painless procedure.

When proofreading, focus first on the sentences, and read the three main elements of each sentence: the subject, verb, and third element. Ask the following questions:

>> Is the message powerful?

>> Is the message clouded by too many extraneous elements?

>> Is the sentence constructed and punctuated properly?

>> Do the adjectives and adverbs describe what they're intended to describe?

If the answer to any of these questions is no, rework the sentence.

Next, examine the paragraphs by asking the following questions:

>> Does each paragraph contain one main topic?

>> Is the sentence structure varied?

>> Do the paragraphs flow together well?

>> Is the writing interesting?

>> Would a reader who is unfamiliar with the information understand what is written?

If the answer to any of these questions is no, structure the paragraphs more carefully.

Next, check the document for errors in spelling and typing. Spell-check programs are excellent tools for the busy paralegal, but don't rely on them exclusively. Spell-check programs will miss errors in forming plurals and verb tenses. After spellchecking the document, reread it to make sure you didn't miss anything. Then have your supervisor or a colleague reread the document. You're less likely to spot your own errors than someone else is.

Avoiding Plagiarism

Plagiarism may not seem to be a big concern in legal writing. After all, much legal writing doesn't seem good enough to warrant theft! Besides, spending hours and hours citing statutes and quoting judicial opinions is not called plagiarism; it's called being a paralegal! Just make sure you properly cite those laws and opinions to help establish the legal authority of your argument.

Sometimes you'll be called upon to cite studies, book, reports, and other copyrighted material. For example, you may cite a scientific report in a brief concerning a tort claim. If you fail to give proper credit to the authors of the report, that's plagiarism.

To avoid plagiarism, be sure to cite the source of all unoriginal material. When using outside sources, put any portions directly quoted inside quotations marks or set off as indented quotations.

You don't always have to quote material word-for-word. Often, you'll want the authority of the source and the conclusion reached, but not the exact wording. In those cases, paraphrase the ideas in your own words. Don't change the conclusions of the court decision, scientific study, investigative report, or book you're citing, and be careful not to credit the judge, scientist, or author with ideas he didn't express. Even when you paraphrase, cite the authority it came from.

TIP

The key to avoiding plagiarism is simple: Give credit to the sources you use. Besides, citing sources has the added bonus of strengthening your arguments.

need to) how computers and
networks work

» Applying cool software applications
in the law office

» Catching the wave of online law
resources

» Taking advantage of technology in
the courtroom

Chapter **17**

Using Technology in Law

Recent technological advances have forever changed the way that law offices function. A typical law office 30 years ago communicated with telephones plugged into the wall. Without the invention of voicemail, office assistants took written messages and put them in the appropriate receiver's office box. Legal secretaries took dictation and typed up letters and legal documents on typewriters until the 1980s when word processors finally eliminated the need for correction fluid and carbon paper. Almost every law office contracted with a local courier service to file legal documents with the courts before e-filing allowed for almost instant delivery.

One of the more significant technological advances involves the way legal professionals conduct legal research. In 1973, Lexis Advance began offering computerized legal research as a subscription service. In 1975, West Publishing began a competing service called Westlaw. Prior to these innovations, attorneys and law clerks researched the law in law libraries using multivolume series of statutes and cases, the way it had been done for more than a century. Only in the last few decades have these computerized legal research resources been made widely available through a friendlier pricing structure.

In this chapter, we introduce you to the ways that computer technology has enhanced the efficiency of law practices. We show you how cloud networks, specialized software, Internet resources, and laptop computers and tablets have revolutionized the way law offices conduct business.

Operating Computer Hardware and Networks in the Law Office

In addition to the computer that occupies your desk (and the ones that occupy the desks of everyone else in your office), your office probably has access to a *server*. The server may be actual computer hardware with a powerful processor and large storage capacity, or your firm may store files and backups in the cloud. Firms use servers to store large amounts of data that can be accessed by all members of the firm.

TIP

A company server provides three important services:

>> **It's a place where you can save files.** The server is a place to store important files that's safer than your PC's hard drive.

>> **It allows multiple users to access a file that's saved to the server.** For example, if you're working on a memo with another paralegal, you could begin the document and save it to the server. Later, your colleague could access the document and finish writing it. You could make any necessary changes and alert the attorney working on the case that you're finished. The attorney could then view the document and request changes, if necessary. The document moves among multiple staff members, but in reality it always resides in a central location on the server.

>> **It provides updated virus protection and a firewall.** When you're working on your home computer, you have your own virus protection. Your Internet provider usually gives you the pipeline to the Internet but doesn't protect you from the things that might come down that pipe. Law firms invest thousands of dollars in computer equipment and have to protect confidential information, so they install firewalls and advanced virus protection software on their servers to keep viruses and hackers from infiltrating the system.

WARNING

If you work for a small firm that doesn't use a server, you're probably responsible for backing up data and updating virus protection software on your own computer. Make sure that you keep on top of these tasks, or you could lose very valuable information or expose confidential information to hackers.

Getting Savvy on Software Applications for the Law Office

Computer hardware doesn't vary much, so if you're familiar with your own PC, you'll be comfortable with any office's setup. You may not be completely familiar with the kinds of software that are loaded on the law office computer, however. Attorneys make wide use of traditional, well known software programs (such as the Microsoft Office programs and Google products) for most of their daily office activities. But just as an engineering firm may use a special drafting program and a medical office takes advantage of specialized software for managing patients' accounts and records, law firms may have unique software programs that handles client records and billing, conflict detection, filing deadlines, and other matters that are crucial to the successful practice of law. Potential employers expect you to know the basics of standard software programs and may be more apt to hire you if you're familiar with the law-office-specific software programs.

Sticking with standard office software

In addition to law-specific software, law offices trust the more familiar programs that are absolutely essential to the practice of law. You use these tried-and-true programs for standard activities like these:

>> Word processing

>> Working with data

>> Sending emails

>> Making presentations

>> Keeping track of deadlines

Processing lots and lots of words

Probably the most important computer application for law offices is the one that has replaced the typewriter: word processing. Word processing offers the same advantages to law firms that it does for everyone:

>> **You can make changes to a document without retyping it.**

>> **You can save commonly used forms and clauses as templates to use over and over again.** In most areas of law, you apply the same wording repeatedly in standard documents, so this feature comes in handy.

Law offices commonly use Microsoft Word to process their documents and some offices use Google Docs. The features of the word processing programs resemble each other, so if you're familiar with one, you should easily be able to pick up the attributes of the others.

TIP

Become familiar with word processing programs and their important features, like creating templates, which allow you to automatically format commonly created documents like memos, filings, motions, wills, and bankruptcy forms. If you take the time to create a template for each type of document you produce, you can save yourself valuable time and the clients valuable dollars in terms of hourly billings. Who knows? You may share your templates with lawyers and other paralegals and become the toast of your firm!

If you're not already familiar with commonly used word processing programs, take the time to read the latest edition of *Microsoft Office For Dummies* by Dan Gookin (John Wiley & Sons, Inc.).

Organizing data

Spreadsheets and databases systematize information so that it's easily assessable. You can store data like billable hours and client contact information in either type of program. Spreadsheets (like Microsoft Excel or Google Sheets) tend to be easier to set up and use, but database programs (like Airtable) allow for more flexibility. The advantages of both programs are simple:

» **They organize and make accessible essential facts.** And they do a better job of it than a paper file system, because the data are at your fingertips instead of in a file cabinet.

» **They save space.** Storing paper files can get out of hand, but handling a growing database is as easy as adding more memory to the server.

» **They save time.** You can import information like addresses directly from a database or spreadsheet into documents, which helps you avoid typos. You enter data only once and then transfer it where it needs to go.

Because many law offices rely on standard spreadsheet and database programs, you may be able to get by just knowing how to use Microsoft Office programs or Google apps. However, specific software created for law firms manage client information even more efficiently than standard spreadsheets and databases. We talk about these programs in the "Navigating special software for law firms" section, later in this chapter.

REMEMBER

You can find out more about the Office programs in *Microsoft Office For Dummies* by Wallace Wang (John Wiley & Sons, Inc.).

Communicating online

Email can be a great timesaver in the modern workplace. It can also be a great timewaster. Communicating by email instead of telephone allows you to respond to and contact people on *your* time schedule. You don't have to wait for that person to get back from lunch to ask a question, and you can wait until you've enjoyed your lunch to answer someone else's questions of you. Plus, email gives you a written record of your correspondence, so you have proof of what other people have said.

REMEMBER

The emails you transmit may be saved by your law office (or the people you send the messages to) forever, so make sure you think carefully before you send. (For tips on writing professional emails, see Chapter 16.)

For all its benefits, email has some drawbacks. You can be bombarded with a ton of emails every day, and without a system to organize them, you may find yourself wasting away the time that online communication is supposed to save you.

To maximize the advantages and minimize wasted time, you need a convenient program to maintain control of your email messages. Spam control on your office's email server allows you to automatically filter out pesky advertisements and other unsolicited communications. And your email system should allow you to sort email in categories (for example, by client) and mark emails that require future attention. Again, standard email software like Microsoft Outlook does an adequate job of filing emails and keeping track of contacts. But many law offices, especially the larger ones, incorporate their email programs into the client management database so that communications by clients become part of the case history.

Presenting the evidence

Other common programs, such as Microsoft PowerPoint, Google Slides, and Prezi, provide paralegals with an easy way to display and analyze tangible evidence. You can easily create impressive presentations of evidence, complete with sound, to inform your clients and supervising attorney and display to the court during the trial process.

REMEMBER

For more information on how to use presentation software, check out *Microsoft Office For Dummies* by Wallace Wang or *Prezi For Dummies* by Stephanie Diamond (both published by John Wiley & Sons, Inc.).

Maintaining calendars

A law practice requires following a series of deadlines, so you must maintain an accurate and reliable calendar to keep track of important cutoff dates mandated by your supervising attorney and imposed by the court. Missing a deadline by even a little bit can jeopardize the client's case. The legal team you work for may use computerized calendars, paper ones, or a combination of both. (You can find out more about law office calendars in Chapter 18.)

Computerized calendars appear in many types of software programs, like Google Calendar or Microsoft Outlook, but, again, many firms make the calendar part of their case management software. More sophisticated computerized calendars set deadlines automatically based on preprogrammed case schedules and customized due dates for each member of the legal team.

TIP

One of the first tasks to master when you start working within a legal team is the office calendar system. When you have the calendar system down, you stay on top of crucial office deadlines.

Navigating special software for law firms

Unique software created just for law firms brings together the functions included in other separate software programs so that everything works together. You can manage law office responsibilities — such as client billing, conflict detection, and case management — with one complete program tailored not only to the practice of law in general but also to particular areas of law. Legal professionals enter important data in one place and the software applies to all the applicable areas. The specialized software programs usually integrate with standard word processing and accounting software so that the entire computerized operation runs smoothly.

Here are just a few of the tasks a complete legal software program can accomplish:

>> **Managing billable hours:** A law office bills the client for the hours that attorneys and paralegal spend working on a case. Special software programs keep track of the duties you perform for a particular case and transfer the total hours to accounting software for client billing. You then verify the hours before the software generates an invoice.

>> **Providing case management:** The case manager inputs the duties required for the successful development of each case and assigns these duties to the responsible member of the legal team. The software alerts each team member of her duties and deadlines and allows the case manager to check everyone's progress. The software also links together databases containing case notes, client files, and documents so you have integrated access to the materials involved in the case — a great help when you're researching a case or drafting memos and motions.

- >> **Detecting conflicts of interest:** Because the program controls and links all office data, you can search the system for conflicts involving former or current cases you're involved in. An important ethical consideration for you as a legal professional is to avoid conflicts of interest. This feature is especially important for large firms who deal with many cases. You may find yourself working on a case where one of the opposing parties happens to be a former client.

- >> **Keeping track of important dates:** Specialized software programs contain calendar systems developed specifically for legal professionals and the areas of law they work in. Often, these programs set deadlines automatically depending on the procedural rules of your state and legal specialty.

TIP

Although learning all the possible specialized legal programs will probably help you land your dream job, it's probably not practical. If you have a good understanding of standard word processing, database, spreadsheet, email, and accounting programs, you can quickly pick up the ins and out of specialized legal programs.

REMEMBER

If you want to introduce yourself to some of the law software programs currently available and maybe try a demo or two, check out the links at www.dummies.com/go/paralegalcareer2e.

Surfing the Net: Online Resources for Legal Professionals

You likely access a vast quantity of information from the Internet on your phone, tablet, or laptop continually throughout the day to shop, plan travel, or resolve the dispute with your friend over which musical group sang that hip hop hit from the 90s. The legal profession takes advantage of the Internet in specific ways, like conducting investigation and research and communicating face-to-face over long distances.

Researching the globe

Attorneys present two kinds of information in court: the facts of the case and the applicable law. To find out the facts of the case, you have to act like a private investigator. You may interview witnesses, gather evidence, and piece together the events that make up your client's case. (You can find more about how you do this in Chapter 11.) Through legal research, you'll also assist with uncovering the law that applies to the client's case, the law that demonstrates why the client should prevail. You can use the Internet to uncover both the facts and the law.

PLAYING ON THE INTERNET: DON'T DO IT

Searching the Internet plays an integral role in conducting business, but some employees undoubtedly abuse it. Estimates are that some employees spend a substantial portion of work hours doing personal business. The practice of going to work and using company equipment to conduct personal business, such as paying bills, making love matches, and shopping online even has a name. It's called *reverse telecommuting*, because instead of using technology to work from home, employees engage in activities at work that should more appropriately be conducted in their own homes on their own time. Fortunately for law firms, most paralegals are far too busy to waste a lot of time on online dating sites!

The hours you spend at work will be billed to specific clients. That means that you focus your attention on the case of the particular client who's paying for that portion of your time. Billing hours to a client for time you spend checking personal email, posting pictures on Facebook, doing your taxes, downloading music, or any of the other crazy things people are known to do at work is unethical. In fact, false billing is actually a crime for legal professionals. So, take care of your personal business at home or during breaks, and don't bill clients for time unless you actually worked for that client during those hours!

Websites give you information about a person's assets and current residence. The Web also provides you with free and paid access to federal and state statutes and case law, which makes your job as a paralegal much easier than it was in the days before the Internet.

For instance, as we discuss in Chapter 13, attorneys need to validate every case they find through legal research to find out if it's still good law. This job usually falls in the lap of the paralegal. With the help of online law libraries, like Westlaw and Lexis/Nexis, you don't have to leave the law office to find out whether the valuable court opinion the client's case is hinging upon has been overruled. Online legal resources provide the most up-to-date source of this kind of information available.

Online legal services assist you with actual legal research as well. You can use them to search for and find cases and statutes and secondary sources, such as law reviews, journals, and newspapers. If you already know the case citation or statute you're looking for, you can enter that information as well. (For specific advice on how to use these valuable research tools, turn to Chapter 13.)

WARNING

Don't rely solely on online resources for conducting legal research. You may decide to work in a small law office that can't afford to use pricey online services for its standard legal research assignments. Make sure you know how to use the bricks-and-mortar law library as well as the virtual one, so you're ready for any position that you're offered.

Meeting over the miles

Technological advances have enabled people in distant locations to see and hear each other in real time. Web conferencing (or video conferencing) allows people to converse over the Internet similarly to a conference phone call, but with pictures. Attorneys can use video conferencing to cut travel costs.

Conference phone calls involving multiple parties have been possible for many years. However, calls among three or more persons can be awkward, because the lack of visual cues leaves everyone wondering when to talk and whether the other parties are listening. You also can't view charts, photos, or other visuals that often play an important part in a typical meeting. For this reason, conference phone calls can be a poor substitute for face-to-face meetings.

By contrast, video conferencing provides a reasonable substitute for many in-person meetings. Certainly, traveling to conduct a meeting, conference, or interview in person still has its place. But in many circumstances, you can conduct face-to-face meetings over a high-speed network.

Special applications of Web conferencing can improve a law firm's efficiency. Although other types of businesses may use Web conferencing primarily to conduct meetings with employees based in other regions of the country, law firms use the technology to save money for their clients and add an additional level of service.

Attorneys may conduct depositions using Web conferencing. Because attorneys for both parties to a case can see and hear the witness, they can conduct examination and cross-examination of an out-of-town witness without being in the room. Web conferencing probably wouldn't be used to interview the key witness in a multimillion-dollar lawsuit, however, because, although Web conferencing is a very good substitute for in-person interaction, it may lack the nuances gained from being in the room with a witness. It's a matter of weighing the time and expense of travel with the advantage of communicating face-to-face with the witness.

Carting Computers into the Courtroom

The use of tablets and laptops in the courtroom make it easier for lawyers to advance their cases during trial, and electronic exhibits are overtaking printed posters as the way to convey evidence, like photographs, to the jury.

Cutting the cords: Wireless technology

Smart phones, laptops, and tablets seem ideal for use in a court of law. Attorneys and paralegals make the most of the portability in court for a number of purposes:

>> To organize and access client files

>> To access a voluminous trial notebook online rather than in multiple binders

>> To conduct spontaneous legal research or view laws and statutes saved to the cloud

>> To present evidence to the jury in multimedia presentations

>> To keep notes of witness testimony, oral arguments, and evidence presented during trial

>> To request information from staff in the law office by phone, text, or email

A paralegal is even more likely to have access to wireless technology in the courtroom than the lead attorney is. The lead attorney focuses on what's happening in the courtroom at the moment, but attorneys or paralegals assisting with the case scurry to keep notes and obtain urgent information. For example, during trial, you may aid your supervising attorney by taking notes on and providing your opinion of the testimony presented. Your legal knowledge and heavy involvement in the case prepares you for what to observe during witness testimony. Your observations may include discrepancies in a witness's testimony that you can verify by checking your phone or tablet for a summary of that witness's prior deposition testimony. Or you may watch for juror reactions that you can analyze using your notes during jury selection. Or you may be in charge of managing and displaying the evidence and exhibits through a slide presentation of photographic evidence you helped to develop.

Recognizing the downside of technology

WARNING

Technology in the courtroom sounds great, and it is. But watch out for possible problems inherent with relying on your laptop in the courtroom:

>> **Ignoring the proceedings:** When you work on a laptop or tablet, avoid the danger of getting so engrossed in what you're doing that you miss important elements of the trial itself. This may be especially difficult if you're working online. Don't make the mistake of reading your personal email while the most important part of the case passes unnoticed!

>> **Alienating the jury:** In most cases, juries appreciate the accessibility of multimedia presentations, but be careful that your presentations don't overwhelm the jury. If you're dealing with serious or sensitive evidence, don't use flashy graphics or fonts that the jury may consider inappropriate.

Watch your reactions in the courtroom. Another reason to refrain from checking Instagram during trial is that you may read something funny and begin smiling or, worse, laughing at an inappropriate moment, which could easily alienate the jury and lose the case for the client.

>> **Compromising confidentiality:** People behind you and adjacent to you may be able to view your laptop screen, so position your laptop so that it's not visible to others. Keep your tablet with you at all times just like would confidential paper documents. And protect access to files with a password just in case your computer falls into the wrong hands.

>> **Depreciating the decorum of the courtroom:** Judges guard the respectability of their courtrooms very carefully. Avoid doing anything that annoys the judge or shines a bad light on the paralegal profession. For example, your typing may distract the judge, the jury, or an attorney. If someone requests that you stop typing, you must oblige. *Remember:* You're representing your firm as well as the paralegal profession, so don't compromise your client's chances in the case by your behavior.

>> **Forgetting the basics:** Technology plays an increasingly important role in the legal profession, but remember that technology doesn't win cases — hard work does. Technology is just another tool to allow lawyers and paralegals to work more efficiently for the clients. Just because you can do legal research online doesn't mean you can get sloppy. Consult all important sources, including those that may not appear online, and make sure you bring along backup paper documents and exhibits in case you experience a hardware or software problem during a hearing or meeting.

Even with technology, your job remains the same: to work zealously on behalf of the client. That's the heart of the legal profession and your primary duty as a paralegal. Technology just makes that job a whole lot easier!

Chapter 18

Law Office Management 101

How much time you spend engaged in law office management depends on the type and size of firm you work for. Most large firms employ a separate staff to take care of the majority of the daily organization activities. But no matter what size firm you work for, as a paralegal you'll probably end up doing some managing and organizing of the law office. If you work for a small firm, you could be responsible for the management of the entire office. In a larger firm, you'll probably be responsible for just your own schedule and maybe that of your supervising attorney. Although it may seem pretty mundane, proper office management is crucial to the productivity of any law environment, so this chapter focuses on proper management of time, files, and monthly billings.

Buying Time: Management Systems

When you think about it, law firms sell their time to their clients, so the value of managing minutes, hours, and days is absolutely crucial. The legal process consists of a series of deadlines that you must meet if you don't want to jeopardize a client's case. Good time management produces efficiency and profit, but poor time management can terminate legal careers. If you have trouble organizing your time, now's a great time to learn and practice time management skills.

Putting together a good time management system isn't complicated. It just requires an interactive use of simple devices, such as lists, calendars, and records. You can keep track of time with pen and paper or on the computer, but you'll probably find that a combination of both is the most efficient.

Marking the days: The calendar system

Keeping track of time begins with a good calendar system. If you've never used a daily planner before, you'd better get used to using one. Calendars are absolutely essential to the smooth running of any law office.

Many malpractice insurance companies require a specific calendaring system with more than one person handling the information. So, consult the insurance policy or contact the agent before you initiate any changes to the way your office keeps a calendar.

The master calendar

Every law office must maintain a master calendar that the attorney, legal secretary, paralegal, and other staff can easily access. It's usually available on the computer network for everyone to see. The main calendar keeps track of all the important events for the entire office, including the following:

>> Court appearances

>> Important filing deadlines

>> Appointments

>> Meetings and conferences

>> Vacations and personal days of all staff members

Figure 18-1 shows a sampling of two weeks of a master calendar.

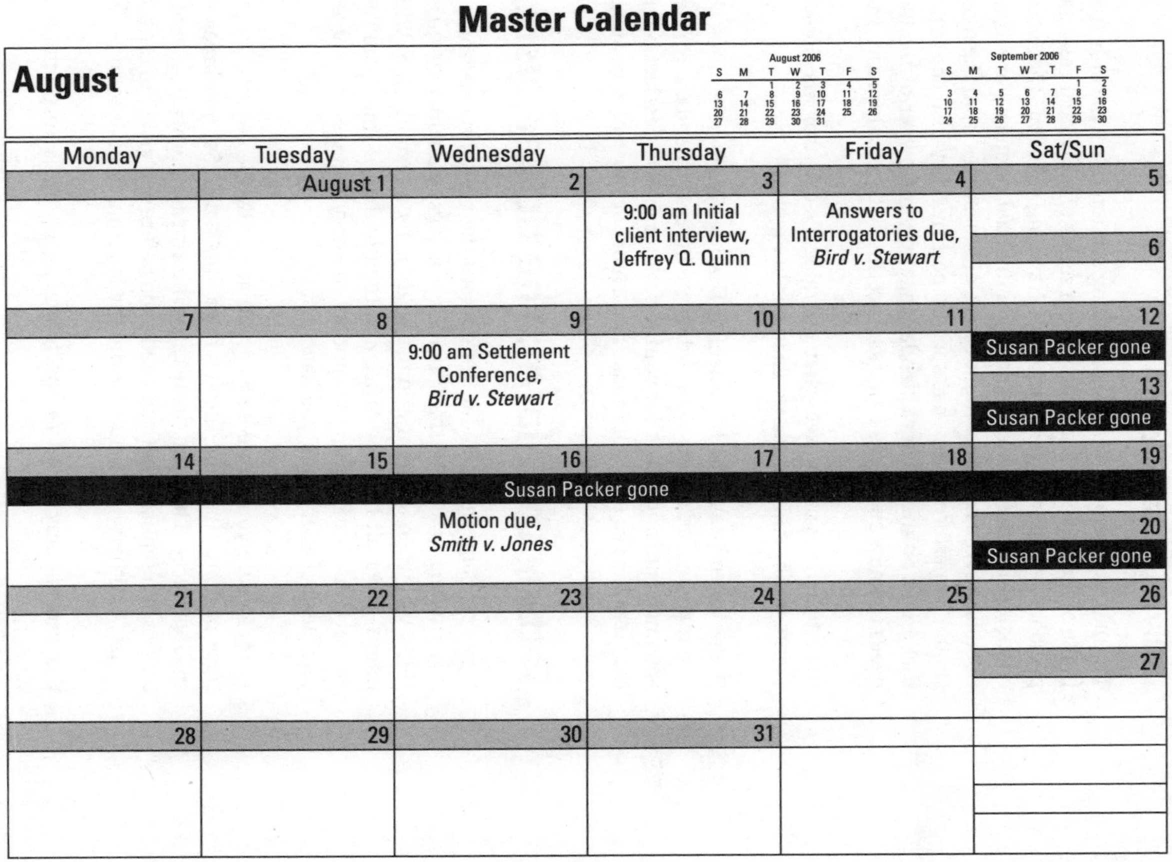

Master Calendar

August

Monday	Tuesday	Wednesday	Thursday	Friday	Sat/Sun
	August 1	2	3	4	5
			9:00 am Initial client interview, Jeffrey Q. Quinn	Answers to Interrogatories due, *Bird v. Stewart*	6
7	8	9	10	11	12
		9:00 am Settlement Conference, *Bird v. Stewart*			Susan Packer gone
14	15	16	17	18	13
					Susan Packer gone
		Susan Packer gone			19
	Motion due, *Smith v. Jones*				Susan Packer gone
21	22	23	24	25	20
					26
					Susan Packer gone
28	29	30	31		27

August 2006
S M T W T F S
6 7 1 2 3 4 5
13 14 8 9 10 11 12
20 21 15 16 17 18 19
27 28 22 23 24 25 26
29 30 31

September 2006
S M T W T F S
3 4 1 2
10 11 5 6 7 8 9
17 18 12 13 14 15 16
24 25 19 20 21 22 23
26 27 28 29 30

© John Wiley & Sons

FIGURE 18-1: A master calendar such as this one is where you record all the key events for the entire office.

Individual calendars

The master calendar (see the preceding section) isn't the only time keeping device in the office, though. You'll also use a series of individual calendars, like your own personal calendar or the attorney's traveling calendar, that you regularly cross-check against the master calendar. Individual calendars are also called *redundant* calendars because they contain copies of the entries from the master calendar that should be performed by that specific person. They also contain events and tasks that aren't on the master calendar that only the owner of the individual calendar needs to know about (like a lunch meeting with a malpractice insurance agent).

In Figure 18-2 you can see what a paralegal's calendar may look like based on the events on the sample master calendar in Figure 18-1.

TIP

Online calendars allow for calendar sharing. The whole office shares the master calendar and can view other staff members' calendars to view all upcoming appointments and check for conflicts. You can also deselect calendars to simplify the view and see only your tasks and events or those of your supervising attorney.

Setting the alarm: The tickler system

If you're using the calendar system (see the preceding section), you can set up a *tickler system* (a system that "tickles," or jogs, your memory) that automatically alerts you when something must be done by a certain time. With the number of things going on in a law office and the number of times you're interrupted in a day, even if you have an exceptional memory you won't be able to keep track in your head of everything you have to do.

To make sure you complete a certain action by the day it's due, you have to keep track of more than just the final deadline dates. So, you break each project into smaller pieces. Then you tickle those interim assignments, giving yourself enough time to accomplish what you need to do before you give it to the attorney to review, revise, or otherwise handle before the looming final deadline.

You can use any or all of the following methods to produce a reliable tickler system.

>> **Enter deadlines on the office's master calendar with an appropriate lead time.** So, if something is due on the 15th of the month, you also enter a reminder entry on the 10th.

>> **Use a *document control register* to track deadlines.** In this system, you give a document control number to every document that leaves or comes into the office. Then you construct a register that lists the status of all documents by their control number, which you consult regularly for unfinished business and approaching deadlines.

Individual Calendar

August

Monday	Tuesday	Wednesday	Thursday	Friday	Sat/Sun
	August 1	2	3	4	5
	Complete research of answers to interrogatories, *Bird v. Stewart*	Draft questions for settlement conference, *Bird v. Stewart*	Set up file for J. Quinn	Answers to interrogatories due, *Bird v. Stewart*	
	Make sure SP's calendar is clear during vacation	Give interrogatories research to SP	9:00 am Initial client interview, Jeffrey Q. Quinn	Draft motion, *Smith v. Jones*	6
				Submit questions for settlement to SP	
7	8	9	10	11	12
Submit motion to SP, *Smith v. Jones*		9:00 am Settlement Conference, *Bird v. Stewart*		Make sure SP returns and signs motion, *Smith v. Jones*	Susan Packer gone
14	15	16	17	18	13
					Susan Packer gone
		Susan Packer gone			19
21	22	23	24	25	Susan Packer gone
File motion, *Smith v. Jones*		Motion due, *Smith v. Jones*			20
					Susan Packer gone
28	29	30	31		26
					Susan Packer gone
					27

© John Wiley & Sons

FIGURE 18-2: An individual calendar helps you keep track of your own schedule or the attorney's schedule.

>> **Note deadlines through the use of a *tickler file* (also known as a *suspense file*).** If you want be absolutely sure you never miss a deadline, you can supplement your management system with a paper-based tickler file. You create 31 separate file folders for the days of the current month, 31 separate file folders for the days of the next month, and 12 file folders for the months of the year. Then you make a copy of the first page of every document that requires a response or action. These pages go into the file folder for a day that's five or ten days before the action deadline. All you have to do is check the tickler file every morning and enter the required actions on your personal work schedule or to-do list.

The key, of course, for any of these methods is to check them daily and to have a personal tickler system to transfer information to. For example, if you know you're responsible for gathering information to be used to answer interrogatories that are due at the end of the following week, you'd tickle this project much earlier on your own calendar than it appears on the master calendar. The tickler gives you ample time to gather the information and present it to your supervising attorney in time for the answers to be drafted, reviewed, signed, and sent.

TIP

Individual ticklers are also quite handy if you're out of the office unexpectedly and another person has to temporarily handle some of your workload. With your awe-somely organized tickler in hand, your co-worker will have no doubts about what has been accomplished and what remains to be done.

Getting it in writing: The to-do list

From the tickler system (see the preceding section), you move to the daily *to-do list*, which, not surprisingly, is a list of all the things you need to accomplish that day, transferred from your tickler system. You'll definitely create one for yourself every day, and you may have to make a daily to-do list for your attorney, too.

Each individual worker in a law office should have a separate to-do list. This list can be a handwritten list of things to do today, which requires a daily review of pending work and priorities, or it can be a similar list kept in the computer. Different members of the staff may use different types of lists. The best lists are ones that don't list more than you can do in a day and that prioritize your activities so you know what you need to do first. You can easily prioritize your list by designating each activity with an A, B, or C. You do all the A activities first, then the Bs, and finally the Cs. Anything you don't finish one day just goes on the next day's list, probably with a higher priority than before.

Figure 18-3 shows what a to-do list would look like for Friday, August 4, based on the sample calendar (refer to Figures 18-2 and 18-3) with a few last-minute assignments added in.

To-Do: Friday, August 4			
✓ Priority	Client	Time	Activity
✓ A	Marissa Bird	9:00-9:15 15 minutes	Send answers to interrogatories in Bird v. Stewart
B	Larry Smith		Draft motion for Smith v. Jones, due 8/16. (Est. 1 hour.)
✓ A	Marissa Bird	9:15-9:30 15 minutes	Review and submit questions for settlement conference to SP.
A	Jeffrey Quinn		Draft a demand letter for Jeffrey Q. Quinn requesting damages in the amount of $50,000 for injury. Submit to SP by 5:00 today. (Est. 1 hour.)
C	N/A		Reorganizing filing cabinet to accommodate more files. (Est. 30 minutes)
	Larry Smith	10:00-10:20 20 minutes	Phone call re: confirming details for motion in Smith v. Jones
B	Larry Smith		Review Stevens depo 7/3 re: Steven's demeanor/how credible as witness? Smith v. Jones. (Est. 30 min.)

FIGURE 18-3: Your daily to-do list helps you prioritize your tasks and work toward your goals.

© John Wiley & Sons

Of course, in addition to the events listed on the master and individual calendars, your supervising attorney will give you other daily assignments. When you get an assignment, write it on your calendar and/or to-do list right away, along with the exact instructions provided by the attorney. Estimate the time involved and enter any deadlines. Take a look at the fourth entry in Figure 18-3 for an example.

TIP

Remembering everything about an assignment would be a challenge even if you never experienced an interruption, but unfortunately, most people aren't so lucky! Most law offices are a bustle of constant activity. The last thing you want to do is waste your employer's time by asking to have an assignment repeated, so get it all down the first time: take written note or text or email yourself the information. And, if the instructions are unclear, ask questions until you feel comfortable with the assignment.

If you keep your to-do list with you throughout the day (in written form or on your phone), you have evidence of your assignment in sight at all times. You can easily get distracted and lose sight of what you're doing, especially when you're conducting research or even doing something simple like searching for a document in a file. You'll save a lot of time if you only have to glance at your notes to remind you of your purpose.

Checking off completed activities on your list is one of the best feelings in the world! As you cross things off, keep a log of how much time you spent on each item and the name of the client so you'll be prepared for billing when the time comes (see the next section). Then, at the end of each day, you just have to review your list to see what you've finished and what remains to be done. If you're in the middle of an activity that you can't finish, note where you are on your to-do list for the next day and put away the file — this clears the clutter from your desk and gives you a starting-off point for the next day.

TIP

Your to-do lists are important documents, so you'll need to save them for later reference. You can keep them chronologically in an expandable file, or you can keep your lists in a bound day-planner notebook or three-ring binder.

Keeping Account: Billing Systems

A paralegal's time may be billed to the client at an hourly rate lower than the attorney's, so you'll need to keep track of every minute you spend working on a client's case. You then have to provide documentation of your time to the accounts receivable department of the firm so it can generate invoices. You need to keep track of your time even if your office handles a client on a *contingency fee* basis (where an attorney gets paid by receiving a portion of the client's settlement). That way you have an accounting in the billing records if there's ever a question of what duties you've performed for a client and when.

If *you're* the accounts receivable department as well as the office paralegal, you need to generate invoices to clients on a set schedule. The invoicing process involves recording billable hours and fee, compiling those hours and fees by client, creating an invoice for each client, and keeping track of unpaid balances.

Recording time

Time is the element in an attorney's inventory that has a direct dollar value, so a law practice should keep track of it just as a jewelry store keeps track of its diamonds. A number of commercial systems exist that keep track of time, some computerized and some manual. Some of the most popular accounting software programs, such as QuickBooks and Peachtree, contain stopwatches that you can set while you're conducting a billable activity to keep track of your time. The program then computes the value of the activity based on your hourly billable rate, associates the time with a specific client, and keeps track of it until you're ready to invoice the client. You don't need special software, though. Most word processing programs have the invoice templates and merge features you need to set up a billing procedure.

Regardless of the medium you use, both you and the attorney keep track independently of the time you each spend on each task for each client throughout the month. Even if you use a software program that records time for you, keeping track of your time on your personal calendar or to-do list is a good idea. You can also keep track on your to-do list of how long you spend on the phone, as shown in the sixth entry in Figure 18-3.

On the designated monthly billing day, the accounts receivable department at your firm will either transfer your activities to invoices in the accounting software or you'll submit a chronological list of the tasks you've performed for each client. If you're responsible for the billing, you'll compile the billable hours and fees for each client, prepare invoices, and usually submit them to the attorney for approval before you send them out.

Creating invoices

Recording time accurately is the first vital step in operating a profitable law office. The second vital step is to actually bill the clients for this time. The most efficient method for sending out bills on time is a simplified approach. Billing procedures vary widely depending upon the size and type of practice and the number of accounts receivable the firm has. Some firms may have a department dedicated solely to billing; others may use an independent firm to prepare their billings. Small firms usually rely upon the paralegal to perform this task.

The easiest way to manage accounts receivable in most law offices is through an accounting software program. The most popular programs, such as QuickBooks and Peachtree, allow you to compute time, record time, enter fees and other costs, and create invoices. You can enter time manually through a timesheet or you can have the software record time for you with its integrated stopwatch. You give the software a detailed description of the activity, associate it with a particular client, provide the hourly rate, and the software stores the information until you're ready to invoice. You can also associate filing and recording fees and other billable costs to a client whenever you record the firm's payment of those fees in the accounting software. Then, when you're ready to send out periodic invoices, you just pull up the invoice form, enter the client's name, and click a button. The software provides you with all the hours and fees associated with the client. You pick the ones you want to bill for and — abracadabra! — the invoice appears. It's that simple. If you're regular about entering time and fees into the accounting software, periodic billings can take only a few hours to complete!

REMEMBER

The online content at www.dummies.com/go/paralegalcareer2e provides a sample timesheet and its resulting invoice as generated by QuickBooks accounting software.

A Place for Everything: File Management

One thing's for sure: Law offices generate tons of paper documents. So, setting up and using a well-organized filing system is crucial to good law office management.

Maintaining a filing system

Odds are the law office you work for will already have an efficient filing system in place when you're hired. Large firms likely store most documents digitally by scanning them and saving them on their servers, but they may still need to hang on to original paper documents, so a paper-based filing system is also necessary. The main purpose of a filing system is to make important papers instantly accessible. Generally, law firms keep files in alphabetical order by client, but some firms use a numeric system. Although assigning numbers to clients requires a cross-reference index (usually kept on computer), the number system is helpful because it provides a way of aging cases chronologically and makes filing completed cases much easier than an alphabetical arrangement. Color-coded labels or folders help to distinguish types of cases, and colored dots or other symbols identify whether a client's case is in the pre-trial, trial, or post-trial stage.

Organizing documents in a file folder

In addition to a system for storing files, you also need a way to arrange papers within a file. The simplest procedure is to place the file's documents in chronological order with the latest information on top. This system makes for easy setup, but as the file grows, its earlier contents become less accessible. Therefore, most offices that use the chronological method also keep a log in the file as an index, usually adhered to the inner left side of the folder. Maintaining the index requires extra time for the one who oversees the files but makes finding specific documents easier.

TIP

Another system is to subdivide the folder into subject areas. This method requires the law office clerk to determine just where a filed document should go, but it eliminates having to log a document every time you take it out or put it in. This system is helpful for the attorney and paralegal because a file organized by subject provides the foundation for the trial notebook that the attorney and paralegal rely on during trial.

The kinds of subject areas you'd choose in this kind of system vary depending on the type of case. For instance, in a personal injury case, you may organize the file according to the following subjects:

>> Intake information (client interview; facts investigation; photos)

>> Initial pleadings (summons and complaint; responsive pleadings)

>> Discovery

>> Depositions

>> Notices

>> Correspondence

>> Notes

Subject areas in a domestic relations file would more likely include the following:

>> Initial pleadings (summons and petition; custody affidavit; response)

>> Temporary orders

>> Discovery

>> Financial affidavits and support worksheets

>> Property division

>> Notices

>> Correspondence

>> Notes

Storing old files

There's no law that says you have to keep closed case files, because the court maintains the legal record. But there are a few reasons to hang on to old files:

>> Closed cases can be valuable reference tools for new cases.

>> Old cases may reopen, particularly in domestic relations disputes.

>> Sometimes a client requests information contained in an old case file.

So, most law offices keep case files indefinitely, especially if they have the space. To conserve space in the work area and make frequently used files easy to get to, the main file cabinets only contain files for cases in progress. You can scan documents and store them online and/or keep files for closed cases in a convenient location either at the office or in a separate storage facility. In most law practices, the size of the active file system remains constant, but the closed file system continues to grow over time.

TIP

If you organize your active files alphabetically, changing to a numeric system for storing closed files is probably a good idea. Numeric filing lets you box up closed files and avoid the constant shuffling of files when you need to file newly closed ones alphabetically.

5

The Part of Tens

Examine crucial ethics standards essential to the paralegal career.

Review fundamental paralegal skills so you're a leg up on other paralegals.

Ensure a healthy paralegal career by observing important survival tips.

Chapter **19**

The Ten Most Important Rules of Ethics

Because ethics are so crucial for the profession, the legal community takes ethical violations by lawyers and paralegals very seriously. Avoiding the kind of ethical problems that can cause difficulty for you and the lawyers you work with is important. Luckily, you can avoid most ethical problems by paying particular attention to some important rules. Here are the ten most important rules of ethics.

Avoiding the Unauthorized Practice of Law

One of the easiest mistakes to make is also one of the most serious. Although many ethical violations are the result of a deliberate decision to do something wrong, the unauthorized practice of law often results when a paralegal tries to do too much. You may want to help a client so much that you begin performing tasks that only a licensed attorney may perform.

REMEMBER

You aren't allowed to have your own clients and you must work under the supervision of a licensed attorney. As long as you're properly supervised, you can perform numerous tasks on behalf of the client. The things paralegals are allowed to do vary slightly from state to state, so make sure to keep current on the rules of the state where you work.

Maintaining Client Confidentiality

As a legal professional, you have access to your office's clients' personal, private information. Your duty is to protect the confidentiality of that information. You may not share confidential information from any client with anyone, including members of your client's family, the judge, opposing lawyers, or the media. The only person you can discuss this confidential information with is the attorney who represents the client and supervises your work.

Disclosing Your Paralegal Status

You must clearly indicate that you're a paralegal when dealing with any client so no client mistakenly believes that you're a licensed attorney. You may not use business cards or other materials that create the impression that you're a licensed attorney (no matter what your mother tells her friends while playing mahjongg). Make sure that the clients you work with understand your role and responsibilities in the case, to avoid any possible misunderstandings.

Reporting Ethics Violations of Other Legal Professionals

When you have knowledge of fraud, deceit, dishonesty, or misrepresentation on the part of another legal professional, your duty to the legal profession requires that you disclose the information to the proper person, who in most cases is your supervising attorney. (If the person committing the ethical violation *is* your supervising attorney, you may report the problem to her superior; absent that option, report it to another trusted attorney or the state bar association.) Unethical behavior is so serious a threat to the legal profession that your failure to report such behavior, in itself, constitutes misconduct.

Disclosing Information to Prevent Death or Serious Bodily Harm

An exception to the client confidentiality rules occurs when you have confidential information that, if disclosed, may prevent a client from committing an act that could result in death or serious bodily harm. Your ethical duty to preserve a client's secrets is considered to be subordinate to the duty to prevent death or serious bodily harm to a client or others.

In other words, if your client says, "Hey, I'm planning to bump off my boss Monday morning," you have to tell someone — hiding behind the confidentiality rule won't cut it. Again, that "someone" is your supervising attorney.

Sharing Information with Your Supervising Attorney

Your duty to preserve your client's confidences doesn't extend to keeping secrets from the attorney who's supervising your work.

REMEMBER

You aren't allowed to actually have clients of your own, which means you must share all information with the attorney who represents the client. One way to get into serious ethical and professional trouble is to establish a secretive and improper relationship with a client that results in your coming between a client and his attorney.

Avoiding Conflicts of Interest

As a legal professional, you're in a special position of trust in relation to the client. As a result, you must always work for your client's benefit and avoid any actual (and potential) conflicts of interest. You must be free of compromising influences or loyalties arising from legal, business, or personal considerations. You also have to avoid working on cases that would conflict with your previous assignments.

This issue comes up more frequently with paralegals who work on a contract basis for several different attorneys. You can't provide work for an attorney for the defendant and an attorney for the plaintiff in the same case, for instance.

Obeying All Applicable Attorneys' Ethics Rules

In addition to the ethics rules that apply specifically to paralegals, you should adhere to the rules of ethics regarding attorneys. As a legal professional, you may perform tasks that are normally performed by a licensed attorney. Because you're doing the work of an attorney under attorney supervision, you have to follow the rules that govern attorneys.

Giving Something to the Community: Pro Bono Services

As a busy paralegal, you may feel as though you never have enough time. However, if at all possible, you should find some time to devote to assisting those who can't pay for legal work. Some paralegal codes of ethics call for paralegals to aspire to contribute a certain number of hours per year of *pro bono* (volunteer) work for persons of limited means or the organizations that help them.

Making Your Voice Heard: Supporting Efforts to Improve the Legal System

Many aspects of the U.S. legal system can be improved. Perhaps the most important of these is the lack of access to the court system for people with limited financial means. Throughout your career, you may find other aspects of the legal system that could use some reform. As a responsible legal professional, be sure to support efforts to improve the legal system. Some of the ways you can achieve this goal may be as ambitious as lobbying politicians to pass laws that enhance victims' rights or as simple as burning the midnight oil to make sure you've done all you can to strengthen a client's case.

Chapter **20**

Ten Things Every Paralegal Should Know

No paralegal knows everything. One of the great things about the legal profession is that you face new challenges all the time. Most of what you need to know as a paralegal you learn on the job as you gain experience. There are a few things, however, that you're expected to know when you start the job. If you know these ten things, you can start off your paralegal career on the right foot!

How to Ask for Help

At the top of the list of things you need to know as a paralegal is what to do when you *don't* know something. Throughout your career, you'll encounter concepts, tasks, and aspects of the law that you're not familiar with. There may even be times when you realize that you won't be able to complete an assignment on time. When this happens, you need to be able to ask your colleagues and your supervisor for assistance.

TIP

People who choose the legal profession are often confident go-getters, with a strong sense of their own abilities. If this is you, just remember that you're working for a client and billing that client for the hours that you work. So when you're tempted to try to do it all yourself, refrain! Everyone needs help — after all, the reason that you're working on the case in the first place is because the attorneys couldn't do it without *your* help!

Your Role

Legal professionals, including both lawyers and paralegals, work for clients by zealously representing the interests of those clients. As a paralegal, you have a more specific role. You perform tasks that would otherwise have to be performed by an attorney. However, you're always working under the supervision of a licensed attorney, and there are certain things that you're not allowed to do.

REMEMBER

The attorney is the one who gives out legal advice and who ultimately must make the decisions on how best to represent the client. You can certainly share your opinions with your supervising attorney, but you must not interfere with the attorney's ability to represent the client.

How to Communicate Effectively

Paralegals need to communicate effectively, both verbally and in writing. Whether you're meeting with the client, interviewing witnesses, or discussing discovery with opposing counsel, you must have good verbal communications skills, including grammatically precise phrasings. If you have any doubts about your ability to communicate correctly, check out *English Grammar For Dummies* by Geraldine Woods (John Wiley & Sons, Inc.) or take a grammar class.

The law is a written profession. Although some paralegals may not do much verbal communication, almost every paralegal has to know how to write effectively. Whether you're writing a memo to your supervising attorney discussing an element of the case, writing a letter to a potential witness, or preparing a document that will eventually be submitted to the court, you need to be able to use standard written English effectively. If your writing skills are lacking, enroll in a basic expository writing course.

The Value of Being Organized

Attorneys and clients don't care what your sock drawer looks like or if you have sports equipment piled up in your basement. But if you lose a client file, your supervisor will care! Paralegals need to be organized to work successfully. You can't afford to misplace client files or miss deadlines. Being organized means keeping your paper and computer files in order, as well as keeping track of your schedule and deadlines. You may have missed some deadlines in school, but you can't miss deadlines in the law office without serious ramifications.

Your Limitations

You can't do everything, and no one can work 24 hours a day! You need to have a sense of your own limitations and be able to respect those limits. Include in your daily life time to sleep, exercise, and enjoy your family and friends. You certainly want to be a team player and work as hard as possible for the client, but don't continually push yourself beyond your limits. Know what kind of schedule you're willing to work, and respect it as you choose an area of the law, look for work, and accept assignments.

Knowing your limits also means knowing what you're able to do. If you're asked to do something that is far beyond your level of experience or that you can't complete before the deadline, ask for assistance immediately.

WARNING

If you take on a task that you can't complete, the firm and the client suffer along with you!

How to Research

Eventually you'll become an expert in conducting the specific types of research that are common in your chosen area of law. You aren't expected to begin a job with a faultless knowledge of how to analyze and research intellectual property case issues, but you should start a position with a basic understanding of how to find statute and case law. Practice researching with printed volumes as well as on computers.

How to Use Technology

Modern paralegals are expected to have the ability to use current technology. Familiarize yourself with standard word processing and spreadsheet programs, as well as online scheduling, cloud file storage, and possibly even website management. As a legal professional, you use technology to conduct research and keep track of hours worked and client files. If you have limited computer skills, take short courses to improve them, and make a point of learning about computerized research during your paralegal training. Your employer won't expect to have to teach you how to use a computer (and you may find yourself guiding your supervising attorney's computer skills!).

The Rules of Professional Responsibility

Paralegals hold positions of trust, so know and observe the rules of ethics. Chapter 15 discusses the importance of attorney-client privilege, honest billing, reporting of ethical violations, and other ethical rules.

REMEMBER

Your behavior reflects on your firm, your client, and your profession, so dress and act professionally.

How to Draft Fundamental Legal Documents

You should enter any new paralegal position knowing how to draft demand letters, basic pleadings, internal memos of law, and motions. These fundamental documents form the basis for other documents you'll learn to draft as part of the specific area of law in which you work.

How to Weigh the Value of Paralegal Organizations

You should know that there are organizations specifically for paralegals. These local and national paralegal associations offer great networking, career development, and other services for members. (Chapter 2 has more information on the major players.)

TIP

Depending on where you live, you'll probably find you get more benefit from local organizations than you do from national ones.

Chapter **21**

Ten Survival Tips to Thrive in the Legal Environment

After you secure a paralegal position, you can do — and avoid doing — a few key things to make sure your career is successful. Here are few tips from working paralegals.

Continue Your Education

The practice of law changes, especially in specialized areas, like bankruptcy and estate planning, so keep on top of your profession by enrolling in continuing legal education courses periodically throughout your career. You'll not only gain valuable information but also good friendships with other paralegals. Local colleges, bar associations, and paralegal organizations are good sources for specialized paralegal courses.

Keep a Good Legal Dictionary Nearby

Legal terminology can seem like a foreign language (and in many cases it is — Latin!). To ensure that you understand every document you read and apply the correct terminology to the documents you draft, have easy access to a comprehensive and comprehensible legal dictionary, such as *Webster's New World Law Dictionary* (Wiley) or *Black's Law Dictionary*, Pocket Edition. websites such as `https://thelawdictionary.org/` and mobile apps provide immediate sources of legal definitions.

Maintain the Integrity of Your Profession

The paralegal profession requires strict adherence to moral and ethical codes and a strong sense of responsibility for the welfare of your office's client. Discipline yourself to maintain a sense of decorum when you work with attorneys, clients, and the courts. If you allow your integrity to slip, you've lost the trust of your supervisors, co-workers, and clients, and when your integrity is gone, getting it back is difficult.

Be Polite and Patient with Court Clerks

If you're in charge of scheduling hearings and filing documents with the courts, you may be dealing with court clerks. They're good people to have on your side, so be kind to them regardless of how frustrated they may make you. You'll probably need a favor from them later on, and you know the old saying about honey and vinegar. . . .

Take a Mind Reading Course

Most paralegals concur that their supervising attorneys expect them to know what they want before they express it. One paralegal even bought a crystal ball for the office to see if it could tell the staff what the boss was thinking!

You won't be able to literally read your supervising attorney's mind, but in the high-stress environment of the law office, having a sense of humor — and getting to know the operations and your supervisor's style well enough to anticipate needs before they arise — is a huge help.

And if you come across a good mind reading course, let us know!

Enjoy Problem Solving

Analyzing legal issues requires law professionals to think creatively. To be a good paralegal, you have to enjoy tackling tough problems. Legal problems are a lot like puzzles: You have to search for the smallest details and try pieces in different arrangements to solve them. Sometimes the frustration tries your patience, so it helps if you like playing detective.

Refrain from Badmouthing Other Paralegals and Attorneys

Just like court clerks, you'll end up relying on all the members of the legal staff eventually, and it's amazing who can catch wind of an offhand unkind comment you make about another. The same advice applies to attorneys and paralegals who work in different law firms. You never know when you may end up working with them (or *for* them!).

Never Act as though You're Irreplaceable

Although the attorney you work for would be lost without you, don't act as if you know that! If you cop a diva attitude, and treat others without respect, you may find yourself replaced in a hurry.

Don't Count on a Normal Work Schedule

Paralegals who work for litigation attorneys can expect late hours and lots of overtime. No matter how prepared the legal team may be for deposition or trial, something always needs attention at the last minute. Paperwork is so voluminous, it may require days (and nights) to comb through it all. And, you may be asked to attend an eleventh-hour settlement conference on a Saturday afternoon. If you'll only be happy with a 9-to-5 schedule, stick to areas of law like estate planning and intellectual property that traditionally don't involve a lot of litigation. But be warned. Every area of law is subject to long hours at unusual times.

Resist the Urge to Gossip about Clients

It's inevitable: The characters you meet in the practice of law will amuse and baffle you. And talking about them with your co-workers and family can be tempting. To maintain your respectability, don't chat about client idiosyncrasies with the rest of the office staff. And to uphold your ethical duty, *never* discuss clients with anyone outside the law office, even your closest friends and family members.

Appendixes

Access important terminology in a glossary.

Experience examples of legal documents and forms.

Visit pertinent websites for paralegals.

Appendix A

Glossary of Important Legal Terms: A Mini Legal Dictionary

As you read through this book, you probably see some terms that look like stirred-up alphabet soup. That's because the language of the law in the United States incorporates lots of Latin terms and uses some common expressions to mean uncommon things. This glossary is here to help you sort through some of the definitions you need to know to make sense of the work you do as a paralegal.

TIP

If you don't find the word you're looking for in this list, consult a legal dictionary such as *Webster's New World Law Dictionary Online www.yourdictionary.com/about/websters-new-world-law-dictionary.html)*; *Black's Law Dictionary Online* (https://thelawdictionary.org/).

acquittal: A finding of not guilty, an absolution of guilt, or a jury verdict of not guilty in a criminal action.

action: A lawsuit brought in court.

***ad damnum* clause:** *See* prayer for relief.

additur: An amount of money conferred by the judge in addition to the damage award provided by the jury. The judge grants a new trial unless the losing party agrees to add a certain amount to the damage award. *See also remittitur.*

ad hoc: For a specific purpose. An ad hoc committee organizes to achieve a particular goal and then disbands.

adjourn: To end or postpone to a later time.

administrative agency: An agency of the executive branch of government whose duty is to carry out statutes and executive orders and that is responsible for the control, supervision, and regulation of specific activities. In many cases, paralegals may represent clients at administrative-agency hearings under the authority of the Administrative Procedure Act, 5 U.S.C. section 555 (1967).

administrative regulation: A regulation that binds agencies and the public in certain areas. It consists of administrative agency rules designed to explain and carry out the statutes and executive orders that govern the agency.

admissible evidence: Evidence that has been declared admissible by the judge for usage in an action. The evidence is admitted for consideration by the judge or jury as to its truth or falsity.

admission: An out-of-court statement made by a party to the litigation that is inconsistent with the position the party is adopting in the litigation. An admission by a party-opponent is not considered to be hearsay, which makes these statements admissible. For example, let's say Jacob sues Samantha for injuries that he sustained when the car Samantha was driving hit him while he was crossing the street. At the time of the accident, Samantha admitted to Jacob that she sped up to beat the red stoplight and didn't see him in the crosswalk. At trial, Samantha alleges that she saw Jacob in the crosswalk but could not stop because her brakes failed. Samantha's prior admission to Jacob that she sped up and didn't see him would be admissible because a party-opponent, Samantha, made the admission.

admission and denial: After the defendant reads the facts that the plaintiff alleges to be true in the complaint, the defendant prepares and files an answer in which he or she may decide to admit the truth of some of the facts and deny the truth of others. When in doubt, the defendant often states that he or she "is without sufficient information to admit or deny the allegation and therefore denies same." The admission and denial is the most critical portion of the defendant's answer to the plaintiff's complaint.

adversarial hearing: A hearing where both parties are present to argue their respective positions. The hearing gives both sides in the controversy a chance to be heard. The adversarial system places the burden of proving or disproving legal arguments on the parties to the litigation rather than on the judge.

adverse judgment: A judgment or decision against the party that you and your attorney represent.

affiant: A person who swears or affirms under penalty of perjury to the truthfulness of a written statement. The person who signs an affidavit.

affidavit: A written statement of fact in which the affiant swears under penalty of perjury that the written statement is true. Those who don't swear under oath affirm the statement rather than swear to it.

affidavit of service: A written statement sworn to by the affiant, saying that a party has been served with papers and stating the time and place details of the service. This document is usually notarized and returned to the court after service has been effectuated.

affirm: To uphold or establish.

affirmative defense: A new factual allegation by the defendant not contained in the plaintiff's allegations. An affirmative defense is usually contained in the defendant's answer to the plaintiff's complaint. Common examples of affirmative defenses are contributory negligence and assumption of the risk. The affirmative defenses for federal proceedings are found in Rule 8(c) of the Federal Rules of Civil Procedure.

allegation: An assertion, representation, or averment. A statement of fact that the party intends to prove.

alternate: An extra juror who sits with the regular jurors and who may take the place of a regular juror if one becomes biased or otherwise incapacitated during the trial.

answer: The pleading filed by the defendant responding to or answering the allegations of the plaintiff's complaint. May also contain the defendant's affirmative defenses, cross claims, and counterclaims.

appeal: An application to a higher court to correct or modify the judgment of a lower court.

appeal as a matter of right: An appeal for which an appellate court has no discretion as to whether to hear the appeal and is thus required to review the decision below, as in capital punishment cases.

appearance: When a party appears in court as a party to a suit, whether as plaintiff or defendant, or when that party files a document called a notice of appearance. In general, entering an appearance voluntarily submits a party to the court's jurisdiction. In a special appearance, the party enters the court only to object to the court's attempted exercise of jurisdiction over that party.

appellant: The party initiating an appeal. Usually, the losing party in the lower-court decision becomes the appellant before the appellate court.

appellate brief: A written argument presented to the appeals court by the appellant indicating the issues on appeal and the appellant's positions on the claimed errors and improprieties that occurred during the trial. Alleged trial-court errors about how the lower court interpreted and applied the law provide the bases for the appeal.

appellate court: A higher court within the same judicial system as the trial court that hears the appeal from the trial court. Appellate courts are traditionally supreme courts and courts of appeals.

appellate jurisdiction: The power of a superior, appellate court to review and modify the decision made by an inferior, trial court.

appellate review: A judicial reconsideration of the proceedings of a court or other body. The appellate court examines or reviews the record of a lower court concentrating upon errors of law and errors in procedure that may have been made by the lower court.

appellee: The party against whom the appeal is brought. Usually, the victorious party in the trial court action.

arbitration: The submission of a controversy to the judgment of another whose decision may then be binding on both parties. One of many alternatives to litigation.

arraignment: A court proceeding in which the defendant is advised of the charges and is required to enter a plea admitting or denying the offenses.

arrest: The seizing of a person and the detaining of that person in custody by lawful authority.

assigned counsel: The attorney appointed to represent an indigent defendant in a criminal action. Most states and counties have indigency standards based upon a party's income, assets, and liabilities.

at issue: *See* in issue.

attorney of record: The attorney who has filed a notice of appearance and who is consequently mentioned in the court records.

attorney work product: Material collected and prepared for a case by counsel that is not subject to disclosure through discovery by opposing counsel. Examples of material that is generally protected by the attorney work product rule include correspondence between the attorney and client, interoffice legal research memos, and the trial notebook.

attorney-client privilege: The privilege of a client to refuse to disclose any confidential communication made with his or her attorney that relates to legal services. Also, the attorney can't disclose the communication without the permission of the client.

authentication: An attestation made by the proper officer certifying that a record is in due form of law and that the person who certifies it is the officer appointed to do so.

bail: The property or sum of money deposited with the clerk of court to insure that the defendant will reappear in court at future designated times. The bail is generally returned to the defendant if the defendant satisfies its conditions.

bar: An organization responsible for promulgating rules regarding attorneys, as in the American Bar Association. Attorneys collectively are called the bar.

below: Term used to refer to the court below the appellate court.

bench: Term used to refer to judges collectively or the actual place where the judge or judges sit in a court.

bench conference: A discussion between the judge and the attorneys held at the bench so that the jury can't hear what's being discussed. Usually the conference is held off the record and concerns the admissibility of evidence.

best evidence rule: A rule applied to documents introduced as evidence at trial that states that the original document should be produced unless it's shown to be unavailable for some reason other than the fault of the proponent of that evidence. For example, in an action for a breach of an apartment lease, the original lease must be produced to avoid speculation that the evidence could have been altered.

beyond a reasonable doubt: The degree of proof required of the state in a criminal prosecution. It is considered to be fair doubt and not imaginable doubt, and it is usually measured by 100 percent agreement on the part of the jury.

bias: The potential for a judge, juror, or party to make unfair judgments because of prior knowledge or involvement in the matters of the case.

bill of particulars: A formal motion or request made to a party requesting greater factual detail about some aspect of the pleadings. It's designed to assist the defendant in preparing an answer to the complaint.

body of the complaint: The portion of the pleading that presents the plaintiff's claims or causes of action.

bond: A sum of money deposited with the court to assure compliance with some requirement. The premium necessary to procure a bond is usually 10 to 15 percent of the face amount of the bond in either a criminal or civil action.

brief: Most commonly, a written argument presented to the court in support of a party's motion. A trial brief consists of legal arguments submitted to the trial court. An appellate brief is filed with the appellate court and contains arguments regarding the trial court's improper application of law or errors in procedure.

brief of a case: A synthesis of the major elements of the case. A case brief usually includes a brief statement of the essential facts, a listing of the issues, the resolution of those issues and the holding, and the subsequent procedural history. Paralegals and law clerks frequently brief cases for their supervising attorneys. Also known as a brief of an opinion.

brief of an opinion: *See* brief of a case.

burden of proof: The responsibility of proving something at trial. Generally, the party making an allegation has the burden of proving it. For instance, in a criminal case, the prosecutor has the burden of proving beyond a reasonable doubt that the accused committed the crime charged. In a civil proceeding, the plaintiff has the burden of proving by a preponderance of the evidence that the defendant caused the plaintiff's harm.

business entries: An out-of-court entry made in a business record that's compiled in the regular course of business by someone whose duty it is to make such entries. Business entries constitute admissible hearsay. Examples include nurses' notes, accountants' records, and automobile maintenance records made by mechanics.

caption of pleading: The pleading's heading. Contains the name of the court, the names of the parties, and the docket number assigned by the court.

case brief: *See* brief of a case.

cause of action: A legally acceptable reason for suing. Also known as a claim for relief.

challenge for cause: A party's request to a judge that a particular prospective juror not be allowed to be a member of the jury for specified reasons, such as bias. These challenges are unlimited as long as the party requesting the challenge is able to demonstrate to the judge that the prospective juror has knowledge of the parties to the suit or is involved in a business that's represented in the litigation. Thus, a police officer is usually omitted from sitting on a jury in a criminal case under a challenge for cause.

challenge to the array: An initial challenge to the selection process and composition of the jury pool. For instance, if a jury pool doesn't reflect the ethnic composition of a community, a successful challenge to the array may be brought that would require a new jury pool to be summoned for duty.

change of venue: A change in the location of a trial. The defendant usually requests a change of venue if, for example, there was too much pretrial publicity by the media. *See also* choice of venue.

charge to jury: Jury instructions on the standards that the jury should apply in reaching its verdict.

charter: The law of a municipality or other local unit of government authorizing it to perform designated governmental functions.

choice of venue: The process of finding the fairest place for trial's location. An impartial venue can be helpful in providing due process in a trial. *See also* change of venue.

circumstantial evidence: Evidence of one fact from which another fact can be inferred. Circumstantial evidence is less persuasive than direct evidence. For instance, the 50 feet of skid marks left by an automobile preceding the point of impact with a school bus is circumstantial evidence of the automobile's speed based on the direct evidence of the actual skid marks on the roadway.

civil law: The legal means by which the rights and remedies of private individuals are enforced and protected. Crime is not an issue for civil litigation, and the responsibility of pursuing a damage remedy in civil law rests with the person harmed.

civil suit: An action that enforces rights and redresses wrongs in the civil arena.

claim for relief: *See* cause of action.

clergy-penitent privilege: The privilege of a penitent (one who confides in a clergy member) to refuse to disclose any confidential communication with his or her priest, minister, or cleric that relates to spiritual counseling or consultation. Neither can disclose the information without the consent of the other party.

clerk: An officer of the court who files pleadings, motions, orders, and judgments; issues the process of the court; and keeps the records of legal proceedings.

closing statements or arguments: The final statements of the attorneys summarizing the evidence that they think they have established and the evidence that they think the other side has failed to establish.

codefendant: An additional defendant sued in the same litigation.

collection of judgment: Effectuation and enforcement of the decision of the court, which, in many cases, is one of the most difficult aspects of litigation.

competency: Legal capacity to testify, determined by (1) an understanding of the obligation to tell the truth, (2)ability to communicate, and (3)a knowledge of the topic of the testimony.

complaint: The initial pleading served and filed by the plaintiff stating his or her version of the facts and law concerning the defendant's alleged wrongdoing. In some states, like Texas, a complaint is called a petition.

concurring opinion: A judge's opinion that agrees with the result of the majority of the court but disagrees with the reasons the majority used to support that result.

Congress: The legislative branch of the federal government with the primary function of enacting law.

constitution: The document that sets forth the fundamental laws that create the branches of government and identify the basic rights and obligations of citizens. There are 50 state constitutions and one federal constitution in the United States.

contempt: A willful disregard for or disobedience of a judge.

contest: To challenge.

corporation counsel: Attorneys who exclusively represent one corporation in-house.

corroborate: To add weight or credibility to testimony.

counterclaim: A claim or cause of action against the plaintiff stated in the defendant's answer.

criminal law: The law concerning an offense that harms the entire community and whose remedy is a fine or imprisonment imposed on the offender. The responsibility of pursuing a violation of criminal law rests with the state. A person may be charged criminally and sued civilly.

cross claim: A claim by one codefendant against another codefendant.

cross examination: The questioning of the witness during a hearing or trial after the other side has completed direct examination. Generally, the person conducting the cross examination must limit himself or herself to the topics raised during the direct examination of the witness by the other side.

damage hearing: A separate hearing sometimes held after the judge or jury has found a party liable. The hearing is limited to deciding how much the losing party should pay the winner and the time period the losing party has to pay the damages.

damages: An award of money paid by one who has been found liable by a judge or jury to compensate the person who has been harmed. Types of damages include general/actual/compensatory, special, punitive/exemplary, nominal, consequential, and liquidated.

declaration against interest: An admissible, out-of-court statement made by a non-party against the interest of the non-party when he or she is no longer available for comment. For instance, Joan sues Betty for the fraudulent use of Joan's credit card, but Betty introduces a signed confession from Susan, who is now dead, stating that Susan was the person who used Joan's credit card. Susan's statement would be admissible hearsay because it's a declaration by Susan, who is unavailable, against Susan's interest.

declaration of bodily feelings: An admissible form of hearsay where a spontaneous declaration was made out of court regarding the person's present bodily condition. For instance, Zachary could be called to testify that his sister told him that she had "a headache" during a heavy-metal concert.

declaration of mental state of mind: An admissible form of hearsay that involves an out-of-court statement about a person's present state of mind. For example, in a slip-and-fall trial, Robert could testify that the supermarket manager told him that she was aware of the slippery surface in the produce aisle and that she would "carpet that area in the morning."

declaration of present sense impression: An admissible, out-of-court statement detailing an event while it's being observed by the person making the statement. For instance, Andrew could testify that Sharon exclaimed to him, "The plane is flying too low!", seconds before it came into contact with power lines.

declaratory judgment: A court's decision that declares the rights and obligations of the parties but does not order the parties to do or refrain from doing anything. It does not seek any damages from the opposing party but merely requests a declaration of the respective rights of the parties.

default judgment: A court order deciding the case in favor of the plaintiff because the defendant failed to file an answer or otherwise plead within the statutory time allowed for that purpose, which is usually 20 to 30 days.

defendant: A person or entity against whom a plaintiff brings an action. The defendant may also be known as a respondent in a domestic or probate court action.

defense: A response made by one party to the claims or allegations of another party. The defense may be a denial of facts or a more elaborate response, like an affirmative defense, and is usually contained in the defendant's answer.

demonstrative evidence: *See* physical evidence.

deponent: The person being questioned in a deposition.

deposition: A pretrial discovery device where one party asks oral questions of the other party or of a witness for the other party. Depositions are usually conducted under oath outside of the courtroom. Paralegals assist during a deposition by taking notes and by providing the supervising attorney with questions to ask the deponent.

digesting a document: Synthesizing a document, like a deposition or court reporter's transcript. Paralegals frequently digest depositions by summarizing the most important elements of the deponent's testimony so that the supervising attorney can quickly review them.

direct evidence: Evidence that tends to establish a fact without the need for making an inference. Direct evidence is preferred over indirect, or circumstantial, evidence.

direct examination: The initial questioning of the witness during a hearing or trial. The attorney who calls the witness to the stand usually conducts the direct examination of that witness, which is then followed by the cross examination of that witness by the adverse party. After cross examination, the attorney may conduct redirect examination of that same witness.

directed verdict: An order entered by the trial court judge in favor of the party requesting the verdict because the opposing party has failed to establish a prima facie cause of action or an adequate defense to that cause of action. Defendants may request a directed verdict after plaintiffs have rested their cases, and plaintiffs may request a directed verdict after defendants have completed their defenses.

discovery: Pretrial devices that can be used by one party to obtain evidence and information about the case from the other party in order to prepare for trial, prevent surprise, and facilitate settlement of the controversy. The most common kinds of discovery are interrogatories, depositions, requests for admissions, requests for production of documents, and requests for mental or physical examinations.

dismissal with prejudice: An adjudication on the merits of the case that bars the right to bring a subsequent action on the same claim. A dismissal with prejudice can only be appealed to a higher court.

dismissal without prejudice: A dismissal of a case based on a procedural error. The case can be filed again so long as the procedural error is corrected in the amended action.

dissenting opinion: An opinion that disagrees with the decision of the majority of the appellate court.

diversity of citizenship: Diversity of citizenship is the federal court's power to hear a case based upon the fact that (a) the parties to the litigation are from different states and (b) the amount of money involved in the lawsuit exceeds a statutory minimum, which changes frequently and is, as of this writing, $75,000.

docket: The court's calendar of pending cases. The docket, which is posted outside of the courtroom, will specify the kinds of cases that are being heard in that courtroom on that day.

doctor-patient privilege: The privilege of a patient to refuse to disclose any confidential communication made to his or her doctor about medical care. The information can't be disclosed without the consent of both parties.

domicile: A physical presence in a state with the intent to reside there permanently.

draft: To write, as in the writing of a document. Paralegals draft letters, pleadings, discoveries, motions, and briefs for their supervising attorneys to proof and sign.

due process: The evaluation of a case based upon the judgment of a disinterested objective party. Due process is a fundamental constitutional right, which means that the judicial system has to give parties notice and opportunity to be heard, confront witnesses against the parties, examine evidence presented, be represented by counsel, defend themselves, and receive a determination.

dying declaration: An admissible hearsay consisting of an out-of-court statement concerning the causes and circumstances of death when made by a person whose death is imminent.

eminent domain: The power of the state to take possession of private property for public use without the consent of the property owner. The state must provide reasonable compensation to the property owner.

en banc: When all of the members of the court decide a case, that decision is said to be rendered en banc, as opposed to a decision made by a panel of judges, which usually consists of only three of the appellate-court judges.

equal protection: The Fourteenth Amendment right that states that no person should be denied the same protection of law enjoyed by others.

escheat: When a person dies without a will (referred to as intestate), or when there is no other person who is competent to inherit, the state may take possession of that person's estate under the state's escheat powers.

estate: All property that's left by the decedent from which any obligations or debts of the decedent must be paid. It also may refer to the surviving representatives of the deceased.

evidence: Written or unwritten proof of allegations at issue between the parties to a lawsuit. Types of evidence include tangible, or demonstrative, and testimonial, or oral.

executive branch: The branch of government that enforces the laws created by the legislative branch.

ex parte hearing: A hearing where only one party to the action is present. A request for a temporary restraining order (TRO) is heard ex parte. To ex parte a judge is to talk to a judge about a case without the other side being present, which is unethical.

examiner: *See* hearing officer.

excited utterance: *See* spontaneous declaration.

exhibit: In a trial, items of tangible evidence that are to be or have been offered to the court and jury for inspection and consideration. Paralegals frequently prepare and mark exhibits for trial.

expert witness: A person who has been qualified as an expert and who then will be allowed (through answers to questions) to assist the jury in understanding complicated and technical subjects that are not generally within the jury's understanding. Medical doctors, accountants, and scientists commonly testify as expert witnesses.

failure to state a cause of action: As common grounds for a dismissal of an action or response to the plaintiff's complaint, defendants frequently allege that the plaintiff has failed to allege sufficient facts to constitute a cause of action against the defendant. This means that even if the plaintiff were to prove all of the facts alleged in the complaint, those facts would not establish a cause of action entitling the plaintiff to recover against the defendant. Grounds for dismissals in federal proceedings may be found in Rule 12(b) of the Federal Rules of Civil Procedure.

Federal Rules of Civil Procedure: The rules governing the manner in which civil cases are brought in and progress through the federal courts.

felony: A crime that is punishable by a sentence of one year or more and by a fine exceeding $1,000. Felons are usually required to serve their time in the state penitentiary as opposed to a county jail.

filed (in court): Paralegals frequently present documents to the clerk of the court, which means that these documents have been filed with the court. If the court clerk's office is closed, paralegals may then attempt to file the documents with the judge or the judge's clerk.

forum: The court or tribunal with jurisdiction over a particular matter.

forum non conveniens: Even if the venue of the court is proper, that court may be an inconvenient forum within which to litigate the action. So, if it appears that for the convenience of the litigants and witnesses and in the interest of justice the action should be heard in another forum, the court may act on its own or may grant a litigant's motion to change venue on this basis. *See also* change of venue *and* choice of venue.

foundation for evidence: What must be established for a party seeking to admit evidence into court. By laying the proper foundation for evidence, the party attempts to establish a prima facie case, which is usually done by the attorney's asking questions of the witness on direct examination.

garnishment: A method of executing judgment where part of the judgment debtor's salary is automatically turned over to the court, which in turn gives the money to the judgment creditor until the judgment is satisfied. Garnishments involving a child-support arrearage may be as high as 65 percent of the debtor's net monthly take-home pay and 25 percent for judgments that don't involve child support arrearages.

general verdict: A jury's verdict that simply says who wins the case and the amount to be paid to the winning party, if anything.

general verdict with interrogatories: The same as the general verdict with the addition of answers that the jury provides to a series of specific, factual questions concerning important aspects of the case.

good time: Time deducted from a prisoner's sentence for good behavior while incarcerated. Good time is usually calculated differently for state and federal convictions.

grand jury: A group of persons, traditionally not fewer than 12 nor more than 23, whose duty is to decide, upon hearing the evidence for the prosecution in each proposed bill of indictment, whether a sufficient case is established to hold the accused for trial. If the grand jury feels that the prosecution has presented sufficient evidence, it will return an indictment or true bill confirming that it is satisfied with the truth of the accusations presented by the prosecutor. The prosecutor may then file the complaint and make the arrests as deemed warranted. Evidence developed during a grand-jury investigation is usually not admissible in the subsequent court proceeding.

hearing: A proceeding, usually formal but sometimes informal, where the judge or hearing officer examines some aspect of a dispute and renders a decision or determination.

hearing officer: A member of an administrative agency's staff who presides over hearings and either makes findings of fact or recommends such findings to someone else in the agency. Also known as the referee or examiner.

hearsay: Hearsay is a statement that is based not upon personal observation but on what has been said or written by someone else who isn't in the courtroom. Hearsay is inadmissible unless it can be shown to fall within one of the hearsay exceptions, which we discuss in Chapter 7.

impanel: To select, swear in, and seat, such as impaneling a jury.

impeach a witness: To discredit that witness by introducing evidence that the testimony of the witness is not credible.

in camera: A discussion or meeting held in the judge's chambers, usually not on the record.

infra: A signal used in legal writing to indicate that a citation to an authority appears subsequently.

in issue: The truth of facts in a case that must be established at trial. A judge must rule on the applicability of law in question or issue in a case. Also known as at issue or in question.

in personam jurisdiction: A court's jurisdiction over a person.

in question: *See* in issue.

in rem jurisdiction: A court's jurisdiction over property or a controversy.

indictment: A formal charge by a grand jury accusing the defendant of a crime.

indigent: A person who is destitute of property or means of comfortable subsistence. By proving indigence, a person may be entitled to taxpayer-supported defense in felony charges.

information and belief: When a party qualifies a statement made in a pleading not as fact but as believed to be true from information available to the party. This standard legal phraseology in complaints protects a plaintiff who isn't absolutely certain of the existence of facts set forth in the complaint.

initial appearance: A court proceeding for the defendant charged with a felony, during which the judge advises the defendant of the charges against him or her and of his or her rights, decides on bail and other conditions of release, and sets the date of the preliminary hearing.

intent: Probably the most important word in law. It refers to a "determination of the mind," which is very difficult to prove and usually up to the jury to determine.

interlocutory appeal: An appeal to a higher court made during the progress of a case requesting temporary relief rather than a final judgment. This appeal usually takes the form of a motion made to a higher court requesting a review of the action, or inaction, of the trial court. For example, when a court grants a defense motion to suppress evidence obtained during a search of the defendant, the prosecution often appeals the trial court's granting of that motion. An interlocutory appeal is requested before final judgment.

interrogatories: Discovery techniques consisting of written questions about the case submitted by one party to the other party. The answers to interrogatories are usually provided under oath.

introduce into evidence: To formally place evidence before the court so that it will become part of the record for consideration by the judge and jury.

issues on appeal: The claimed errors of law or in procedure committed by the trial judge provide the basis for the issues on appeal. Allegations of errors of law and errors in procedure committed by the trial court are the only issues on appeal. The appellate court does not retry the case and no witnesses are called.

joint and several liability: Responsibility together and individually. For example, let's say Mary, Greta, and David borrow $10,000 from Alison under a contract that provides for joint and several liability. If David and Greta file for bankruptcy and become judgment-proof, Alison can attempt to collect the entire $10,000 debt from Mary under the joint and several liability provision.

judgment: The final decision of the court that resolves the dispute and determines the respective rights and obligations of the parties.

judgment creditor: The party that wins the judgment award.

judgment debtor: The party that loses and, therefore, owes the judgment award. *See also* judgment-proof.

judgment *non obstante verdicto* (JNOV): A judgment ordered by the court in favor of the plaintiff that's contrary to the jury's decision in favor of the defendant. This is also known as a judgment notwithstanding the verdict, because the court's decision opposes the verdict reached by the jury and, in effect, overrules the jury.

judgment notwithstanding the verdict: *See* judgment *non obstante verdicto.*

judgment on the merits: The preferred form of judgment because it is based on the legal rights of the parties as distinguished from mere matters of practice, procedure, and jurisdiction.

judgment-proof: Term used to describe a judgment debtor who does not have any assets out of which to effectuate a judgment. Often a judgment debtor will attempt to become judgment-proof if he or she is not already.

judicial branch: The branch of government that interprets laws created by the legislative branch and administrative laws produced by the executive branch and creates common law (judge-made law) by issuing opinions.

jurisdiction: A court's power to hear a case and decide the outcome.

jury: The group of citizens who decide the issues or questions of fact at the trial. Members of the jury are summoned from sources such as motor vehicle registration lists, driver's license lists, voter registration lists, and property ownership lists. Most juries consist of either 6 or 12 jurors.

jury charge: The jury instructions after the judge reads them to the jury. *See also* jury instructions.

jury instructions: Guidelines and law given by the judge to the jury that the jury is to use in deciding issues of fact at trial. Paralegals can be instrumental in preparing jury instructions. *See also* jury charge.

jury panel: The group of citizens who have been called to jury duty from a jury list.

leading question: A question asked of a party or witness that (a) suggests the answer desired, (b) assumes to prove a fact that has not been proved, or (c) embodying a material fact, admits of an answer by a simple negative or affirmative. "Isn't it true that you bought drugs with the money that you stole?" is an example of a leading question because either a yes or no answer indicates guilt. Leading questions are not admissible in court.

legislative branch: The branch of government that creates law. Congress is the legislative branch of the federal government.

liable: To be responsible or accountable in law or equity.

lis pendens: A notice of *lis pendens* is filed in the public records for the purpose of preventing any transaction that would thwart the purpose of the pending lawsuit. For example, in a quiet title action, where title to real property is being contested, the party who isn't listed as the owner in the public records might file a *lis pendens* to prevent the sale of the property prior to the resolution of the quiet title action.

litigation: An action or lawsuit.

magistrate: A judicial officer with limited jurisdiction in criminal and civil matters, such as a justice of the peace.

majority opinion: The decision of the majority of the members of the appellate court, which is often recorded in written form.

mandate of court: A command or order, usually from a superior court to an inferior court.

marital communications privilege: The privilege that prevents one spouse from disclosing confidential or private communications made to the other spouse during their marriage. One spouse can prevent the other spouse from making these disclosures, and both spouses must agree to the disclosure in order for it to be admissible.

misdemeanor: Any crime or offense not amounting to a felony or petty offense. Misdemeanors are crimes generally punishable by a sentence of less than one year and a fine of less than $1,000. Misdemeanants serve their sentences in the county jail as opposed to the state penitentiary.

motion: A request made to a court. Although most motions must be submitted in writing, some trial motions (like a motion to suppress) may be presented orally.

motion for a new trial: A request that the judge set aside the judgment and order a new trial on the basis that the trial was improper or unfair due to specified prejudicial errors that occurred during the trial.

motion for summary judgment: A pretrial request by a party that a decision on an issue be made on the basis of the pleadings and discovery without having to go through an entire trial. A party who requests summary judgment attempts to convince the judge that there are no issues of material fact disputed between the parties and so a decision should be rendered by the judge without the necessity of jury consideration.

motion *in limine*: A pretrial request to exclude potentially prejudicial evidence at the subsequent trial. Gruesome photographs are often excluded in response to this motion, or black-and-white photos may be substituted for objectionable color photos.

motion to dismiss: A request by a party to end a case without going through a trial.

motion to suppress: A request by a party to the court requesting the suppression of particular piece of evidence.

movant: The person or entity who requests relief from the court or administrative tribunal, usually through oral or written motions.

move into evidence: To request that the court declare that specified items be admissible as evidence.

nolle prosequi: A statement by the plaintiff or prosecutor of an unwillingness to further prosecute the case. At that point, some or all of the charges or allegations are dropped.

nolo contendere: A no-contest plea. It has the effect of a guilty plea without actually admitting guilt and allows the judge to sentence the defendant as though he or she pled guilty. A defendant will often be counseled to plead no contest to a criminal accusation so that the plea can't be used as an admission of liability in a related civil suit.

notice of appeal: A document announcing an intention to appeal filed with the appellate court and served on the opposing party.

nunc pro tunc: When a court allows the entry of an order, judgment, or other act so that it has a retroactive effect, that court is said to have acted *nunc pro tunc*, or "then for now."

off the record: Term used to describe court proceedings that the court reporter does not include in the official transcript. *See also* bench conference.

objection to evidence: A challenge to the evidence that the other side tries to introduce.

opening statement: Each attorney's presentation to the judge and jury outlining the facts and issues involved in the litigation and the position of each party to the litigation.

opinion evidence: Evidence a witness believes or infers to be true regarding facts in dispute. An inference from a fact is generally inadmissible. Opinion evidence should be distinguished from personal knowledge of the facts, which would be more likely to be admissible.

opinion of the attorney general: Legal advice provided by the attorney general to governmental officials on legal issues like the interpretation of a statute or new legislation.

opinion of the court: A court's explanation about why it reached a certain decision. The written decision of the court often includes the reasons for the decision, and these opinions are often collected in official and unofficial reports.

parol evidence rule: Oral evidence. Oral representations about the terms of a written agreement must be integrated into that agreement to be admissible and enforceable.

peremptory challenge: Usually the final juror challenge exercised by each litigant where no cause or reason need be provided to the court for the dismissal of potential jurors. These challenges are usually limited to three per side.

personal recognizance: One who is criminally accused may apply for a personal recognizance bond, which consists of a sworn promise to return to court at designated times without having to post cash or collateral bail. Various criteria are considered by the probation department in granting personal recognizance bonds including the accused's prior criminal record, the accused's family and job contacts in the community, and the magnitude of the crime alleged to have been committed.

personal service: Service of process upon an individual, or the designated agent of an individual or corporation, by delivering, or attempting to deliver, a copy of the summons and complaint to that individual or agent. A subpoena should also be served in the same way.

petition: A formal request that petitions the court to take some action. *See also* complaint.

petitioner: The person who brings a petition. *See also* plaintiff.

physical evidence: Evidence that can be seen or touched. Physical evidence is also known as tangible evidence or demonstrative evidence.

plaintiff: The person bringing the lawsuit. A plaintiff may also be known as a petitioner in some states and in domestic and probate actions.

plea bargaining: The process whereby the accused and the prosecutor negotiate a mutually satisfactory disposition of a criminal case. The defendant usually agrees to plead guilty to a lesser charge in return for the state's willingness to drop the more serious charge(s).

plead: To formally admit or deny the charges made by the prosecutor in a criminal case.

pleadings: The initial documents filed in a lawsuit that state the positions of the parties pertaining to the causes of action and the respective defenses. The most common pleadings are complaints, answers, replies, third-party complaints, cross claims, and counterclaims.

poll the jury: To question each juror individually in open court as to whether he or she agrees with the verdict announced by the jury foreman.

prayer for relief: A request contained in the complaint or petition (usually right before the attorney's signature) that asks for the relief that the plaintiff thinks he or she is entitled to. Common wording after the request is the phrase "and such other and further relief as to the court may seem just and proper." This enables the court to grant whatever relief it feels is appropriate in addition to what was specifically requested. Also known as a wherefore clause or *ad damnum* clause.

preliminary hearing: The means in a criminal case of determining the question of whether probable cause for the arrest of a person existed. The preliminary hearing is held shortly after arrest and before trial, and the prosecution must produce enough evidence to satisfy the judge that the defendant committed the crimes as charged.

preponderance of the evidence: The standard of proof that must be established to win a civil case. This standard is met when a party's evidence indicates that it's "more likely than not" that the fact is as the party alleges it to be. A majority of the jurors must agree for a plaintiff to prevail in a civil action.

presumption: An inference regarding the truth or falsity of any proposition of fact. A presumption may also indicate the weight to be given to evidence by law.

pretrial conference: A conference held between the judge or magistrate and the attorneys to prepare the case for trial. At this conference, the presiding judge sometimes tries to encourage the parties to settle part or all of their dispute.

prima facie case: A case sufficient on its face that's supported by the requisite minimum evidence and free of palpable defects. This must exist to prevail under any cause of action.

privilege: The right to refuse to testify or the right to prevent someone else from testifying on a matter.

privilege against self-incrimination: The privilege that holds that an accused can't be forced to testify in a criminal proceeding or to answer incriminating questions that directly or indirectly connect the accused to the commission of a crime.

pro se: When a party appears in an action without representation by an attorney.

probable cause: A reasonable basis to believe that a defendant has committed a wrong or is guilty of the crime charged.

probation: An alternate to imprisonment where the court releases a defendant found guilty of a crime to the supervision of a probation officer subject to conditions imposed by the court.

procedural law: The rules setting forth the steps required to conduct a lawsuit. Distinguishable from the substantive law, which governs the rights and duties of the parties.

process: Summons and complaint.

proof: The evidence offered to prove or disprove a fact or issue. In civil cases, it's defined as a preponderance of the evidence and in criminal cases as beyond a reasonable doubt.

prosecute: When the government, through the office of the attorney general or district attorney, files criminal charges against an accused, the government begins the prosecution of the accused.

qualify a witness: Before testifying in court, witnesses often must be qualified to testify. The court must be convinced through a demonstration of background and experience that the witness has expertise to testify in a particular area.

***quasi in rem* jurisdiction:** A court's power to resolve a personal claim against the defendant with the judgment being satisfied out of property or assets that the defendant has in state.

quasi-judicial: Term used to describe an agency that acts similarly to a court.

recidivist: A person who makes a trade of crime, who is a habitual criminal.

record: The official collection of all the trial pleadings, exhibits, orders, and word-for-word testimony that took place during the trial. The trial court record must be ordered and prepared as a prerequisite to prosecution of an appeal.

redirect examination: Examination that takes place after questioning the witness on cross examination. The attorney who conducts the direct examination conducts the redirect examination.

referee: *See* hearing officer.

relevant: Something that tends to prove or disprove a fact in issue is declared relevant by the court and is admissible for consideration by the judge and jury.

remand: To send back to an inferior court for further consideration.

remittitur: The procedural process by which the verdict of a jury is diminished by subtraction. It's a device the judge uses to tell the winning party that a new trial will be granted unless the party agrees to decrease the damage award reached by the jury.

reply: A defensive pleading that may be filed by the plaintiff in response to new allegations raised by the defendant in the defendant's answer. Or, an appellant may file a reply brief that responds to new matters set forth in the appellee's answer brief.

request for admissions: Discovery techniques consisting of written statements of facts concerning the case that are submitted to an adverse party and that that party is required to admit to or deny.

request for physical or mental examination: A form of discovery that requires court approval unless the parties agree, or stipulate, to it. A defendant usually wants to conduct a physical or mental examination of the plaintiff in an effort to verify the damages and injuries complained of by the plaintiff.

request for production and inspection of documents: A discovery technique that asks a party to produce, at a specified time and place, documents or other things in that party's possession or control.

res gestae: An evidentiary term that applies to exceptions to the hearsay rule involving statements that are made close to or concurrently with the happening of a transaction or occurrence.

res judicata: The legal doctrine that a judgment on the merits will prevent the same parties from re-litigating the same cause of action because the parties have already had their day in court and the controversy has already been judicially decided. It's similar to the doctrine of double jeopardy in a criminal case.

respondent: The party who is required to answer a petition or a writ requesting that the party take some sort of action as opposed to provide money damages. *See also* defendant.

restitution: The restoring of property or a right to a person who has been unjustly deprived of it. Restitution is often a condition of sentencing in a criminal case.

retainer agreement: A contract between an attorney and client stating the nature of the services to be rendered and the cost of those services.

review: *See* appellate review.

rule on witnesses: The rule that requires that all witnesses be removed from the courtroom until it's time for their individual testimonies so that they won't be able to hear others' testimonies. Either party may invoke this rule.

rules of court: Laws governing practice before a particular court and the procedures to be followed in litigation before that court. Paralegals should be aware of the nuances in practice and procedure among the various federal and state court systems in which they practice.

satisfy: To comply with a legal obligation. A release and discharge of an obligation is the satisfaction of that obligation.

sentence: The punishment ordered by the court to be assessed upon a person convicted of a crime.

serve: To present legal papers to a party notifying that party of a lawsuit.

service of process: The delivery of a summons and complaint to a defendant ordering that defendant to answer the allegations made by the plaintiff. Service of process is a prerequisite to the court's acquisition of personal jurisdiction or power over the defendant.

set for trial: To schedule a date for a trial to begin on.

settlement: A compromise reached by the adverse parties in a civil suit before the final judgment where they agree between themselves about their respective rights and obligations, thus eliminating the necessity of a judicial resolution of the controversy. Judicial statistics indicate that 90 percent of filed civil actions settle prior to trial, and paralegals can be instrumental in the preparation of settlement demands, or brochures, that are used to achieve a settlement.

special verdict: A form of verdict submitted to the jury that requests that the jury answer specific factual questions in addition to rendering its verdict for plaintiff or defendant.

spontaneous declaration: An exception to the hearsay rule consisting of an out-of-court statement or utterance made spontaneously by the observer of an exciting event during or immediately after the event. This admissible hearsay is also known as an excited utterance.

standard of proof: A statement of how convincing the evidence must be in order for a party to comply with his or her burden of proof. In criminal cases, the standard of proof is "beyond a reasonable doubt" and in civil cases the standard of proof is "by a preponderance of the evidence."

stare decisis doctrine: The doctrine that the court is obliged to stand by decided cases and to follow set precedent. As long as the facts and issues presented and decided in prior cases are substantially similar to the case being considered, an inferior court must apply that prior precedent in resolving its case.

state a cause of action: To include all the relevant facts and law in the complaint so that if those matters are successfully proved at trial, the plaintiff will be entitled to win.

statute of limitations: The law establishing the period within which a complaint must be filed before it is no longer permitted to be litigated.

stay execution of the judgment: To delay enforcement of a court's judgment.

stipulate: A fact agreed upon by the parties is said to be stipulated. A stipulation of fact won't be contested or disputed so that no evidence need be presented at trial concerning the truth or falsity of that fact.

subject-matter jurisdiction: A court's power to hear the type of case being presented. A bankruptcy court would not have subject-matter jurisdiction over a child-custody case, for example.

subpoena: A writ issued under authority of a court to compel the appearance of a witness at a judicial proceeding. Generally, a subpoena must be served personally and can't be served by substitute service on a person not named in the subpoena.

subpoena *duces tecum*: A writ issued under authority of a court to compel the appearance of a person at a judicial proceeding and to command that person to bring specified documents with him or her. The primary objective of the subpoena *duces tecum* is to order that a person produce documents at a deposition, hearing, or trial so that those documents can be reviewed and considered.

subscription: On a complaint document, the signature of the attorney who prepares a complaint and who represents the plaintiff. If the plaintiff prepares the complaint and is acting as his or her own attorney in the case, the plaintiff signs "pro se."

substantive law: The positive law that creates, defines, and regulates the rights and duties of the parties and that may give rise to a cause of action. It represents the nonprocedural rights and duties imposed by law.

substitute service: Service of process upon a designated agent of the party. Paralegals often consult the secretary of state's office to ascertain the name and address of the registered agents for corporations against which their offices are filing actions.

summary: A compilation of the crucial points of fact and law contained in a document. Paralegals often provide summaries of lengthy discovery documents, like depositions.

summons: A formal notice from the court ordering the defendant to appear in court or to answer a complaint in lieu of appearing.

supra: A signal in legal writing indicating that a citation to authority appears previously.

Supremacy Clause: The popular title for Article 6 of the United States Constitution, which states that federal laws are above state and local laws.

sustain: To support, approve, or adequately maintain a motion.

take under advisement: When a court delays its ruling on a matter, usually a motion, until a later time.

tangible evidence: *See* physical evidence.

testimonial evidence: Evidence that can be heard and considered by a judge and jury.

third-party complaint: A pleading filed by the defendant against a new, third party that alleges that the third party is or may be liable for all or part of the damages that the plaintiff attributes to the defendant.

tickler system: A common filing system that allows the secretary and paralegal to alert the attorney of approaching deadlines. Tickler systems are important for keeping the law-office staff aware of court dates, filing deadlines, and other important dates.

tort: Generally, a tort refers to a civil wrong committed against another that results in damages and doesn't emanate from a breach of contract. Most civil actions are tort actions.

tortfeasor: The wrongdoer; the person who committed the tort.

transcript: The written record of proceedings; the verbatim transcription of everything that was said on the record during the hearing or trial.

trial court: The court where the trial is held. Trial courts are generally the only forums that allow for a trial by jury.

trial de novo: A totally new fact finding hearing.

tribunal: a quasi-judicial court or judicial body.

United States Court of Appeals: An appellate court of limited jurisdiction. The jurisdiction is limited to appeals from the United States District Court.

United States District Court: The federal trial court where the litigants are entitled to a trial by jury. This court's jurisdiction is limited to cases where the United States is a party, a federal question is at issue, or diversity of citizenship exists between two or more of the parties and at least $75,000 is at stake.

United States Supreme Court: The court of last resort. It is the nation's highest court and selects certain appeals referred to it from the United States Court of Appeals and state supreme courts. It also has original jurisdiction in cases involving ambassadors, public ministers, and consuls and those cases in which a state is a party. The United States Supreme Court has a chief justice and eight associate justices.

venue: The place where a trial is held. An impartial venue is critical to a fair trial. *See also* choice of venue.

verdict: The final decision of the jury.

verification of pleadings: An affidavit that is submitted with a pleading and signed by the party on whose behalf the pleading was prepared. The affiant swears that he or she has read the pleading and that it's true to the best of his or her knowledge, information, and belief. A verification is much more likely to be filed with a complaint for breach of contract, where the facts are relatively certain, than with a complaint for negligence, where the facts are less certain. Furthermore, attorneys who may be skeptical of their clients' allegations often request that their clients verify their complaints to protect themselves if the complaint later proves to be frivolous.

voir dire: The jury-selection process; the examination of prospective jurors by the attorneys and the court. It may also refer to the examination of the qualifications of a prospective witness prior to allowing that witness to testify.

warrant: An order from a judicial officer authorizing the arrest of an individual or the search of property.

wherefore clause: *See* prayer for relief.

writ: A written order from a court.

writ of certiorari: An order by an appellate court concerning the review or reexamination of what a lower court did. If the writ is denied, the higher court refuses to hear the appeal and the judgment below stands unaffected.

Appendix B

What You'll Find Online

A bonus feature of this book is the online material, which you can access for free at www.dummies.com/go/paralegalcareer2e. Here you can find all kinds of documents, links, and tools that you'll find useful in your paralegal career.

These files are in Adobe PDF and Microsoft Word formats:

>> **Adobe Reader:** Adobe Reader is a freeware application for viewing files in the Adobe Portable Document format. Download it free at www.adobe.com.

>> **Microsoft Word:** You can download a free basic version of Word at www.office.com even if you don't have Microsoft Word.

Documents Online

In this appendix, we let you know what you'll find on the website. The following sections are arranged by category and provide a summary of what you'll find online.

Paralegal associations

National and State Paralegal Associations and Related Organizations (ParalegalAssoc.pdf): You're bound to find an organization to join with this comprehensive list of national, state, and local paralegal associations.

Job search

Sample Cover Letter (`CoverLetter.pdf`): Here's a sample of a professional cover letter you can use to introduce yourself to prospective employers.

Sample Resume Highlighting Skills (`ResumeSkills.pdf`): This sample resume is best used when you have more education than you do law office experience.

Sample Resume Highlighting Employment (`ResumeEmployment.pdf`): This file gives you an example of a resume to use if you have more law office experience than you do advanced education.

Sample Freelance Rate Sheet (`FreelanceRates.pdf`): This file gives you an example of the type of rate notification you can send out to prospective clients if you choose to open your own freelance paralegal business.

Legal process

Branches of the Federal Government (`FedGovernment.pdf`): If you need to know what offices and agencies make up the branches of the federal government, this is the chart for you.

Map of the Federal District Courts (`DistrictCourtsMap.pdf`): The U.S. District Courts system is laid out for you in this map.

Fundamental legal documents

Sample Demand Letter (`DemandLetter.pdf`): This letter shows a sample of the way an attorney may initiate a civil case.

Sample Complaint (`Complaint.pdf`): One of the first pleadings a plaintiff files in a civil case is a complaint.

Sample Summons (`Summons.pdf`): The complaint is served with a summons that generally looks like the one in this file.

Sample Answer (`Answer.pdf`): The defendant responds to the complaint with an answer.

Sample Answer and Third-Party Complaint (`Answerand3rdComplaint.pdf`): Sometimes a defendant brings in another party. This sample answer and third-party complaint shows you what that pleading looks like.

Sample Answer to a Third-Party Complaint (Answerto3rdComplaint.pdf): The third party has to respond to the allegations against it, and this pleading gives you an example of how that's done.

Sample Internal Memo in Support of a Motion (InternalSupport.pdf): Here's an example of a memo a paralegal may write to respond to a specific legal research assignment provided by the supervising attorney.

Sample Motion for Summary Judgment (MotionSummJudg.pdf): Based on the paralegal's recommendations in the internal memo, the attorney asks the paralegal to draft a motion for summary judgment.

Sample External Memo in Support of a Motion (ExternalSupport.pdf): To let the court know why it should grant the motion, the attorney submits with the motion a memo that supports the motion.

Sample Notice to Set (NoticetoSet.pdf): To accompany the motion, the paralegal drafts a notice to set the hearing on the motion.

Sample Order (Order.pdf): In anticipation of the court's granting the motion, the paralegal prepares an order for the judge to sign.

Sample Jury Instructions (JuryInstruct.pdf): Each side may suggest to the judge the kinds of things it wants the jury to consider during deliberations. This document contains some sample instructions.

Sample Internal Memo of Law (InternalMemo.pdf): Because writing good internal memos is an essential skill for paralegals, we've provided you with another example.

Discovery

Sample Interrogatories (Interrogatories.pdf): Interrogatories require the other party to answer questions.

Sample Request for Admissions (RequestAdmissions.pdf): A request for admissions asks the party to admit to or deny specific allegations.

Sample Request for Production (RequestProduction.pdf): Requests for production of documents list items that one party requires the other party to supply.

Investigating and interviewing

State and Federal Agencies (`StateFedAgencies.pdf`): This list of state and federal agencies can help with an investigation project.

Client Interview Checklist Divorce (`DivorceChecklist.pdf`): You should begin every interview with a checklist of what you need to accomplish. This file contains the kinds of information you're seeking in the initial client interview for a divorce action.

Legal research

These files guide you to the kinds of information that constitute primary and secondary authority and non-authority:

>> **Types of Primary Authority** (`PrimaryAuthority.pdf`)

>> **Types of Secondary Authority** (`SecondaryAuthority.pdf`)

>> **Types of Nonauthority** (`Nonauthority.pdf`)

Trial procedures

Sample Criminal Trial Notebook Checklist (`TrialNotebookChecklist.pdf`): This file contains a comprehensive list of the kinds of information you should include in a trial notebook for a criminal case.

Jury Panel Seating Chart (`JurySeatingChart.pdf`): You can use this file to create your own seating charts for the jury selection process.

Sample Master Witness List (`WitnessList.doc`): To keep track of witnesses, use this handy chart as a springboard for your own creation.

Law office administration

Sample Timesheet (`Timesheet.pdf`): This file shows you what an individual timesheet looks like using QuickBooks accounting software.

Sample Invoice (`Invoice.pdf`): With QuickBooks, you can generate invoices like this one automatically from individual timesheets.

Links to Websites

The links listed are accessible using an Internet browser. You can either click on the Web addresses or type them into your browser to get to the sites.

Paralegal associations

National Federation of Paralegal Associations (`www.paralegals.org`)

National Association of Legal Assistants (`www.nala.org`)

NALS (`www.nals.org`)

Ethics rules

American Bar Association Model Rules of Professional Conduct (`www.abanet.org/cpr/mrpc/mrpc_toc.html`)

National Association of Legal Assistants Model Standards and Guidelines for Utilization of Legal Assistants/Paralegals (`www.nala.org/certification/nala-code-ethics-and-professional-responsibility`)

National Federation of Paralegal Associations Model Code of Ethics and Professional Responsibility and Guidelines for Enforcement (`www.paralegals.org/files/Model_Code_of_Ethics_09_06.pdf`)

NALS Code of Ethics (`www.nals.org/page/history`)

Job search

National Federation of Paralegal Associations Legal Career Center (`www.paralegals.org/i4a/pages/index.cfm?pageid=3293`)

LawJobs.com (`www.lawjobs.com`)

Legal Staff (`www.legalstaff.com/`)

FindLaw.com (`http://careers.findlaw.com`)

Lawyers Weekly Jobs (`www.lawyersweeklyjobs.com`)

Law Match (`https://lawmatch.com`)

Law Crossing (www.lawcrossing.com/)

Paralegal 411 (www.paralegal411.org/jobs/)

NALP (www.nalp.org/jobs)

Gibson Arnold & Associates (www.gibsonarnold.com)

Monster.com (www.monster.com)

Career Builder (www.careerbuilder.com)

Indeed.com (www.indeed.com)

Rules of evidence and procedure

Federal Rules of Civil Procedure (www.federalrulesofcivilprocedure.org/frcp/)

Federal Rules of Evidence (www.rulesofevidence.org/table-of-contents/)

Links to State Rules of Procedure (www.law.cornell.edu/wex/table_civil_procedure)

FirstGov.gov State and Territorial Governments (www.usa.gov/states-and-territories): Most state government sites provide access to statutes, cases, and legal forms. Use this site to link to your state's homepage.

Online investigation and asset searches

For a fee, you can search for background checks, assets, and other personal information on the Internet. Here are just a few of the sites that provide these services:

>> Asset Records Search (https://recordsfinder.com/asset/)

>> InfoTracer (https://infotracer.com/asset-search/)

>> Docusearch.com (www.docusearch.com)

>> Black Book Online (www.blackbookonline.info/assetsearch.aspx)

>> People Records Asset Search (www.probateresearch.net/asset-search/)

>> Asset Searches Plus (www.assetsearchesplus.com/)

>> Public Record Center (www.publicrecordcenter.com/)

Online research

If you want to become familiar with online legal research before you begin your career, this section provides some of the best sites on the Internet.

The following websites offer free searches:

>> **Cornell University Law School Legal Information Institute (`www.law.cornell.edu`):** Cornell University Law School's Legal Information Institute is an excellent resource for legal research available to the public. Law schools and other legal sites link to Cornell's thorough and ambitious collection. Use this site to find the exact text of laws, as well as judicial opinions and even articles from law reviews and journals.

>> **FindLaw (`https://lp.findlaw.com/`):** This site provides legal information pertinent to legal professionals.

>> **Internet Legal Research Group – Public Legal (`www.ilrg.com`):** The Internet Legal Research Group organizes, categorizes, and indexes more than 4,000 law-related Web sites. It's designed to provide the user with downloadable files and legal forms.

You can only go so far with free Internet legal research. To access everything, you'll need to pay for the services of an online legal research database. **Westlaw** (`https://legal.thomsonreuters.com/en/products/westlaw`) and **Lexis Advance** (`www.lexisnexis.com`) are the two most popular. They're the original computerized research sites that revolutionized the practice of law. Many legal professionals will tell you that they're still the best. Each site is constantly improving with new services designed to save valuable research time. Neither site has an extensive free service for the public, but you can tour the sites and learn a little about the services they offer. Chances are, whatever the area of law you choose, you'll rely heavily on one of these two sites.

Other paid computerized research sites giving Westlaw and Lexis a run for their money are **Bloomberg Law** (`www.bna.com/bloomberglaw/`), **Casemaker** (`https://public.casemakerlegal.net/`), **Casetext** (`https://casetext.com/`), and **Fastcase** (`www.fastcase.com`).

Law firm software

Beyond word processing and spreadsheets, a wide range of software has been designed to help make the practice of law more manageable. If you want a preview of some of the software designed specifically for law firms, check out the links below:

- » **AbacusLaw** (`www.abacusnext.com/software/case-management/abacuslaw`): AbacusLaw software does everything except put the stamp on the envelopes. It keeps track of hours worked, automatic billing, client conflict monitoring, scheduling, and a whole lot more.

- » **Actionstep** (`www.actionstep.com/us/`): In addition to managing finances and clients, Actionstep includes document management in its software system.

- » **Clio** (`www.clio.com`): Clio is a popular system for managing accounting, clients, time tracking, calendars, and more.

- » **CosmoLex** (`www.cosmolex.com`): This cloud-based platform combines accounting, document assembly, client management, and more.

- » **MyCase** (`www.mycase.com`): This case management system emphasizes its organization features.

- » **Perfect Practice** (`www.perfectpractice.com`): Perfect Practice tailors its products to the specific needs of clients. There are different packages for different types of practices and different areas of the law.

- » **PerfectLaw** (`www.perfectlaw.com`): PerfectLaw offers what it calls an "all-in-one" solution. Like the previous two software packages, this software offers an integrated system that allows you to enter information once and have that information work in a calendar, case tracker, client manager, and billing system.

- » **PracticePanther** (`www.practicepanther.com`): This software is dedicated to make taking care of law office finances and case management easier and more efficient.

Index

A

ABA (American Bar Association), 21, 26, 235
AbacusLaw, 344
acceptance of offer, 77
accounting software, 280, 294, 295, 340
acquittal, 315
acquitted, 64
act, 45
action, 315
Actionstep, 344
active voice, 259
actual written law, 120
ad damnum clause, 158, 273, 315
additur, 315
adjourn, 315
adjudicatory hearings, 45–46, 60
administrative agencies, 45, 58–63, 315
administrative law, 57–60
Administrative Procedure Act (APA), 58–59
administrative regulations, 45, 119, 122, 316
admissible evidence, 80, 108, 112, 316
admission, defined, 316
admission and denial, 316
admissions, request for, 95, 97, 109–110,
    151, 170, 171, 332, 339
Adobe Reader, 337
adoption, 126
adversarial hearing, 316
adverse judgment, 316
advocacy, 60–62
affiant, 316
affidavit, 104, 150, 180, 297, 316
affidavit of service, 316
affirm, 99, 316
affirmative defenses, 64, 94, 106, 148,
    160, 162, 316
aggravated assault, 66

Airtable, 278
allegation, 90, 94, 106, 129, 148, 149, 157,
    158, 160, 317
alphabet soup, use of term, 45
alternate, 317
amend judgment, motion to, 151
amended pleading, motion to file, 150
American Bar Association (ABA), 21, 26, 235
American judicial system
    becoming familiar with background
        concepts of, 39–40
    importance of legal precedence, 40–42
    levels of, 46–54
    U.S. jury system, 54–56
American Jurisprudence, 2d., 201, 204, 205
American Jurisprudence Proof of Facts (POF)
    series, 178
American Law Reports (ALR), 201, 203, 205
Annotation History Table, 206
annotations, 205–206
annulments, 126
answer
    to complaint, 160
    defined, 94, 317
    sample, 338
answer and third-party complaint, 253, 338
answer to a third-party complaint, 160, 339
APA (Administrative Procedure Act), 58–59
appeal
    in civil law, 99
    defined, 49, 317
    notice of, 88, 99, 153, 329
    in state judicial systems, 51, 52
appeal as a matter of right, 50, 52, 53, 317
appearance, 317
appellant, 52, 53, 88–89, 99, 317
appellate brief, 89, 145, 153, 317

C

cabinet departments, 58

Caher, James P. (author)

Personal Bankruptcy Laws For Dummies, 132

Caher, John M. (author)

Personal Bankruptcy Laws For Dummies, 132

calendar system, 288–290

calendars, 279–280, 288–291

California, regulation of paralegals in, 16, 21

caption, in complaint, 157

caption of pleading, 319

Career Builder, 342

case administrator, paralegal as, 9

case brief, 319

case citators, 208

case law, 40, 46, 123, 124, 207, 212, 282, 307

case management, technology for, 280

case of first impression, 41, 118

Casemaker, 343

cases, citing of, 215

Casetext, 343

cause of action, 69, 75, 90, 93, 94, 95, 101, 239, 319

cc (courtesy copies), 155

ceremonial marriages, 126

certificate of mailing, 157, 160

certificate of service, 160, 168

certification, 22–24

Certified Legal Professional (CLP) exam, 23

Certified Paralegal (CP), 20, 22–23

challenge for cause, 223, 224, 319

challenge to the array, 223, 224, 319

challenge to the venire, 224

challenges

to the array, 223, 224, 319

for cause, 223, 224, 319

peremptory challenges, 98, 223–224, 330

to the venire, 224

change of venue, 93, 319

change of venue, motion for, 149

charge to jury, 320

charging documents, 80–81, 218

charter, 320

checklists

in legal interviewing, 189–194, 196

in legal investigation, 177–179

for trial notebook, 220

checks and balances, 42–46

The Chicago Manual of Style, 15th Edition, 264

child custody matters, 8, 12, 50, 126

child molestation, 66

child rape, 66

choice of venue, 93, 320

Circuit Court of Appeals, 49, 121

circuit courts, 49, 50, 51

circuits, 49

circumstantial evidence, 320

citation format, 214–216

city courts, 53

civil case, carrying through of, 90–99

civil law

contract law, 76–78

defined, 57, 320

enacted law also known as, 120

equitable relief and money damages, 68–69

injunctions, 68

monetary damages, 69

overview, 68

specific performance, 69

tort law, 69–76

civil procedure, 102–111

distinguishing between procedural law and substantive law, 102

civil process

conducting pre-trial conferences, 97

dealing with discovery, 95–97

deciding on venue, 93

determining jurisdiction, 90–93

initiating of, 90–93

plodding along in post-trial, 98–99

Rules 8, 11, and 12, 105–107

sending demand letter, 90

traveling through trial, 97–98

M

About the Authors

Scott and Lisa Hatch have prepared students for careers in the legal field for more than 35 years. While in law school in the late '70s, Scott Hatch taught LSAT preparation courses throughout Southern California to pay for his education. After graduation, he went out on his own and, at the urging of one of his students, added paralegal courses to his course offerings. Using materials he developed, he then prepared thousands of eager career seekers to work as paralegals, legal nurse consultants, legal secretaries, legal investigators, mediators, and victim advocates.

Scott and Lisa kindled their romance in the classroom. Lisa took one of Scott's LSAT preparation courses at the University of Colorado and improved her love life as well as her LSAT score. Lisa's love for instructing and writing allowed her to fit right in with Scott's lifestyle, teaching courses and preparing course materials. They married shortly thereafter.

Since then, Scott and Lisa have taught students worldwide. Currently, more than 300 universities and colleges offer their courses through live lectures, correspondence, and online, and Scott and Lisa have written the curriculum for all formats. The company they built together, The Center for Legal Studies, provides courses for those who desire careers in the field of law (including paralegals, legal secretaries, legal investigators, victim advocates, and legal nurse consultants) and who need preparation for the gamut of standardized tests.

Scott has presented standardized test and legal career courses since 1980. He received his undergraduate degree from the University of Colorado and his Juris Doctorate from Southwestern University School of Law. He's listed in *Who's Who in California* and *Who's Who Among Students in American Colleges and Universities,* and he was named one of the Outstanding Young Men of America by the United States Jaycees. He was a contributing editor to *The Judicial Profiler* and the *Colorado Law Annotated* series and has served as editor of several award-winning publications.

Lisa has been teaching standardized test courses since 1987. She graduated with honors in English from the University of Puget Sound, and received her master's degree from California State University. She and Scott have co-authored numerous law and standardized test texts, including *Paralegal Procedures and Practices; A Paralegal Primer;* and *LSAT For Dummies, GMAT For Dummies, ACT For Dummies, Catholic High School Entrance Exams For Dummies, SAT II U.S. History For Dummies, SAT II Biology For Dummies,* and *SAT II Math For Dummies* (John Wiley & Sons, Inc.) and *The Legal Guide to Family Law* and *The Legal Guide to Probate Law* (B & B Publishers).

Dedication

We dedicate our *For Dummies* series books to our children Alison Hatch and Dan Welch, Andrew Hatch, Zachary Hatch and Miarra Jackson, and Zoe Hatch and John Gilchrist and our grandchildren, Paige and Ryan Welch. Rather than file missing persons reports on us with local law enforcement agencies, they demonstrate extreme patience, understanding, and assistance while we write these books.

Authors' Acknowledgments

This book wouldn't have been possible without the extensive research and writing contributions of Martin Rollins, JD, David Newland, JD, and Zachary Hatch. Their efforts greatly enhanced our information gathering, and we're deeply grateful to them.

We also need to acknowledge the input of the thousands of paralegal, legal secretary, legal investigator, and legal nurse consultant students who've completed our law career certificate courses over the last 35 years. The classroom and online contributions offered by these dedicated learners have provided us with lots of input about what prospective paralegals want and need to know most.

The editing professionals at Wiley Publishing greatly facilitated our writing process. Our thanks go out to Chad Sievers for his support and attention to detail, David Dougherty, JD, for his insightful technical edits, and Lindsay LeFevere for initiating the process and being available whenever we had questions.

Finally, we want to acknowledge our literary agent, Margo Maley Hutchinson, at Waterside Productions in Cardiff for introducing us to the innovative *For Dummies* series.

Wiley has to be commended for its pioneering efforts to make finding out about new careers fun. We thrive on positive reinforcement and feedback from our students and encourage our readers to provide comments and critiques at feedback@legalstudies.com.

Publisher's Acknowledgments

Executive Editor: Lindsay Lefevere

Project Editor: Chad R. Sievers

Technical Editor: David Dougherty, JD

Production Editor: G. Vasanth Koilraj

Cover Image: © Alexander Kirch/EyeEm/ Getty Images

Take dummies with you everywhere you go!

Whether you are excited about e-books, want more from the web, must have your mobile apps, or are swept up in social media, dummies makes everything easier.

Find us online!

Leverage the power

Dummies is the global leader in the reference category and one of the most trusted and highly regarded brands in the world. No longer just focused on books, customers now have access to the dummies content they need in the format they want. Together we'll craft a solution that engages your customers, stands out from the competition, and helps you meet your goals.

Advertising & Sponsorships

Connect with an engaged audience on a powerful multimedia site, and position your message alongside expert how-to content. Dummies.com is a one-stop shop for free, online information and know-how curated by a team of experts.

- Targeted ads
- Video
- Email Marketing

- Microsites
- Sweepstakes sponsorship

20 MILLION PAGE VIEWS EVERY SINGLE MONTH

15 MILLION UNIQUE VISITORS PER MONTH

43% OF ALL VISITORS ACCESS THE SITE VIA THEIR MOBILE DEVICES

700,000 NEWSLETTER SUBSCRIPTIONS
TO THE INBOXES OF
300,000 UNIQUE INDIVIDUALS EVERY WEEK

# of dummies

Custom Publishing

Reach a global audience in any language by creating a solution that will differentiate you from competitors, amplify your message, and encourage customers to make a buying decision.

- Apps
- Books
- eBooks
- Video
- Audio
- Webinars

Brand Licensing & Content

Leverage the strength of the world's most popular reference brand to reach new audiences and channels of distribution.

For more information, visit dummies.com/biz

PERSONAL ENRICHMENT

Staying Sharp
9781119187790
USA $26.00
CAN $31.99
UK £19.99

Facebook
9781119179030
USA $21.99
CAN $25.99
UK £16.99

Guitar
9781119293354
USA $24.99
CAN $29.99
UK £17.99

Investing
9781119293347
USA $22.99
CAN $27.99
UK £16.99

Beekeeping
9781119310068
USA $22.99
CAN $27.99
UK £16.99

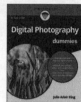

Digital Photography
9781119235606
USA $24.99
CAN $29.99
UK £17.99

Meditation
9781119251163
USA $24.99
CAN $29.99
UK £17.99

Pregnancy
9781119235491
USA $26.99
CAN $31.99
UK £19.99

Samsung Galaxy S7
9781119279952
USA $24.99
CAN $29.99
UK £17.99

iPhone
9781119283133
USA $24.99
CAN $29.99
UK £17.99

Crocheting
9781119287117
USA $24.99
CAN $29.99
UK £16.99

Nutrition
9781119130246
USA $22.99
CAN $27.99
UK £16.99

PROFESSIONAL DEVELOPMENT

Windows 10
9781119311041
USA $24.99
CAN $29.99
UK £17.99

AutoCAD
9781119255796
USA $39.99
CAN $47.99
UK £27.99

Excel 2016
9781119293439
USA $26.99
CAN $31.99
UK £19.99

QuickBooks 2017
9781119281467
USA $26.99
CAN $31.99
UK £19.99

macOS Sierra
9781119280651
USA $29.99
CAN $35.99
UK £21.99

LinkedIn
9781119251132
USA $24.99
CAN $29.99
UK £17.99

Windows 10
9781119310563
USA $34.00
CAN $41.99
UK £24.99

SharePoint 2016
9781119181705
USA $29.99
CAN $35.99
UK £21.99

Fundamental Analysis
9781119263593
USA $26.99
CAN $31.99
UK £19.99

Networking
9781119257769
USA $29.99
CAN $35.99
UK £21.99

Office 2016
9781119293477
USA $26.99
CAN $31.99
UK £19.99

Office 365
9781119265313
USA $24.99
CAN $29.99
UK £17.99

Salesforce.com
9781119239314
USA $29.99
CAN $35.99
UK £21.99

Coding
9781119293323
USA $29.99
CAN $35.99
UK £21.99

dummies.com

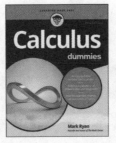

Small books for big imaginations

GETTING STARTED WITH **Coding**

Get Creative with Code!

Camille McCue, PhD

9781119177173
USA $9.99
CAN $9.99
UK £8.99

MODDING *Minecraft*™

Build Your Own Minecraft Mods!

Sarah Guthals, PhD
Stephen Foster, PhD
Lindsey Handley, PhD

9781119177272
USA $9.99
CAN $9.99
UK £8.99

MAKING *YouTube* VIDEOS

Star in Your Own Video!

Nick Willoughby

9781119177241
USA $9.99
CAN $9.99
UK £8.99

DESIGNING *Digital Games*

Create Games with Scratch™!

Derek Breen

9781119177210
USA $9.99
CAN $9.99
UK £8.99

GETTING STARTED WITH *Raspberry Pi*®

Program Your Raspberry Pi!

Richard Wentk

9781119262657
USA $9.99
CAN $9.99
UK £6.99

EXPERIMENTING WITH **Science**

Think, Test, and Learn!

9781119291336
USA $9.99
CAN $9.99
UK £6.99

CREATING *Digital Animations*

Animate Stories with Scratch™!

Derek Breen

9781119233527
USA $9.99
CAN $9.99
UK £6.99

GETTING STARTED WITH **Engineering**

Think Like an Engineer!

Camille McCue, PhD

9781119291220
USA $9.99
CAN $9.99
UK £6.99

WRITING *Computer Code*

Learn the Language of Computers!

Chris Minnick and Eva Holland

9781119177302
USA $9.99
CAN $9.99
UK £8.99

Unleash Their Creativity